Waking Up In Jamaica

Printed in the United Kingdom by Butler & Tanner Ltd, Somerset

Published by Sanctuary Publishing Limited, Sanctuary House,
45-53 Sinclair Road, London W14 0NS, United Kingdom

www.sanctuarypublishing.com

Copyright: Stephen Foehr 2000 (as *Jamaican Warriors*). This edition © 2002.

Photographs: all courtesy of the author. Cover photograph © Nik Wheeler/Corbis.
Author photograph by Lucian Foehr.

ISBN: 1-86074-380-3

Waking Up In Jamaica

Stephen Foehr

Sanctuary

Acknowledgements

Thanks to Richard Haight, mentor and dear friend, for reading the text and making corrections so that I didn't make a public fool of myself; to Jah Earl, who took me to places in Kingston I didn't know I had to go and introduced me to people I didn't know I had to meet; to all of the Jamaican musicians, for making themselves so easily accessible and speaking so openly without hidden agendas; and to Jamaica – thanks for being so beautiful and contradictory and complex and for welcoming me with an open heart and a warm smile.

Contents

1 Nine Mile

11 May, Bob Marley's deathday. On this date in 1981, shortly before noon, he died of cancer of the brain, liver and lungs at the age of 36. A person's deathday is equally important as his birthday. It is the day you live for, work all your life for, and when that day comes you hope that you did alright. The deathday is when you can do no more. You've made your mark, be it good, bad or mediocre. On that day, you toe the line and say, "Yeah, that's right, I did that. Yeah, right, I chose not to do that. Yeah, well, what can I say? No excuses. I did what I did." Bob Marley spread the word of liberation reggae around the world. His lyrics, more than the beat, made the music an anthem for freedom fighters and oppressed people. He did alright. This was a good day to pay homage to a musician who was a terrific writer.

Jah Earl took me down to the intra-island bus terminal, on the edge of Tivoli, behind a huge local market of open stalls and street stands. "When you come back, get off at Three Mile, at the edge of the city, and catch a taxi from there," he advised. "It can be a bit rough down here." Always my guardian, Jah Earl. I thanked him for it. The bus compound, enclosed by a high cement wall, seemed a bastion of security. Inside, buses were lined up in ordered ranks. The majority were vanilla-white vans which held 15 passengers, used for runs in the Kingston area. The cross-island buses were equally nondescript, without the elaborately gaudy paint jobs or twinkling Christmas lights around the windscreen, or shrines to the Virgin Mary or Che Guevara above the dashboard, as sported by buses in Central and South America. Jamaican buses are workhorses, not rolling art projects.

A man asks me where I'm going.

"Nine Mile in St Ann's."

He points. "That one to Brown's Town." The driver was behind the wheel, and the bus nearly full of passengers – a good sign. The buses are individually owned, so the owner/driver won't leave until he has the maximum payload on board. Schedules are not posted, but operate approximate to the hour. I found a seat and settled next to a large woman, who did not acknowledge me, although we were nearly cheek by jowl. Vendors came to the open windows hawking peeled oranges, cartons of juice, snacks, sunglasses and dishtowels. My seat companion bought a towel and stuffed it down her ample bosom to soak up the sweat.

The bus was configured so that there were two seats, then the aisle, and then one seat. As more passengers got on, jump seats were pulled up, filling the aisle with a solid row of passengers. We were jammed four across, thigh-to-thigh, shoulder-to-shoulder, which I discovered is actually a good thing. On the windy mountain roads, the closeness minimised the way we were tossed back and forth as the driver took the tight curves at full speed.

We pulled out, clearing the city within 20 minutes, although not the industrial sprawl that extends west almost as far as Spanish Town, Jamaica's first capital. Originally known as Villa De La Vega – "the town on the plain" – and later renamed St Jago De La Vega, Columbus' son Diego laid down the town's foundations in 1534. The Spanish planted mulberry trees, and a silk-spinning industry gave the town a commercial base. However, the population of Villa De La Vega never reached more than 500. Today, 90,000 people live in Spanish Town, making it the third-largest city on the island.

The English captured the city in 1655 and renamed it Spanish Town. Why not British Town? The city flourished as the administrative centre, with a prison, gallows, slave market, synagogues, theatres and a lively social scene. There is still a prison there. During the "dead season" on the sugar plantations (October to December), planters and their families flock to the city. In 1755, upstart Kingston merchants strong-armed a bill through the local legislature which transferred the seat of government to their city. King George II, when petitioned by the outraged citizens of Spanish Town, declared the bill illegal, and so the government archives returned to Spanish Town. By the 1850s, however, the city was on the decline. Kingston became the new capital in 1872.

The bus left the highway and wound into the city centre, where remnants of British Georgian architecture border the modest square. Little of Spanish Town's colourful past remains in the form of historical buildings, or in any form that attracts tourists. In 1988, Hurricane Gilbert did considerable damage to the historic town centre, which has never fully recovered.

The driver blasted Jamaica's proudly independent radio station, Irie FM, from the bus speakers. Between songs, the velvet-voiced announcer asked that we "light a candle for Bob". The next announcement said that, "Having sex with a virgin won't cure your sexual disease. If you have gonorrhea, for example, don't have sex with a little girl. It won't help you, and it will do great harm to her. Go to a doctor and get medical help. Leave the little girls alone."

We left the plains and climbed into the mountains. The road there was so narrow that the over-the-road tractor trucks, for which this is the main coast-to-coast route, had barely three feet to spare between them when passing. The bus driver, true to the entrepreneurial conviction that time is money, gave a credible imitation of a Formula One driver pushing a 50-passenger bus to a photo-finish Grand Prix victory. I concentrated on the lush tropical hillsides, the sweet farmland and the soothing peace of the deep-green everywhere. Brown cows grazing in the fields were sleek and solid. The woman on the jump seat fell asleep on my shoulder.

We crested the mountains and began a slow twist to the North Coast. At Claremont, I saw a sign to Nine Mile, but a helpful man told me to stay on the bus. "You can only get there by taxi from here. Cheaper to take the bus to Alexandria. I'm going there. Stay with me."

At each fork in the road we took the smaller path, skirting along the shoulder of the mountains like a surfer hanging onto the side of a glass-green 40-foot wave. I could just make out the sea a couple of thousand feet below on the hazy horizon. As we approached Brown's Town, a market town and transportation hub, passengers passed their money to the conductor, Fish, who had been standing at the door for the two-and-a-half-hour drive. (The fare was $120 JA, about $3 US.) Passengers folded their bills lengthways. Fish tucked the bills between the fingers of his right hand, which, as he collected the fares, resembled a geisha's fan tracing patterns in the air.

At the bus plaza, my new helpmate handed me his antique-quality Singer sewing machine and picked up his other two bundles. I followed him to a jitney van for the 20-minute drive to Alexandria ($25 JA), truly deep in the Jamaican countryside. Raw patches of red-soil fields, where yams and plantains grow, made the green hillsides look like a child's knee scraped in a bicycle fall. Camel-hump hills pressed close, sealing this rural living away from the tourist-poster vision of Jamaica.

When I stepped from the van at Alexandria, a young man asked, "Nine Mile?" Where else would a white person be going on this road so far from the beaches of Negril and Montego Bay?

"How much?" I asked, showing that I'm a savvy traveller not to be fleeced.

"Four bills." My helpmate had told me to expect a charge of between $300 and $400. Compared to the bus fare, it's a soaking, but there's no bus to Nine Mile. I got into the unlicensed station-wagon taxi, which suddenly filled with other people, as if they had been waiting for someone to come along and subsidise their ride. First was a mother with chubby twins, then two young boys, and at the last moment a sweet-faced little girl carrying a bag of oranges, who squeezed in next to the driver on his seat. The driver, Curtis, dropped the passengers at hamlets along the nine-mile drive to Nine Mile. I was the last passenger remaining when we reached the Bob Marley hilltop shrine and mausoleum compound.

As soon as I was out of the taxi, a Rasta approached with a big smile. "Hello. What's your name?"

"Stephen."

"I'm Steve, too." Steve is not a Rasta name, but I accepted his Salesman 101 bonding as a friendly gesture. He gave me the closed-fist salute and we bumped knuckles. The closed fist is a symbol of unity, of oneness, as opposed to the separation of the five fingers. A Rastaman once explained this to me, showing the "V" peace sign with two fingers split. "This is two." He closed his fist. "This is one." At the time, I thought that this guy should learn some history. Winston Churchill boosted his nation's sagging morale during the dark days of World War II by flashing the V-for-victory sign, and the hippies of the '60s adapted the gesture during the Vietnam War to signify peace. The shibboleth became much like the early Christians' fish logo, a way of recognising fellow believers. This history of the "V" sign as a white man's symbol helps explain the closed fist, a way of greeting widespread among those of African descent. The fist signifies a political and cultural bond within the black experience.

I expected a hustle from Steve, but he simply explained that I should go through the door in the wooden fence, buy a ticket in the gift shop for $400 JA, and a guide would give me a tour. Just a few years ago visitors weren't kept out by a wooden fence, and didn't pay an entry fee. It was possible to spend the night in Marley's boyhood home at the top of the hill if you slipped his cousin, the caretaker, a few bills. The hotel across the road from the shrine had not been constructed, and there was nowhere else to spend the night.

My guide, Orville, his dreads under a colourful tam, offered the closed fist, bumped the top of mine, and said, "Peace." He bumped the bottom of my fist with his. "Love." We went knuckle to knuckle. "Unity." Our thumbs touched and we twisted our fists apart. "Respect." I felt as though I had just gone through the ritual handshake of the Masonic House Of The Raccoon.

Our first stop was a look at the roof of the house of Omeriah, Marley's grandfather, hard against the balcony of the restaurant/gift shop. "This is where Bob was born, 6 February 1945," Orville explained. "It was destroyed by Hurricane Gilbert and since rebuilt, so it looks better than it was." Indeed, with its yellow walls and dusty rose trim, it looked like the colourful Caribbean cottages seen in slick travel magazines.

We walked up the hill, the Mount Zion made famous in Marley's songs, to the shrine site itself. On the right was a small stone house, and on the left, ten feet away, Marley's mausoleum.

"Bob moved up here from his grandfather's house with his mother when he was six months old," Orville said. "He lived here until he was 13, when he went to Kingston to learn to be a welder." Orville didn't mention Marley's father, Captain Norval Sinclair Marley, a white man and son of a second- or third-generation planter. He once worked as a merchant marine, and so was given the honorary title Captain. Captain Marley, who was never a strong positive force in young Marley's life, died on 20 May 1955. Here, at his son's shrine, the father doesn't exist.

We stepped into the house, approximately ten feet wide by 20 feet long. Marley spent his boyhood in this one-roomed house without running water or electricity. Orville pointed to an exposed band of rock at the baseboard. "The walls are plastered now, but when Bob lived here they were exposed rock like that. This was all one room, but we put up the partition" – we walked through a doorway – "to keep the original bedroom separate."

In the room there was a single bed, with an iron bedstead that was painted white. A bunch of vividly red fake roses had been stuck into the curlicues of the headpiece. A bedspread covered the four-inch-thick foam mattress. We stood on the original plank floor, painted a deep red. "In the front room we put cement because the floor was rotten," explained Orville.

He suddenly started singing, in a tremulous tenor. "Roof right over my head/we share a single bed," from Marley's song 'Is This Love?'.

"This is the roof," Orville gestured to the ceiling. "And this is the single bed."

I had always taken the song to be about lovers, perhaps in tribute to the early days when Marley and his wife, Rita, were a struggling poor couple. However, it has sweeter poignancy as a love song from son to mother. I easily imagined young Marley and his "Ciddy" curled on the bed sharing a laugh or a restless night, or mother and child play. Suddenly, for me, the international superstar reverted back to a little boy whose ambition was to love his mother. Later, I listened to the song again. It is clearly a love song for a woman.

We stepped out of the house and walked a few feet to a large rock cemented in place and painted in concentric rings of red, yellow and green, the colours of the Ethiopian flag. "Red for blood. Yellow for sun. Green for vegetation," Orville said. "This was Bob's meditation rock. He'd lay on the ground with his head on the rock to think about music."

Orville again broke into song. "Cold ground was my bed last night/and rock was my pillow too," from Marley's 'Talkin' Blues'. "This is the rock he used as a pillow."

"Talkin' blues, talkin' blues, they say your feet is just too big for your shoes," I sang to myself. I consider the song one of Marley's writing masterpieces. It starts off sounding like the old familiar "woe is me" blues. The line "I've been down on the rock so long I seem to wear a permanent screw" echoes centuries of slave oppression and the suppression of spirit; but standing next to Marley's meditation rock, the place where he sat in contemplation, the "permanent screw" took on another level of metaphor. Anyone familiar with the meditative sitting practice experience – unsupported spine straight, legs crossed, shoulders squared, and hands resting lightly on the knees while you breathe relaxed, focusing on the exhale, letting thoughts rise and flow out until an inner peace and serenity fills you – anyone who has spent even only 20 minutes doing this knows what torture it can be. The back throbs, the shoulder muscles stiffen, the knees ache and, worst of all, the undisciplined mind becomes a stick-up man robbing you over and over of the least coin of calm you can find. You start to hate the sitting practice. You feel like you're screwed in place, and permanently screwed if you prematurely leave the interior place of seeking. Marley knew from experience what he sang. The honed insights of his lyrics didn't come without the hard work of sitting still and looking, eyes wide open, inward and outward.

"But I've gotta stare in the sun/let the rays shine in my eyes," goes the song. Yes, and sit there and stare into the light of truth, however painful, until you find the true way of looking at things. Then the woebegone bad-luck kid isn't going to take how it's been, no matter what hundreds of years of history say. There's going to be a new way. Marley kept the blues allusion going for another line: "I'm going to take just a step more/'cause I feel like bombing a church/now that the preacher is lying." Here is the fulcrum of the song, where the weight shifts "just a step more" from blues into the universal view of reggae. The preacher is the teacher, the colonial teacher who taught a false history to the Jamaicans and to all colonised peoples; the preacher teacher who taught that God is white; the Babylon teacher who taught the false values of materialism at the expense of humanity. Enough of that, Marley says. I'm taking the screw out of that rock of oppression and walking my own path. I don't believe the lies that have kept me and my people down for so long. And I'm going to do something about how things work.

"So who's going to stay at home when the freedom fighters are fighting?" Marley asked in the song. Not the warriors, that's for sure. Pick up a small axe and start chopping at the rotten tree. "Don't you take our life for granted knowing where we're bound," Marley warned. Our life. We're on our way. Stand aside because we're not asking permission any more. Marley showed his writing gift for the subtle metaphor in turning the blues song 'Talkin' Blues' into a revolutionary song. He took the blues prototype and pushed it into the liminal space of "We are talking about something bigger than my blues. We're talking about the liberation of the human spirit."

The next song on the *Talkin' Blues* album is 'Burnin' & Lootin', and refers not to buildings and cities but to burning illusions of the Babylon system, putting fire to the false illusions of the capitalistic system that keep people, both rich and poor, in chains. Now Marley's into the full Rasta reggae universal vision that has struck such a deep chord around the world.

Orville led me around the back of the mausoleum, where Marley's mother had her outdoor oven, and pointed to the Star Of David made of red and purple stained glass set in the wall. "When the sun rises from the east, the light shines through that window in on Bob."

We went around the mausoleum, past the avocado tree which Orville said that Marley planted, over to the entrance. We removed our shoes and hats, as if entering a mosque or a church, and stepped inside. Immediately in front of me was a larger-than-life bronze bust of Marley. To my left was a table, where Marley's Bible lay open. Over the table was a painting of a messianic Marley in a long white robe, holding a shepherd's crook in one hand and a lamb in the other. At his feet is a flock of sheep. To my right was the tomb, seven feet high and made of a pastiche of irregular white, or nearly white, Ethiopian marble. A wide band of African cloth, brought by Rita Marley, wrapped the lower section of the tomb. A colourful football hung in a string bag, a reminder that Marley injured his right big toe while playing football. The injury refused to heal, and the subsequent medical investigation led to the discovery of the terminal cancer. The three ears of corn hanging from the ceiling recalled Joseph, of the Old Testament.

"Bob is laid six feet in the air, his feet to the east and his head to the west," Orville said. "His brother Anthony is buried beneath Bob, in the lower half of the tomb. Anthony was shot and killed in 1985 by the Miami police. They said it was an accident."

We walked down the side of the tomb, past the lit candles and an eagle feather at the base. On the rear wall was a large photo of Anthony with his mother, Cedella "Ciddy" Booker-Marley. He had her round face. Bob had the long, thin face of his father. Above the photo, tacked to the ceiling, was a poster of Marley's son Ziggy's 1993 'Joy And Blues' world tour.

After the tomb visit, I walked down Mount Zion to check out the gift shop. Marley's smiling face appeared on T-shirts, bottles of jerk sauce, cans of tea, bars of scented soap, Rasta tams, sandals, dresses, hats. In the adjoining six-table restaurant bar a colour television showed continuous loops of Marley-on-tour tapes. I went out on the back deck, with its two picnic tables and a wide-open view of the countryside.

I'm glad that Marley was laid to rest there, rather than in Kingston's National Heroes Park, where Dennis Emmanuel Brown, the Crown Prince Of Reggae, is interred. Visitors to Jamaica need to get off the beaches and into the hills in order to experience the real country. If you don't venture into back-country Jamaica, you miss an essential understanding of Marley and his music. Bob Marley was a farm boy. He spent his formative years looking at these clumps of hills spread out below me. He cared for the cows and picked the yams. He grew up knowing that you don't reap if you don't sow, and that you should always give thanks to the land and its creator for your blessings and sorrows. When he became famous, Marley still returned to his Mount Zion, lit a spliff and sat on his rock, remembering that life is simple: peace, respect, love, justice, something to eat, a roof over your head and a single bed. Marley learned all of that right here. You have to come to this place, sink into it – and let it sink into you – before you can hear the root spirit of Marley's music.

Even so, of all of the talented singers in Jamaica, how did this country boy – unschooled in music, with no access to the music business when many of his urban peers were cutting their teeth on cassettes – become reggae's international star?

There was only one man to ask: Mortimo Planno. Planno, Jamaica's esteemed folk philosopher, schooled many of the '60s reggae stars, including Bob Marley, Ken Booth, Pipe of The Wailing Souls, Dream, The Abyssinians, Count Ossie – almost the entire roster of the core creators of roots reggae. He is arguably the most influential force in shaping the message of evangelical liberation reggae.

"Brother Planno's work is a major component of our era," Jalaui Niaah told me over lunch in the faculty dining room at the University Of The West Indies. Niaah helps Planno compile his work, analyse it, and prepares Planno's largely handwritten notes for publication. "If you're looking at the decades of the '60s, '70s and a little of the '80s, he was a major influence in those periods."

In the 1998 academic year, Planno was given a year-long fellowship by the university's faculty of social sciences. During that year, Planno gave lectures and consulted with university professors and international scholars, who came to the Mono campus specifically to visit him. He has been on three missions to Africa for the Rastafari movement, and has toured Europe and North America on the lecture circuit.

"The quality of his life's work has given him that level of weight as a thinker," Niaah said. "Someone like Mr Planno, who has a phenomenal mind, is a thinker perhaps more so than a trained academic. His wisdom comes from his intuitive folk philosophy. He has defined a context of describing a new facility of interpretation – that is, intuitively, in the way we perceive ourselves and the world."

Planno coined the phrase "polite violence". In a lecture on the subject, he said that, "By that I mean when one does you wrong and apologises, according to them, politely. Like when one mashes your foot, hurts you, and says, 'Excuse me.' 'Sorry.' 'Please', 'sorry' and 'excuse' are scientific words that entail polite violence. Doing you wrong and asking you to pardon me, and then doing the wrong again and asking to be excused again is polite violence. Colonialism was direct brutality without asking for pardon. The new type of Neo-Colonialism – that is, economic colonialism – really enhances this polite violence."

Neo-Colonialism, according to Planno's definition, includes international corporations that exploit a nation's resources, be it that country's minerals or cultural values, for their own profit. Neo-Colonialism is mining a country's bauxite, for example, for exportation and not contributing directly to the welfare of the country's people. Multinational corporations that push their self-serving interests to the detriment of a society and/or culture do polite violence. Importing chemical-laden food and soft drinks at the expense of locally grown products is Neo-Colonialism. Promoting music that undermines the values of a society is polite violence. Agencies such as the International Monetary Fund, the World Trade Organisation and the World Bank, which force nations to accept policies harmful to their people, exercise polite violence, according to Planno. Globalisation in the name of making the rich richer while keeping the poor in a subservient and powerless position is Neo-Colonialism and polite violence. "You react back to polite violence mystically," Planno said. "The mystic breeze blows, and what goes around comes around. Passive resistance is the proper term. That requires a lot of patience, but it also perpetuates peace at that level."

The only directions I had to help me find Planno was to look on the right-hand side of the road for a blue, single-storey house near the border of the parishes of Manchester and Clarendon when approaching the town of Porus.

Jah Earl and I left Kingston in the early morning and set out on the two-hour drive. Along the way, I noticed people industriously cleaning their yards, fixing the roofs of churches, painting pedestrian crossings on roads and in general sprucing up the place.

"Labour Day," Jah Earl explained. "That's when people all over the island work to clean their yards, clear up cemeteries, whatever, to make things look better."

The well-maintained Sir Alexander Bustamante Highway, named for Jamaica's first prime minister, rolled through the island's most abundant and prosperous agricultural region. There were a good number of large, expensive houses. The roadside restaurants and refreshment stalls were substantial and gaily painted. When we approached the border between the two parishes, Jah Earl stopped a Rasta and asked if he knew where to find Brother Planno.

Rastas treat each other as members of a tribe within the Jamaican population. A fellow dread is someone to trust. That person will have news within the Rasta community and knows where to find a bredren. The hippies of the '60s had the same attitude towards each other. The early Christians, like any oppressed group, developed the same sense of brotherhood and trust for each other.

The dread said yes.

"You don't sound too sure," Jah Earl replied.

"I can find out," answered the dread.

"You know Dago," Jah Earl asked. Dago is Hugh Scott, an old friend of Jah Earl's and an associate of Planno.

"Yes," replied the dread.

A few miles down the road, the dread told Jah Earl to stop opposite the HQ Snacks And Tavern at a crossroads. Next door there was a blue, single-storey house. Jah Earl found his friend Dago inside the bar, which he owns. "Planno is here," Jah Earl reported back.

Dago, a tall, handsome man with a biblical beard, led us to a room behind the bar. The single room reminded me of a crash pad for migrant workers. The room was crowded with two queen beds, a narrow table with a cast-iron garden bench behind it and an open bamboo rack piled with clothes, suitcases and a 15-inch television.

However, it was neat and tidy. Sitting on one bed was Mortimo "Kumi" Planno.

Planno's first lesson that day was one of context. I had expected to see a professorial philosopher, neatly if casually attired, sitting in his book-lined study. Either that or a holy man, a guru with a benevolent smile. Instead, I found this Aboriginal-looking fellow wearing only shorts and with a mass of dreadlocks. A bright blue pen was tucked into the short hair above his forehead. I don't mean to be disrespectful, but he reminded me of a mud-caked frog. He had a big, heavy face. The bridge of his nose disappeared directly under his single-line brow. The right side of his upper lip was puffy, as if swollen by herpes. He was snaggle-toothed, missing several front teeth. He had a huge, distended belly, perhaps as a result of his kidney problems, for which he is scheduled for surgery. His painful right foot kept him bedridden. He was rolling a spliff.

So much for my image of what an eminent philosopher should look like. I introduced myself and stated the purpose of my visit. It was 10am and he hadn't had breakfast. "Let's just chit-chat until I get my stomach settled," he said. He showed me the introduction to the book he was writing with Allan "Skill" Cole and Dago, titled *Filosofies And Opinions Of Rastafari, The Bob Marley I And I Know.*

"Bob was a bad man," he said in his sonorous bass voice. "Did you know that? A very bad man."

"In what way?"

Instead of answering, Planno asked Dago to insert a tape into the VCR. It was a professionally produced slick sales pitch aimed at radio stations to promote a CD and tape compilation of Marley songs. The CD and the tape each contain exclusive songs not previously released, touted the announcer. If you buy both the CD and the tape, you'll get 18 unreleased songs.

Then we watched the hour-long tape *Lion Of Judah*, which documents Italy's 1937-38 invasion of Ethiopia. After a brutal seven-month campaign, during which Italy used illegal mustard gas, Ethiopia was defeated and occupied for five years. Despite Emperor Haile Selassie's pleas for assistance, Western nations did nothing to stop

Mussolini or to help the outgunned Ethiopian forces. When *Lion Of Judah* was over, and his breakfast of dry toast and tea consumed, Planno said, "Now we can talk."

"Did you deliberately school Marley to use reggae as an evangelical music to spread Rastafari?" I asked.

"Yes. I saw that. That was one of the mystic visions, the mystique of the mystic. We took care of moulding Marley as the messenger to take the message of Rastafari throughout the world."

"Why Marley and not Jimmy Cliff, or Toots Hibbert, or Ken Booth?"

"Bob Marley was chosen because I saw a halo around him," Planno replied. "If you look deep enough on those levels, you can see such things. Marley sings, 'Open your eyes and look within. Are you satisfied with the life you're livin'?' Looking inside, you see all deep things. I choose reggae because reggae is the King's message, you know. If you check the lexicon it shows that it's the message from the King. I worked in the music business from 1960 to 1974. It took 14 years really working to get the result.

"When Marley was a youth and just starting, he sounded more like the Americans. Rhythm and blues. He wanted to be an R&B performer when he joined his mother in Baltimore, but he got proper training culturally with Joe Higgs and myself. Joe Higgs helped him musically, and I helped him spiritually."

Planno gave Marley his coming-out song as a Rastafarian, 'Selassie Is The Chapel'. Over the slow Nyabinghi drum track, Marley chanted, "Haile Selassie is the chapel, power of the trinity, conquering Lion of Judah, he's the King of Kings." Only 26 copies were pressed.

Marley joined the Rasta organisation The 12 Tribes Of Israel, founded in 1968 in Trench Town by Vernon Carrington, a juice man who had a pushcart and sold cowfoot, a medicinal drink make from the juice of the cowfoot. He called upon his followers to prepare themselves by mystical means for repatriation, when they would migrate to an area in Ethiopia's Goba Valley called Shashamani.

Carrington, known as Gad (Gadmon) The Prophet, became Marley's instructor. Marley reportedly said that, "Gad revealed back to I and I the secret of the lost 12 tribes."

According to Israel's principal dogma, the human race was divided into 12 scattered tribes, each named for one of Jacob's sons, whom Jah sent down into Egypt. Each tribe was associated with a certain month, symbolised by a certain colour and endowed with a secret blessing. This colour symbolism is common among all of the Rastafari groups. The tribe's month was based on the Egyptian calendar, which pre-dated the "corrupt" Roman calendar. April is the first month, according to the Egyptian calendar. Marley, born in February, belonged to the tribe of Joseph. In 'Redemption Song' Marley identifies himself as the present-day incarnation of Joseph, son of Jacob.

Other prominent musicians who belonged to The 12 Tribes included Dennis Brown, Freddie McGregor and Judy Mowatt, who later became a "church lady".

The 12 Tribes was less radical than the Puritan branches of Rastafari. It represented a respectable version of Rastafari. The 12 Tribes appealed to the middle class, and this signified a shift in acceptance of Rastafari in Jamaica. The middle class was more willing to identify with the African point of reference rather than with the European point of view. This continuing gradual change of perspective was an important sociological shift in national identity.

Planno's guidance helped Marley to realise that the purpose of music was not just entertainment. The music was a channel to tell of the presence of the divinity who lives among us here and now. In the song 'Blackman Redemption', Marley sings, "Coming from the root of King David, through the line of Solomon, His Imperial Majesty is the Power of Authority." In 'Chant Down Babylon', on *Confrontation* (Tuff Gong, 1983), Marley sings, "Music, you're the key/Talk to who, please talk to me/Bring the voice of the Rastaman/Communicating to everyone…"

"Does reggae need another Bob Marley?" I asked Planno.

"I don't think we will have another Marley. Bob can't be dead. The message is in the music. The Rastafari teaching is still happening, but more in the country. In those days, we were more in the city, Trench Town. Now it's spread out all around. The elders are responsible for teaching the younger ones. The message goes around in the music. If you take *mu* out of music, that leaves *sic*. We take the *mu* out of the music, leave them sick, you see? The message continues in the music today. The music of today is a hotter fire. It will get more hot, hot, hot.

"In this realm we live in, it's our job to always evolve. Angelic work, you know? There's always going to be evil and good because that's the evolution. There is never paradise here, but every man must seek his paradise. As I look at Jamaica and the world, I see that the understanding becomes more clear daily."

"Marley sings of the sufferers. What's the cause of suffering?" I asked him.

"Look there." He pointed to the television, which was showing an interview of Rastafarians in Ethiopia. "Put your tape recorder up there and get that information."

After an hour of the video, Planno asked, "In your country, you see suffering?"

"Yes."

"A lot of bloodshed daily?"

"Daily."

"For what?"

"I personally think it's to remind each of us individuals to work against the shedding of the blood."

"That's why I give you this interview, for I think that we are working towards the type of relationships to give the world the peace and love we deserve. In this, the warrior must be compassionate. He must forgive but not forget. We can't forget" – he suddenly shouts in a falsetto – "what the white man doing. The white man's story and our story is his-story. Sociology becomes history."

"When I go to reggae concerts in the States," I replied, "I see mostly young white kids jumping up and down shouting 'Jah' and 'Rastafari' and 'Am I black enough?' I get the impression that they have no understanding of the depth of Rastafari. Does it make any difference if they understand or not?"

"It appears that they don't understand the depths when they shout 'Jah' or 'Rastafari'," Planno answered, "but mystically they are demonstrating it. Our strength comes in the youth."

"Why is it important for black people to have a black god?"

Planno laughed. "The white man teaches us that our god is white, which is a lie. You can have a white god for a white man. I don't mind him saying that his god is white, but I don't agree with him that my god is also white. God made me in His own image, so I look like this."

It took six hours for Planno to show the tip of his iceberg. The place and context was not proper for him to reveal the insights of his mysticism, which is the basis of his knowing as a philosopher. He ended the interview by saying, "I think you have quite enough to work with," and patted me on the head as a father would a small son.

I pondered Planno's concept of polite violence for days. It can be applied to any potentially exploitative situation: male and female, parent and child, employer and employee, and the internal power structure of a country exploiting the rest of the citizenry. I called Kwame Dawes, my reggae singer/professor friend, and asked his opinion.

"One of the things that Jamaica has to recognise is that, after 30 years of so-called independence, the language of who becomes the colonial force changes," Dawes said. "Let's go back to Marley. As early as the 1970s, there becomes a lyrical ambience about what colonialism is. He talks about 'Never let a politician grant you a favour; he will always try to control you forever.' Bob Marley is not talking about the colonial government. He's talking about the Jamaican politician. Sometimes, in his lyrics, when he talks about oppression, he's talking about localised oppression. He's talking about a Jamaican oppression that emerges out of one's own people, and he is speaking against that. The easy language of saying that this is colonialism in terms of how we construct our society doesn't work as easily. It works in economic terms because we can see that the impact of colonialism still remains in the Jamaican society. The society is essentially constructed around an exploitative agenda, and that paradigm cannot change, for Jamaica is a cash country, so we still carry that legacy. But the oppressive forces in the society are also very much rooted in the people who emerge out of the society and become their own oppressors. Reggae doesn't make any bones about articulating that element."

2 Pinnacle

Sweat made me shine, like a fish rising from water. The woman's black eyes were a hymn. She turned her face from my words, then lifted an arm languidly. My eyes moved down the grace of her forearm, lingered on her delicate wrist and then, centimetre by moist centimetre, slipped over her thumb's mound before dropping off her pointing finger. The fingernail was broken and rimmed with dirt, as if she'd been digging.

"You've gone too far, mon."

"We've gone too far," Jah Earl said.

"Turn around," the woman ordered.

Jah Earl pulled a U-turn in front of the Girls Pub. "Take the next right," the woman called after us as we started back down the narrow crack of asphalt between the hills. The next right led to the St Jago Hills, where the ancient seabed was being hacked into residential sites. This didn't look promising. Jah Earl flagged down a blue Toyota pick-up. "We're looking for Pinnacle. We know of it?" he asked the driver.

"You mean the ruins? The old Rasta place?"

"That's it," I replied.

"You have to go back down to Water Loo, take a right, then go around and up."

When I told Jah Earl I wanted to find the old Pinnacle Estate, that morning in Kingston, he had looked at me for a long time. The driver of yellow cab 81A, he was a solid, calm man, a Rasta with a rich white beard and a comfortable paunch.

"Why?" he asked.

"I need to start my journey there if I'm going to understand anything right."

Pinnacle was the first Rasta commune, founded in 1940 by Leonard Percival Howell. On Pinnacle Hill, a transplanted African music burrowed into the consciousness of the people. Thirty years later, that music became a taproot of liberation reggae. From Pinnacle, I was planning to start my journey through the Kingston recording studios; to venture into the Yards to hear new sounds; to hump over the Blue Mountains to find Maroons and coffee; to explore the Cockpit for fife and drum and abeng horn; and to sit on the sands of hedonistic Negril to wait, expectantly.

I'd hoped that, by coming down here, to ground zero, I might gain some understanding as to why the music of this small island – 145 miles long and 53 miles wide, with a population of 2.6 million – attracts millions upon millions of rabid fans from all over the world, from Japan to England, from Finland to Brazil. I wanted to understand why reggae is the most successful evangelical music in the world. I wanted to understand the sorrow and grace and joy and rage of this music; this acceptance and victimhood and *savoir complèxe*; the laid-back good times and aggressive righteousness; the gentleness and love; the wit and faith and optimism; the hopefulness and ganja vision that makes Jamaica the heart of the beat of the music.

When I'd finished talking, Jah Earl said, "I've always wondered about that place."

We drove further down towards Water Loo. At a fork in the road with a few houses and shack stores – junk food, cigarettes, soda, beer – Jah Earl asked a man, "Do you know Pinnacle?"

The fellow, in short locks and a red fishnet top under a loose shirt, flashed a smile brighter and bigger than anything the Cheshire Cat would have thought possible. "I know that place. I was there as a little boy. My grandfather was part of that."

"Can he show us the way?"

"You want to meet Howell's son? He can tell you history of the place."

He climbed into the back seat. "Go down and take a left, then straight to the bamboo factory. I remember Mr Howell from when I was a boy. He didn't have locks but wore long hair. I thought he looked just like Marcus Garvey. He was a kind man." Our guide was Danny Lewis, father of four daughters, who farmed a small plot behind the zinc fence where we had met him.

At the bamboo factory, Danny directed us onto a smaller road, following the sign to the Caymanus Golf Course. We pulled into the parking lot of a country club set in the boonies of Jamaica. Danny got out and disappeared behind the new shiny zinc fence. A few minutes later he returned with a thin man wearing a white faux polo shirt and a baseball cap.

"Hello, sir. I'm Arnold Howell." He extended a calloused hand and took mine softly. He was a lean man, his white moustache and white hair in stark contrast to his dark skin. Like foam on a dark brew, I thought. I told him of my interest in visiting his old home. "We can go up there if you like. It'll be nice to see the view I had as a boy."

We piled into Jah Earl's taxi. Arnold directed us across the golf course, where he worked as a caddy, and through the back fence onto a rough track that no one would have called a road. "My father got the land from an Albert Chang in 1940," Arnold said, "but we lost the land in a court fight in 1980. A Mr Watt sent my father a letter saying that he bought the land from the Boy Scouts. My father scorched the letter at all four corners and sent it back."

Jah Earl went real slow over the rocks to save his tyres. The track eventually petered out at a house under construction.

"We walk from here," said Arnold, and immediately went to the cinderblock shell of the house, where the builder, a small man with a massive knitted hat concealing his dreads, greeted us.

"Nya," Jah Earl replied.

Arnold walked right through the still-imaginary rooms to a back corner. "There." He pointed to a sunken cement tank, eight feet across and 15 feet long, hard against the partially built wall. "That's the original water tank. We used to have barbecues around it." A thicket of tropical brambles now crowded around the tank. Water lilies grew in the bottom. "Over there, where the road goes now, was the milking shed. Here was a trough for the cows to drink. We lived on top of the hill. This way."

Arnold set a fast clip up an eroded old track closed in by bushes and trees. Danny and I trailed behind. How do these people stand it, this heat saturated with humidity so dense I can eat it, like tasteless candyfloss? In another setting, in another context, I would be a performing art piece, a human fountain, but here, on this Jamaican hillside, I was just a white guy out of place.

I asked Arnold about the gong. After a police raid on the compound in 1954, one of many, Howell had posted ferocious dogs at the entrance and menacing-looking dread guards, called the Ethiopian Warriors, and a gong was hung to loudly announce visitors, and to serve as an early warning system for when the police arrived.

"I don't remember anything about a gong," Arnold, 58, replied. He had lived at Pinnacle for 17 years. "We had an iron triangle that we'd bang to call people to eat or to work."

"Gong" was one of Howell's nicknames. "Tuff Gong" was Bob Marley's street name when, as a skinny kid, he won his survival smarts in the Trench Town slum while learning to sing under the tutelage of Joe Higgs. He later named his record company Tuff Gong.

Jamaicans are fond of nicknames: Bread (Lloyd McDonald) and Pipe (Winston Matthews), of The Wailing Souls; Bunny Rugs (William Clark) of Third World; Beenie Man (Moses Davis); Sizzla, Bounty Killer, Yellowman, Lady Saw and Half Pint are just a smattering of current Jamaican musicians. Howell had a number of monikers: the self-given Gangungu Maraj, which he loosely translated as "Teacher Of Famous Wisdom, King Of Kings," Uncle Percy, Counsellor, Prince Regent, and The Bard Of Pinnacle. Howell told his followers to call him God, according to various sources.

I wondered if anyone ever called him Larry. Would that have been like calling Peter the apostle Petey?

I asked Arnold about the God name. "Mr Howell" (he always referred to his father as Mr Howell) "didn't think he was God, and the people didn't think of him as God. He was a leader that the government wanted to get rid of."

At the top of the hill, Arnold pointed into the bushes. "My brother, Cardiff, and I used to play hide-and-seek under that arch." There, framed by leafy green, was a graceful brick arch, the only solid piece left of the great house, which burned down before Howell set up his commune. "We'd sit here with a spyglass and look down on Port Royal." The Littorals plain stretched a couple of thousand feet below, with Kingston and Port Royal, the infamous pirate hangout, 20 miles away on the far edge, where the Caribbean defined the coast.

"A mountain view is a poor person's sentiment," said Arnold quietly. "And there," he pointed ahead to a flat space clear of overgrowth, "is where we had the teeter-totter. This place here," he spun his arms in circles, as if clearing smoke, "here was the playground, where all us kids would run around and around. My father wasn't a man to play ball with his 14 kids. He'd walk and talk with us. Mr Howell was a man who loved to give you lessons in godly ways. He was a strong man, not that he was big or anything. He was only about my size [5' 8"], but he had a strong presence."

Howell must have been quite a guy to get an estimated 1,700-4,000 people to homestead these hills. His followers were the homeless and discarded war veterans, sugar-cane cutters and small farmers, who sold their land and moved to Pinnacle, and women. Women were an important contingent. By all accounts, Howell was a world-class charmer, a common trait among Jamaicans. He was a man with a honeyed tongue who spoke with the conviction of a charismatic street-corner preacher. He was a handsome man with a full, round face. He was also well read, with a large library, and he maintained contacts with European Marxists. Even in his photos, a light of wit and intelligence plays about him.

Howell was the first to proclaim the Ethiopian Emperor Haile Selassie as God and the one and only king of black Africans. This teaching has become a basic tenet of Rastafari, although the Emperor never had the temerity to make the audacious claim of Godhood.

"Mr Howell was born on 16 June 1898, up in St Catherine parish at a place called Pumpkin," Arnold said. "I heard Mr Howell was a soldier in the British Army as part of a Jamaican unit, in Panama and later at the Up Park Camp in Kingston. He returned to Panama and joined the US Army. He was a cook, I believe."

Various sources dispute Howell's military career. It's commonly cited that he served in a transportation unit. The army transferred him to New York in 1918, where he was honourably discharged in 1923, after which he did manual labour and eventually opened a coffee shop specialising in "herbal teas". He claimed to be a Garveyite, and knew Marcus Garvey, the Jamaican who championed pan-Africanism and the blacks' rights of self-determination. However, French journalist Helene Lee, who spent four years researching her book on Howell, *Le Premier Rasta*, found no evidence that Howell had served in the US Army. "He didn't became a US citizen," Lee told me, "although he did file an intent to declare for citizenship. There is no record of him under the Howell name, but he also used the name Honeyman. I believe he *was* a cook on a US military transport ship, but as part of the civilian crew."

Howell claimed to have attended the coronation of Haile Selassie at St George's Cathedral in Addis Ababa on 2 November 1930, but Lee found no evidence to support that claim. "Howell probably got his information from Annie 'The Comet' Harvey, who did attend the coronation," she said. "Harvey was part of the group in the St Thomas parish, where Howell first started his evangelical work. He also stole from Annie a picture of the Emperor at the coronation and used that picture to shore up his legitimacy."

"I remember him telling us about being at the coronation," Arnold said. "He described how Haile Selassie and his queen rode in a chariot pulled by six white Arabian horses. He told me, 'Arnold, Rasta shall grow, shall grow.' He told me that Rasta will grow right over the world. I didn't take it serious. He said that Haile Selassie was a messenger from the father Himself. Mr Howell was a man of God. Mr Howell was a good man. He spoke to his Father."

When Howell returned to Jamaica from the United States in 1932, he took up his mission, proclaiming the newly crowned Haile Selassie as the King of black people, the returned messiah fulfilling Old and New Testament scriptures, the one true God, the Black God. He cited Revelation 5:2-5 as evidence: "And I saw a strong angel proclaiming with a loud voice: Who is worthy to open the book, and to loose the seals thereof? And no man in heaven, nor in earth, was able to open the book, neither to look thereon... And one of the elders saith unto me, Weep not: behold, the Lion of the tribe of Judah, the Root of David, hath prevailed to open the book, and to loose the seals thereof." (Haile Selassie claimed to be of the direct line of King David, of the tribe of Judah.)

To bolster the theory of there being a black king and god, Howell referred to the prophesy of Daniel 7:9: "And I beheld till the thrones were cast down and the Ancient Of Days did sit, whose garment was white as snow, and the hair of his head like pure wool; his throne was like the fiery flame, and his wheels as burning fire." In Howell's reading, fire is synonymous with blackness.

"Mr Howell always said, 'Black people, black people, rise and shine because that the light has now come and the glory of the Lord God of Israel is now risen up anew," Arnold quoted as he walked around his former playground, where large flat stones had been stacked into four seats.

"Sizzla, Bunny Wailer and U Roy come up here for private ceremonies," Danny said.

Howell must have had a righteous fire in his eyes when he preached to his fellow Jamaicans about the indignities of the colonial system under which they lived. He must have shouted out, his words full of heat, "Since slave days, the system has kept us in poverty, powerless, oppressed, sufferers of injustice." Much of the same sentiment is heard in today's Jamaica, which became an independent nation in 1962.

Bunny Rugs, lead singer for Third World and a Rasta himself, told me in a conversation one day that, "Jamaica is still an English colony in many ways, especially in the mindset of the ruling class. We still have a British governor-general, who represents the Queen. The English still have lands here. The Queen would have to come to Jamaica and say that she no longer has anything to do with Jamaica and give back all the Crown lands. Give back the land to the people. All the Roman Catholic schools and churches that belong to Rome, the Pope must give them back too.

"Nothing has really changed since the colonial times," Rugs said. "The change we're looking for is to make that change in Africa. Jamaica isn't ours. Jamaica isn't for the black man. Jamaica is for the Indians. We were taken from Africa, and are now going to reunite Africa. I'm not concerned about the change in Jamaica. I'm mostly concerned about the change in Africa. Africa is mine. I go there every day. The trip to Africa is a trip home. You don't have to actually take up your bed and refrigerator and ship back furniture and cars. It's not about that. We are children of the universe. We live anywhere at any time, but our hearts and our work are designed for the freedom of Africa.

"This is primarily kept alive through the music. The musicians are the cultural warriors. None of this is taught in schools. That's not surprising. It's an English system. If you teach history of the African people in the classroom, you'll make the student too strong. You'll make him a true individual. The ruling class doesn't want that. They want people they can control, so teach them about Christopher Columbus and Jesus Christ, with an image from Europe. They don't teach the student with African heritage about himself or about Marcus Garvey or Cudjoe and other Maroon leaders."

Howell offered a way out from under the thumb of the white authority and their white god. He proclaimed self-determination, black pride, and a rebellion of the underclass. This remains a rallying cry of Rastas and a constant chorus in reggae, a voice that could be heard in the days of Jamaican slave rebellions. Fighters in the 1865 Morant Bay Rebellion shouted slogans still heard in the Rasta lexicon: "Colour for colour, skin for skin", "Lion" and "Black skin, white heart". From that phrase, Rastas and other Jamaicans coined the term "roast breadfruit", meaning black on the outside and white on the inside – an Uncle Tom. The Rastafarian movement didn't spring full-bloom from Howell's head, but he gave it an identity, a focus of cause. He is considered the founder of Rastafari.

Arnold doesn't remember his boyhood home as a religious movement, although he agreed that his father was a revolutionary. "Me, I don't know directly about the spiritual part," he said. "I know that the people who lived here, those people talked with one voice, united. We called each other 'brother' and 'sister'. Outsiders, they never know the love between us. The people were always cultivating, and we lived off our own produce – corn, cassava, yams, oranges, grapefruit, bananas, many things. We had a storehouse where you could go and get whatever food you needed. Mr Howell taught unity and sharing. We all ate in a big mess hall."

He stopped suddenly. "Look there," he said, pointing to a tree. "That's one of the originals." His voice was full of pleasure at finding this old friend still flourishing from his childhood days.

Arnold walked across his old playground unerringly to stone stairs well hidden in the bushes. We climbed the 15 steps to a pole with a tattered Rasta flag. It had three panels, red, green and yellow. In the middle of the yellow panel was the Lion of Judah. Arnold found a path through the tangle of bushes to a bare outline of a ruin.

"This was our house," he said. It was once a large, sprawling place built of brick, judging from the outline of the foundation perched on the hillside. Shards of walls still stood, one bearing a faint rose pigment of the original paint. "Here was the kitchen," Arnold said, and for a moment a hint of nostalgia crept into his voice. "As a boy, I used to scramble up there," he said, pointing behind the wall to a tree, "and hang in the branches. It's good to be home," he grinned.

Arnold gazed out over the 320 acres that comprised the estate. "There we had a big field of corn." He swept an arm over a hillside. "The camp where the people lived was down there, near the fields. We had a valley of corn and lots of herb growing on the south-facing hills. And there," he pointed to a valley about a mile off, "we called that Horse Grave because we had a white horse we kept tied to a tree down there. The horse got tangled up with the tree and broke a leg. We buried him there. And there, that whole hillside was planted with herb." He dropped his arm. "This land was very productive, and now no one is using it." All of the land that Arnold encompassed with his sweeping arm was now wild wood.

Each family at Pinnacle was responsible for its own upkeep, but communal labour was undertaken for the good of the community. A small pond supplied water for plants and livestock. The people lived in thatched huts, like peasants. Cooking, eating, washing and socialising were done in the open yard, a common lifestyle in the hot tropics. There was a parade ground, where rituals took place, and a playing field for the children. On Sundays, after dinner, community members would gather at the parade ground to sing and dance to the rhythms of Nyabinghi drumming. They didn't live in isolation, like some religious cults. The children went to school in the nearby village, where the Howellites bought groceries.

"Everybody who came in connect with Mr Howell benefited," Arnold said. "The people in Water Loo were happy with us because we'd buy water from them. The people in Sligoville were happy because we'd buy their fruit, and pay cash. We started with a horse but managed to buy a truck. That made the government mad because we were succeeding. Our men, when they'd go to town, they wore nice vests and jackets.

"We had drumming at Pinnacle," remembered Arnold. "The Nyabinghi drumming came with the people. Mr Howell would talk about Africa, about Uganda, and Ethiopia. Mr Howell wasn't for luxury. He could have had a business in town and just cared for his family, but he wanted to help people make their own way, grow their own produce. Mr Howell thought that unity and helping others was richness and luxury."

There are differing accounts of the Howellites' good neighbour policy. Some neighbouring farmers complained that the Howellites encroached on their land to plant marijuana, or *ganja*. There were complaints that the Howellites harangued their neighbours with rants against the capitalistic system, the government, the justice system, against nearly everything they didn't like. They refused to pay taxes as an act of defiance against the government, and demanded that their neighbours also should refuse to pay taxes to the government. Instead, the taxes should be paid to themselves, in the name of Haile Selassie.

In July 1941, 173 armed policemen raided the Pinnacle, acting under the Defence Regulations. Howell's connections in high places tipped him off as to the timing of the raid. On the night before the police arrived, he called his people together and said that he'd had a vision. "Visitors will come tomorrow to visit us," he said, "but do not be afraid. No harm will come to you." At about 3:30am, he got dressed and slipped away. Shortly afterwards, his wife heard the loud footsteps of the police approaching.

The police spent the day rounding up the Howellites and pulling up ganja plants. In the afternoon, they discovered that Howell was missing. Search parties were sent out. They'd hear Howell's voice from one hilltop and rush over there, and then they'd hear him from another hilltop and rush over there. He played with them all that afternoon. The police organised a manhunt before darkness fell. While they were co-ordinating the dragnet, Howell rode into camp on a donkey. He wasn't wearing shoes, as usual, and was dressed in peasant clothes, which was unusual. (He normally wore a three-piece suit.) The police didn't recognise him when he joined the manhunt for himself.

Howell was eventually found out and arrested, however, along with 70 Howellites, charged with having committed acts of violence and cultivating a dangerous drug. After a trial, Howell and 28 others were sentenced to two years in prison.

A 1941 court deposition quotes Howell as saying, "I will beat you [the Jamaican government] and let you know to pay no taxes. I am Haile Selassie. Neither you nor the government have any lands here." He was released from prison in 1943 and returned to Pinnacle.

"Mr Howell believed in keeping our money to help ourselves and told others to do the same," confirmed Arnold. "The police would come all the time, like it was a duty. They'd come check about every six months. They never liked to leave him. I don't know why. When I was a boy, the herb was product that brought us money to send the kids to school. When the police burn the herb, we had no money to go to school, so we didn't get much education. That makes us poor now. As a grown man, I took some night school in Spanish Town but that didn't go too long. My mother died, and I had to work. I always worked, ever since I was a boy.

"We sold the herb mostly to people from Kingston. Bluefeather would ride his bicycle up from town and buy four or five bags, then ride all the way back. Gilley would buy, and some East Indians headed by

Coolie Man. Once they came up in their truck and loaded it, but it broke down so they made us unload the truck and haul all the weed back."

Howell was wealthy and owned a Mercedes. He made other people wealthy by supplying them with ganja. He was an important political force, in that he controlled a voting block, although he had no personal political ambitions. Howell also had many friends in high places, both politically and in business. When Garvey returned to Jamaica, he visited Howell at his house.

"I think the police were suspicious because we didn't link to the outside – that is, with their government," Arnold continued. "We were making something outside that system. We were being successful. They said that Mr Howell couldn't make his government amongst their government. I think that was behind all this. Of course, Mr Howell got upset about this constant harassment. We had a good foundation that got mashed up. We had a fullness I didn't realise until I was a grown man."

On 22 May 1954, the police pulled their largest and most destructive raid on Pinnacle. According to a report entitled "Operation Pinnacle", written by the officer in charge, Superintendent CA Mahon, the raid was strictly a drug bust on a "cult known locally as 'Ras Tafari', a cult in itself almost as anti-social as ganja". The raiding force consisted of 116 men, five officers, and five detectives acting as forward scouts to identify wanted criminals.

At 4:15am, the police launched a two-pronged attack on Pinnacle, one group coming up the main road and the other a circuitous route around the hill. The first person arrested by the detectives was a woman on her way to the Spanish Town morning market with a bundle of marijuana in her basket. A man tending his ganja patch and carrying two loaded revolvers was the second arrest.

When the police arrived at the top of the track, they saw 150 huts in the valley below. It was 4:40am. Using a "radio loudhailer...sufficient to awaken the dead", according to Superintendent Mahon, the police roused the villagers, who offered no resistance. In all, 138 men, women and juveniles were arrested. After a hard day spent pulling up marijuana plants and burning them, Superintendent Mahon estimated that, "we had seized no less than three tons", and by his rough count they had uprooted 180,000 marijuana plants. The police worked for another five days, eight hours a day, to destroy another 929,380 ganja plants and 197 nurseries and seedbeds. Of those arrested, 110 were convicted and sentenced to prison terms ranging from nine months to two years of hard labour, including Howell.

Pinnacle was all but destroyed. Some of the Rastas moved into the slums of Western Kingston, primarily Back-O-Wall and Trench Town. Howell made a living running a bakery in Kingston and published a paper, *The People's Voice*, as he attempted to pick up the pieces of his movement. By 1958, he was no longer a player. In 1960, he was committed to Bellevue mental asylum in Kingston. When he was released, he set up office as a healer on East Queen Street, across from the police station. Howell had practised healing arts from the first days of his mission in St Thomas' parish.

"Most of us stayed right around here," Arnold said, recounting the days after the raid. "I lived in Water Loo for three years directly after leaving Pinnacle. Mr Howell lived around here, and then went to Kingston, but after a few years he moved back to Simon Road, at the bottom of Pinnacle. He built a house there and a small church, so people, Rastas, came to live around him. This upset some of the local people. They would rob our people of their goats and money. They tried to kill Mr Howell. One night, men attacked him with knives. I remember the big gash on his hand, and here," says Arnold, pulling back the corner of his mouth to show how a knife went into his father's mouth, "and here," he says, making slashing motions around his neck. "Mr Howell fought those men and they didn't kill him."

There is more to the story. As Helene Lee discovered while she was researching her book on him, although the Rastas were aligned with the JLP (Jamaican Labour Party), Howell was more of a PNP (People's National Party) person at heart. In 1954, the JLP was on the brink of losing a national election. "Perhaps the JLP had a hand in the ganja trade and was using drug money in their politics," she speculates. "Perhaps the PNP decided to put a stop to it before the election. Perhaps the JLP saw the handwriting on the wall and turned Howell out themselves."

There is another political aspect to the 1954 raid on Pinnacle. The police were in the JLP camp and the army were in the PNP camp. The police in Spanish Town – the closest precinct to Pinnacle and friendly to the Howellites – were not included in the raid. Instead, Kingston police conducted the raid, with some assistance from the army in communications.

When Howell moved to Kingston, JLP thugs targeted him as a traitor. Their threats and harassment finally drove him from Kingston and into hiding at the isolated house on Simon Road, where the JLP thugs found him. They tried to cut out his tongue, which is how he received cuts in the cheek and around his neck. His hand was wounded when he grabbed the knife to save his tongue.

As we walked back down Pinnacle Hill, Arnold said, "About nine months after the attack, I heard on the radio, while I was caddying at the golf course, that Mr Howell had died. That was in 1987. He was living at the Sheraton Hotel in Kingston at the time. Pinnacle was captured from us unjustly. All of Mr Howell's kids are living, but we don't have an acre of our own. I don't even own my own house. I'm not educated. I don't know how to go about writing the letter to the government. I've heard that the Jamaican Boy Scouts own the land. I don't know what to do. Do you have any ideas how to help us?"

From 1936 to 1946, Albert Chang held the title to the land. Chang was a wealthy businessman and head of the Chamber Of Commerce. He was also the vice chairman of the Jamaican Boy Scouts. In 1940, he agreed to sell Pinnacle to Howell for £1,200 sterling. Howell paid only £800, which may be why he never got the title. When Chang died, he passed on the property in his will to another businessman, an Indian by the name of Edward Rasheed Hanna, owner of Hanna Enterprises and also a vice chairman of the Boy Scouts.

According to an article in the Kingston newspaper *The Star* on 24 August 1954, the ganja trade was organised and financed by gangs with links to respectable people. The police knew their names but could never get enough evidence to make arrests because the suspects were always tipped off in advance. Perhaps Chang and Hanna were using the Boy Scouts as a front to hide their involvement with the ganja trade at Pinnacle.

In 1957, Pinnacle was sold to Joseph Watt, a Scotsman and real estate developer who owned a great deal of land around Kingston and who was determined to rid the place of all Rastas. In 1958, under his direction and with assistance from the police, the remaining buildings were burned down. The people who lived there had no choice but to leave, although a few Rastas farmed there until 1981.

Several days after my visit to Pinnacle, I had breakfast with Helene Lee, who was in Kingston to conduct further research. "Why the raid in 1954? I don't think we'll ever know the real story," she said. "There is a lot of mystery around Howell."

Perhaps Howell got caught in a political trap. In 1953, Winston Churchill, then England's prime minister, told the two most powerful politicians in Jamaica, the cousins Norman Manley (head of the JLP) and Alexander Bustamante (leader of the PNP, who became Jamaica's first prime minister), that certain conditions had to be met before Jamaica would be granted independence. Curtailing the ganja trade was one of those conditions. Howell was by far the largest and best-organised cultivator of marijuana on the island.

The provenance of the Rasta's outlaw mindset lies in the history of Pinnacle. Rastas were, and continue to be, persecuted for their beliefs and their appearance, although things have now improved. They were denied employment and their children barred from school. Rastas were physically assaulted, jailed and murdered. They saw themselves as separate from Jamaica, a Lost Tribe in the wilderness, who nevertheless did not forsake the basic foundations of their faith – love, unity, and oneness. They regarded themselves, as they do now, as the saviours not only of Jamaica but also of the world. Reggae was the vehicle that would carry their message. The lyrics were written at Pinnacle 30 years before Bob Marley, Peter Tosh, Jimmy Cliff or Toots And The Maytals sang the words.

3 Kingston

Back in Kingston, Jah Earl and I drove down to the William Grant Park, once the site of a British colonial army garrison, parade ground, barracks, headquarters…and gallows for public hangings. Today, it's the bustling heart of Old Kingston, the city centre before sleek, sterile New Kingston sprang up three miles inland, on the site of the old Knutsford racing track and wild bush. According to Rasta cosmology, 72 Rastas – the number of representatives of nations who attended Emperor Haile Selassie's coronation – settled in this part of Kingston after they left Pinnacle.

A block from the square, at 76 King Street, Marcus Garvey established his headquarters for the UNIA (United Negro Improvement Association). The two-storey building, secure behind an iron gate and set back from the street, was being restored with a coat of beige paint when I visited it. The stair's balustrades were painted alternately red, gold, black and green, the colours of Garvey's flag.

Jah Earl let me out in front of the sky-blue, early Art Deco Ward Theater, while he went off in search of a parking place. The theatre was once modern, progressively chic and yet insistent on its wedding-cake decorations. In front of the theatre, the square teemed with people hurrying purposefully; people standing still with no purpose; a constant crowd streaming from the city bus stand of gleaming new, white Mercedes buses, none yet dented or defaced; and mothers towing tots, who were wearing bright yellow-and-red football shirts. One side of the square was curtained by rows of trousers and shirts suspended across the front of roadside stalls, a mummer's pantomime of invisible people hanging in mid-air. Piles of cooking pots, shoes, boxes of detergent and miscellaneous household goods spilled from shop doorways and across the sidewalks. The place reminded me of a DJ hip-hop song, jumpy and jagged, with a steady bottom beat to stop the randomness from overwhelming the fleeting perception of order. The whole square was one big clash, but a harmonic clash at that.

A fellow lounging against the theatre's wall spotted me before I picked up on him, and the sight of this North American pigeon braced him like a pointer on set. He was beside me quiet as a shadow. "Yo, mon, your hat's goin' someplace."

I didn't acknowledge him, didn't glance sideways, didn't slow my step. To stand and chat, like a nice liberal tourist, would invite a plucking.

"That's a Miami hat?" His voice came from his hips, a loose rhythm that pushed seduction, a dance-floor glide to get his partner going backwards. My hat was a black-and-white straw swirl I'd bought specifically for stylin'. Having a style is important where an attitude has currency, especially when there's not much currency in your pocket. An attitude is a safety shield, but you have to strut with your shoulders at just the right angle, with your hands loose but ready, and with enough slowness in your walk to show confidence that you're where you belong. You want everyone to know that you don't feel rushed to get out of their territory. And your eyes, they're the most telling. You have to not look at someone. Like they're not there, not important enough to be up on your radar. And when you do look at them, give them a hard, straight shot through the iris right into the back of the brain, where primordial instincts still linger, so that they feel the ancient fear of a weak prey caught in the stare of a big, hungry T Rex hoodlum.

"You wan ta buy somethin' from me?" I kept my brush-off attitude going, but I knew that deterring this fellow would be as successful as lighting a match in a hurricane. "Maybe I can show you somethin'?" He dipped his head toward me and leaned a shoulder in, an intimate gesture meant to invite. "You wanna smoke?"

"No, man. I want you to stop treating me like a fool." I kept my face straight ahead, talking to the air in front of me.

"A fool. I don't know you're a fool. I don't know you so I don't know you're a fool. I do know you are foolish."

That put a hitch in my step. Foolish about what?

Tivoli Gardens, Trench Town's brethren in arms, borders the South Parade side of the square. When the Rastas moved into this part of town, Tivoli was called Back-O-Wall, a shanty town of plank houses walled off by rusted and torn zinc fences. It was also the town dump. Only the residents could successfully decipher the maze of dirt lanes that connected the warren. This physical barrier, and its well-deserved reputation as a killer neighbourhood, insulated the community. Country practices that dated back to slavery, especially drumming, continued without outside contamination. Its isolation and its outcast status reinforced the Rastas' garrison mentality of always holding off the enemy. If "the others" wandered into Back-O-Wall, they were fair game, which is generally how the people of Tivoli regard strangers today.

I dawdled to let Jah Earl find me, stopping before the higglers sitting on low stools, taking my time to examine their mangos and oranges, neat pyramids of Colgate and Pepsodent boxes, mirrors, combs, cheap plastic trinkets, colourful barrettes, socks, nail clippers and piles of Chinese plastic shoes. The doughty women didn't call out their goods like carnival barkers. If you wanted something, they'd help you make the best selection. I stopped at the mango pile of a large woman wearing a white baseball cap with "Penn State" above the bill. I hoped that the fool-calling man would move on.

"How many mangos do you want?" the higgler asked. "These are three for $100." She pointed to the smaller mangos. "Or these bigger ones, three for $140. Or you can have these sweet-tasting East Indian ones, three for $170. They're the sweetest." She didn't say it as if she was trying to sell me but rather just to be helpful in a neighbourly way.

$100 Jamaican equals a little over $2 US. My dope dealer stayed at my elbow, as if interested in how the deal might turn out.

"I want ripe ones," I said, reaching for an Indian mango, a sleek torpedo of waxy orange fading to pale yellow, blending into green at the blunt end. The higgler started to feel her mangos, searching for the best. I sneaked a glance for Jah Earl. The higgler put her selection in a plastic bag and I handed her the money.

My self-appointed friend glided with me as I moved off. "Where you goin', mon? You should have a guide to keep you safe."

"I'm fine, man, really I am. Thanks for your concern."

"I need some of your concern, ghostly mon. Things are hungry down here. Things have to live." His shoulder nudged mine, a light brush, like a lead-in to a major chord. I glanced around for Jah Earl.

There are two things that Jamaicans dislike in a person, impatience and cowering behaviour, so I paraded my all-pro, eye-gouging, tongue-biting, ball-busting, giant badass attitude. "Why are you fouling my day?" I demanded up close and personal in his face. "I'm here to take a walk, enjoy the place," I said, making a short, jabbing gesture towards William Grant Park across the street, "and you're trying to shake me down. You're a bee buzzing me, not even giving me the peace of day, and that's free. You won't even give me something that's free." I leaned into him, the way Arabs do when they talk, nearly whispering in each other's ears, cheeks and chests almost touching. This can be very intimidating if you speak with the sound of a closed but spring-loaded switchblade.

He didn't give an inch. "You stinky, belly-swelling bloodclot." His words came hard and loud. "You come down here when this is no place for you. You deserve...you deserve to be shaken, see what comes loose. What bounces from your pocket belongs to us because this our place."

In that moment, I woke up to a Jamaica I hadn't truly recognised. I had always indulged in the image of Jamaica as an island of easy-going people, the land of the "no problem" smile. I preferred the tourist bureau's propaganda of the Jamaica of white beaches and tropical idyll. But the vehemence in the man's voice shook me awake to the reality of Jamaica's dark shadow. The island's people are, in general, pissed off at the bitter legacy of injustice that the former colonial masters left them. They are angry at foreigners, at each other and at the country's increasingly desperate economy. In 2001, the murder rate in Jamaica rose by 30 per cent – 1,100 deaths occurred as drug gangs, political thugs, common criminals and ordinary men and women shot each other, hacked each other with machetes and beat each other to death.

"You own this place?" Jah Earl materialised at my elbow.

The fellow didn't miss a beat. "Ya, you better believe it."

"Then you go to that place you own because you don't own the space I'm in, and I'm here." Jah Earl's voice didn't rise above his normal soft drawl. "And my bredren Stephen is here and you don't own his space. So go find that space you own. Come, Stephen, you want to go into the park?" He deftly steered me away from the puffed-up man.

In that moment, I woke up to the reality of the Jamaicans' capacity for gentle strength, their innate compassion for their fellow Jamaicans' pain, their natural sunny disposition that the dark side cannot extinguish. Time after time, during my stay in Jamaica, the people gifted me with kindness, good humour, patience and an abiding faith in goodness.

Actually, I wanted to go into the Jubilee Market, three blocks of street stalls that stretches from the edge of the square along West Orange Street into Tivoli, and to find Eddie Seaga's new One Loaf Studio, buried somewhere in Tivoli. Seaga was once Jamaica's leading authority on folk music and a record producer, before he became a JLP politician and served as prime minister. Now that the rival PNP is in power, Seaga is the leader of the opposition party. Many blame Seaga and his then-opponent, Michael Manley, for importing guns to contest their electoral battles in the late '60s. That time marked the beginning of "garrison politics" and the gun culture that bedevils Jamaica today. Shoot 'em and leave 'em is the national motto.

Seaga created Tivoli Garden in the early '50s, when he was appointed to the government. The area was given to him as his constituency so he wouldn't have a power base of voters. A hardcore and ambitious man, Seaga hit upon an urban renewal scheme to create his power base. He bulldozed Back-O-Wall, over the dismay and vigorous protests of the shantytown dwellers, who had no other homes. Then he built the two- and three-storey tenements all in a row that is Tivoli today. In doing to, he destroyed the yard culture.

Kingston's yards date from the 1770 law that stipulated that, if four slave huts were on the same piece of urban land, they had to be enclosed by a wall at least seven feet high. There could be only one means of entry into the yard. It was an architecture of fear and control. However, the yards evolved into an important social institution. A man's yard was his castle. It was where he took care of his family, including his grandmother, his auntie, and his cousin's family if necessary, along with the neighbours. The poor had no one to rely on but each other.

Seaga destroyed this yard culture and created a slum culture when he re-created Tivoli in 1951, with semi-detached and terrace-type single-room buildings. The government yards of Trench Town in Marley's song were created a decade later. The original government yards were built in the wake of the hurricanes of 1944 to replace the destroyed dwellings with good intentions.

"It's better that we stay on the North Parade side," Jah Earl said as we crossed the street to the island park in the centre of the square. "You go into Tivoli and maybe someone will want to rob. There is much poverty and desperation in there. You're my white bredren. I have a responsibility to see you are safe."

The park felt like a zoo behind the enclosing spiked iron fence. The park was mostly paved with a few patches of grass, as straggly as the fur of a mangy dog. An enormously ugly dead fountain, a monument to Victorian bad taste, occupied centre stage. People skirted the foundation as if it was a garishly painted dowager who didn't have the common decency to die. On the periphery, photographers lounged with 35mm cameras ready to snap a portrait. Bougainvilleas as big as small trees erupted in white, red and rose blossoms, giving their best to add a touch of beauty. An eight-foot-high block of speakers, set up by The Mighty Rock Man, blasted music. It was Saturday morning, and the park was getting ready for the weekend.

When the Pinnacle Rastas came to this square, they fell in with the Burru people. Burru is a generic term for Gold Coast West African slaves, particularly the Ashanti, who brought to Jamaica the dialogue of Burru drums. In the early '50s, severely depressed areas of Back-O-Wall and West Kingston were the melting pot of indigenous African and Afro-European music, religions, mysticism and cultures. Into this social blender went Burru, Kumina, Myal, Revivalism, Pocomania and the aspirations of the still-emerging Rastafari. Common threads tied all of these groups together: frustration with being social outcasts; a smouldering rage against the establishment that squeezed them to the fringe; limited economical, educational, and political opportunities; and an alive connection to their African heritages through music and beliefs.

The Ashanti used the Burru drums in groups of three, the high-pitched atumpan acting as the free-form lead accompanied to the alto apentemma and the bass petia. They were played in concert with rattles, rhumba boxes, shakers and "saxes" (bottle saxophones with mouths covered by a membrane). Burru songs closely parallel the praise songs of original African tradition, which would expose the good or evil of a person or a village. The songs were about current events, and especially about newsmakers in the community who may have been guilty of some misconduct. This is the traditional role of the African *griot*, the singer, who, like the European troubadours centuries later, travelled from town to town carrying the news. The music heard in Kingston's slums follows in this tradition in that it serves as a daily newspaper, a bulletin board and an early warning system.

Burru drumming was one of the few African-derived musical forms to survive fairly intact into the 20th century in Jamaica. The colonial Jamaican planters allowed Burru drumming as a work metronome to keep a rhythmic cadence for the field slaves. With the demise of slavery, many of the slaves and the drummers headed for the notorious slums of West Kingston in search of jobs.

The former rural slaves didn't have much experience in urban survival, although they did bring the tools of practical skills. The drummers, on the other hand, had very few practical skills. Drumming had been their work. What did they know about growing a garden plot, or searching out firewood for resale, or running a hustle? Scamming on the streets was not their natural occupation, but they, and everyone else in the notorious hardscrabble West Kingston, learned and learned fast to compete with the other squatters, discharged prisoners and hoodlums who had also settled in the yards.

The drummers found a special niche in the community. They

drummed for holiday dances and to welcome discharged prisoners back to the community. There was always a big street party on the night when a prisoner returned. The drumming was for rejoicing and to drive away the evil spirits of those who had locked up the people that were being welcomed back, who were greeted as political prisoners, warriors who had struck out against the colonial system, no matter the nature of the crime.

The Rastas and the Burrus became allies. They shared an ideology, common goals and a passion for Africa. Both were anti-establishment. They believed in self-reliance. The Burrus' African-rooted drumming appealed to the Rastas, and the Rastas' communal lifestyle appealed to the Burrus, who had more or less lived that way since slavery. Burru drumming gradually became part of the Rasta ceremonies, especially by the locksmen. Those same drumming patterns can be heard in today's reggae. Lee "Scratch" Perry's tracks 'Cool And Easy' and 'Well Dread', on his album *Africa's Blood*, are one example.

The newly arrived Rastas did whatever they could to make a living, selling ganja, cutting and selling firewood, becoming vendors at fruit and fish stalls – skuffling along, basically, and often on the wrong side of the law. The Rastas earned a widespread disreputable reputation as criminals, thugs, drug dealers and, in general, lowlifes. This was not entirely fair to the many craftspeople and law-abiding bredren who struggled to survive the ghetto's severe poverty.

The Rastas were understandably hostile to the system that made them outcasts. Some took to preaching on the streets, calling down fire and brimstone on the oppressive system. The Rastas' dreadlocks, profane language, wild behaviour and rebellious message shocked the conservative establishment and the aspiring middle class. They were branded as boogiemen, living symbols of the devil. Parents threatened ill-behaved children that, if they didn't behave, the awful "black-hearted mon" Rasta would snatch them away.

The Rastaman – displaced once again, cast out as a black pariah once again, vilified once again, treated as a cur once again, made captive by an exploitative economic system once again – became a potential redemptive figure. In the zealot Rasta's mind, the awakening to his true role – that of saviour – mirrored the suffering and striving for deliverance that is the journey of all men's souls. It is the mystic journey from the bosom of the divine to the suffering of the mortal, who, through faith and moral living, returns to Jah. Keenly aware of their self-appointed function as pathfinders for others, the Rastas preached their spiritual vision.

Their first commandment was that the black man must struggle to remain faithful to Africa, his earthly home. They had an off-beat, Old Testament flair, with their long matted dreadlocks swirling about their heads as they shouted out passages from the Bible. Their voices hot with the flame of righteousness, they called down destruction on the Babylon around them, which is on everyone else. They were weird. Outside the box. Over the top. A disquieting and threatening presence among people still caught up in the colonial pattern that might lead to bourgeois respectability. They were madmen, and the aspiring middle classes didn't want to hear their madness, didn't want to witness it, didn't want to be baited by it. They were crazy boogiemen. Out of their foxy insanity emerged classical reggae, an art form that has steadily marched around the world as a flag bearer confronting injustice and oppression.

The Rastas' fervour and their musical memory leapt beyond the Christian images of Baptist hymns, known as *skanties*, which Howell used to accompany his preaching. There was nothing about Africa in those white-European pieties of a colonial God. The Rastas heard in the rhythms of Nyabinghi, Pocomania, Myal, Kumina, Burru – all African in origin – a beat syncopated to rhythms that their own hearts knew. The Rastas found in those chants and drums patterns from a musical idiom that aroused a visceral memory of ancestral heritage and culture.

I wanted to go to the cliff where that echo was once again given a living voice. "I want to go to Trench Town," I told Jah Earl. "I want to see where Marley and Tosh and Cliff and Livingston and Booth started."

Jah Earl clearly did not relish the idea. Taxi drivers avoid the area in fear of being robbed, just like taxi drivers avoid certain areas of Washington, DC, or New York City. "I should check some bredren to see what's happenin', ya know?"

"Let's cruise the edge to get a feel for it," I urged.

"You want to do that, mon?"

"Yeah. I want to see where Marley lived."

"Maybe we have some cold jelly," Jah Earl countered. Cold jelly is a chilled coconut. The jellyman trims the sides of the coconut shell with a machete and, if he's good, opens a small hole in the top. A too-large hole allows the coconut milk inside to spill out. Coconut milk is much more refreshing and healthy than sugar-laden soft drinks. When you're through drinking, the jellyman hacks a "spoon" from the hard shell and splits the cast open. You use the bit of shell to scoop out the soft membrane of coconut meat. Some people prefer a hot jelly, unchilled, claiming that it tastes more natural.

We had two cold jellies at a street vendor's stand. "You want to go do that, mon?" Jah Earl asked.

"Just check it out."

"If it's cool, I'll drop you off and come back. They won't bother a white man so much as a taxi man. All right, Stephen? I'll drop you off if it looks cool."

4 Trench Town

As we drove down Maxfield Avenue, a major street bisecting Trench Town, Jah Earl carefully scanned the neighbourhoods to read the vibes. We passed through Upper Trench Town, the Jungle, which is the better part of town, then down to Lower Trench Town, Rema, the pit where music brewed. A good number of people were walking around, and cars were on the street. The residents apparently weren't afraid to be in the open. "It's cool right now," Jah Earl said. "It could flare up without warning, but now it's okay."

Jah Earl had lived in Trench Town with his wife and two kids in the early '60s. That was before Trench Town earned its Billy-The-Kid-from-Chicago reputation, a place where gunmen and politicians were equally deadly.

"Back then, it was okay," Jah Earl said, reading the street for signs of trouble. "It wasn't like a ghetto, a slum ghetto people associate with Trench Town now. There were only a few roads for cars, no big streets, just enough room for a couple of bcars to squeeze past. And the rest were lanes, some only wide enough for a bicycle. The houses were wood and plaster with zinc fencing in front. It could look a bit shabby, but it was an okay place to live. You understand? You didn't worry about yourself or people stealing from you. In the mornings, the milkman came around and left your bottle of milk and loaf of bread on the post outside your house. Nobody steals it. People were neighbourly. It wasn't until about 1967 or '68 that things began to change to make it dangerous. That's when the political parties, the Jamaican Labour Party and the People's National Party, came in and put guns in the hands of their supporters. Then the violence started, and more crime, so today you have to watch yourself in Trench Town. Now I don't stop the car in Trench Town unless I see a bredren and he can tell me how things are. Sometimes these young toughs will chase after a car to rob it. You understand?

"Anyway, back then Rita Anderson lived down the block from me. She and my wife were like sisters. Rita was always over. She was singing in the group The Soulettes and starting to do some recording. She met Bob at a studio, and we know the rest. So Bob started coming to hang out because of Rita. Other musicians came around, like Toots Hibbert and Bunny Wailer and Chinna Smith [Bob Marley's lead guitar player, who now plays the same role for Ziggy Marley]. Peter Tosh and Ken Booth and The Heptones all came from the neighbour[hood]. I liked to play the guitar and sing then, nothing professional. Jerry Hinds, the guitar player for The Skatalites, taught me to play. All those musicians, they came over and we sat around playing and smoking a spliff. Ya, mon, back then none of them were thinking about being famous. They just loved music.

"Bob was over at my house the night before he left to spend time with his mother in the United States. We passed the chalice and sipped and passed it back. I don't do the chalice any more. It's too strong that way. Set you right out. Have to give the man some sugared lemonade to bring him around. I just smoke the spliffs now."

We pulled up in front of the Trench Town Culture Center at 6-10 First Street, the first fledging step to turn the Marley/Tosh/Bunny Wailer neighbourhood into a tourist attraction.

"I'll come back in an hour, okay, Stephen? I don't like to hang out here." I didn't blame Jah Earl. The taxi was his livelihood. To lose it to a gang of thugs would be to risk his family's wellbeing.

I stepped through the centre's gate. To the left was a office that used to be a house and a garden of eclectic sculptures meant to express intuitive knowing. To the right was another small house, originally the culture yard of Vincent "Tata" Ford. Tata was Marley's original mentor and the co-writer of 'No Woman, No Cry', for which he holds the copyright. Tata, much revered as a teacher of folk wisdom and the fountainhead of reggae, still lives in the area. He is a double amputee, and can occasionally be seen in front of his house sitting in his wheelchair with his dreads under a large colourful tam and nursing a Guinness.

A gap between the two houses led to a dirt yard the size of a short basketball court. The original five attached single rooms, typical of the homes still found in Trench Town, lined up on each side of the yard. The residents had voluntarily moved into other housing when the community wanted to develop the site as a cultural and tourist attraction. At the end of the yard were two blockhouses with five doors, each opening to the kitchen assigned to a house. Tata's kitchen was the third door on the left. Young Marley had often slept there when he was left in the care of Bunny Livingston, his cousin's father. The uncle and nephew didn't get along. Beyond the kitchen blocks was a rectangular dirt yard with a cement back wall bearing large painted portraits of Bob Marley, Peter Tosh and Bunny Livingston.

Lloyd "Bread" McDonald and Winston "Pipe" Matthews, who made up the duo The Wailing Souls, grew up in the same yard as Marley's sleeping kitchen. (The Wailing Souls have received two Grammy nominations in the Best Reggae category, in 1992 for *All Over The World* and in 1998 for *Psychedelic Soul*. When I was there, a new album, *Equality*, was scheduled for release in June 2000.) Marley's home, where he lived with his mother, was on Second Street, a minute's walk away. Peter Tosh and Bunny Livingston, meanwhile, lived on Fifth Street. Ken Booth, Alton Ellis and Jimmy Cliff were neighbourhood boys. Bread and Pipe played football and cricket with Marley and Tosh and Livingston in the park across the street from their house. When dark came, they'd all congregate in the yards to sing together, the younger kids learning from the older and the older ones learning from those who were already recording. Marley, Tosh and Livington, who were a few years older than Bread and Pipe, had not yet recorded.

The kitchens were a favourite rehearsal space. Six or maybe eight boys would crowd into the eight-by-ten-feet cement cubes to harmonise, the sound reflecting from the hard surfaces. The people didn't much use the kitchens for cooking, preferring instead the relative coolness of the open verandas. The kitchens were always there for the singers. The boys would gather in any tenement yard, and nobody would tell them to go back to their own yards. Everywhere was home.

Bread now lives in the United States. When I spoke with him, he vividly recalled his old neighbourhood.

"Trench Town was the birthplace of reggae, this ghetto right in the heart of Kingston," he said. "Growing up in a place like that, you're exposed to nearly everything good and also everything bad. Quite early, you have to make a decision on where you're going to go, whether you're going with the bad guys or with the good guys, you know what I mean? That basically determines your future. Music and sports were the two ways out of the ghetto.

"Joe Higgs, one the great singers, lived in Trench Town. [Higgs died in 1999.] A lot of the great singers – like Bunny and Scully and Alton Ellis, all of those great Jamaican singers – lived in Trench Town. Singing was something that everyone just did. It was a lot of pleasure. One of those professional singers would always be around when us youth were singing in the kitchens. They would always be singing, and we, the youth, would be singing harmonies, joining in with them.

"Out of that, Bob and Peter and Bunny founded their own group, with Joe Higgs. That was The Wailers, and they started recording. Higgs was living, like, next door to us. After Bob and those guys would rehearse and leave, we – myself and Pipe and others – we would then take over the camp. We were just comin' up, learning to play the guitar and singing. Five, six, seven of us always around. Eventually, we got so good that, when Bob and them guys leave and we were singing, people would come around thinking it was still Bob and them there singing. 'Boy, you guys getting good. We thought it was still Bob and them guys. Time for you guys to start recording now.'

"Ken Booth, Jimmy Cliff and other elders who were out there recording heard us singing. They'd say, 'Man, you guys need to start recording, man.' We started recording when we were still in high school, about 1965-66.

"At that time we were called The Renegades, myself and Pipe and

George, who later on become a Wailing Soul. We went to a studio called Federal Recording. That's where Tuff Gong is now. We did four or five records as The Renegades and did background singing at that time for other established artists. After that, we recorded with Matador, one of the early Jamaican producers. That's when we became The Wailing Souls. But we always had the name Wailing Souls in our minds, me especially. The Wailers were there, right out of our neighbourhood. The Soulettes, with Rita Marley, was there. So we say, 'Wailers, Soulettes, Wailing Souls.'

"When I was growing up, the music they were playing at the time was what they call *mento* – Caribbean music, like calypso and *soca* – along with the American music of the day – R&B, soul, the black music. That was the music of my father and my mother. When I really first heard our own authentic Jamaican music, which then was ska, the first time I heard that type music I couldn't get enough of it. I was a little boy then. I was too young even to go to the dances. Prince Buster, Skatalites, Sir Coxsone, they were the main guys out there, with the sound systems. In Trench Town, we could hear all the music. The guys who were recording most of the music, they come from Trench Town.

"In Trench Town, you had a lot of spirituality. You have the Pocomania. You have the traditional religions, like the Catholics and stuff like that. Then you have the Rastaman, who at that time chant his drums and quote scripts from the Bible. Every word out of their mouth was from the Bible. They speak of love and truth and right. The music evolved out of that. Out of the drums and singing. You could hear the African influence in the rhythms and know it was coming from Africa. Lyrics singing up things in the Bible, speaking of things that happened in the past and is to come in the future.

"There is a spiritual element you can't ever leave out of Jamaican music. The music was built from that spirituality. All that is coming from the Rastaman, the early music. Most of the singers in those days used to go to the meetings of the Rastaman, listen to the Rastaman teachings anyway they can find it and listen. And then that manifests whenever they sing.

"Mortimo Planno played a role in that. In Trench Town, Mortimo

Planno was revered in that he is a very spiritual man. An elder who went to Ethiopia. A man who always stood up for truth and right. He went to jail and got beat up and all sorts of things for his beliefs. Growing up in Trench Town, we looked up to Mortimo Planno. I love Mortimo Planno. He used to live on Fifth Street in Trench Town.

"There were always some Rasta elders there also. The elders would tell us to check out the Bible, to start reading scripts from the Bible, think about humanity and human rights. Then the singing would start. We'd sing for hours, man, hours.

"I definitely think of myself, and other Jamaican musicians, as warriors. We're soldiers, even now. You have a work to do, so you keep soldiering on. This is a music that lacks a lot of support from the structure that controls music, I'd say like marketing – you'll notice that reggae doesn't have big multinational record companies promoting it. Every now and then a reggae artist will get a little break with a record company. Basically, it's just Jah and the love of the music and the people out there that keeps reggae going. The music can only get bigger 'cause the people love this music so much and support this music so much. You have to search the radio dial to find reggae, and people keep finding us.

"We need to get this music to the widest possible audience we can. It takes marketing to do that. This is a business world. You have to go through the system. As long as we're not tying up or compromising our creative ability, you know what I mean? We need to put our foot more in the door to push it open.

"The spiritual message of reggae is still there, even in the DJ music. Not all of the DJs have that sensibility, but fortunately I can see nowadays that more and more DJ dancehall are looking inside themselves to discover that music is a thing here for the enjoyment of the people and for the education of people. A lot of kids listen to the songs and go out there and do whatever the songs say to do, so you have to be very careful what you write and sing. Society on a whole nowadays is more readily willing to hear a lot of filth than the real deal. The filth occupies your mind with filth. You don't look at the real picture.

"The music still deals with the oppression and suffering. I don't think it will change, man. Oppression is still here. The music can change the politics. The music makes people more aware of what is going on outside. The music works on the soul. The Jamaican people are a peaceful people, a religious people. We're not prone to go out there and be too militant physically."

In Kingston, I tracked down Ken Booth and asked him about those early days in Trench Town.

"There was much more sense of a community back in the '60s," Booth recalled. "There is not much of that now. There is music coming out of the ghettos now, but what kind of music? You see the kind of environment around them, this generation. They see violence, all kinds of negative things, so that is portrayed even in the music. I remember, when I was growing up, I was seeing love, so we sing about love.

"Rasta music was there before ska or rock steady or reggae. The Rastaman was singing songs that were revolutionary to the system that's not right. I've been singing these kinds of songs ever since 'Freedom Street'. 'Let's not quarrel/let's not fight/let's together, we all can unite/and take these chains off our feet/because we have to walk/we've go to walk on Freedom Street.'

"Rasta music was there from a long time. We get the Rasta fate because, that period we were growing up, we realised that the music was the key to being positive and knowing that you are in the arms of God, you understand? It was not materialistic.

"I start listening to Mortimo Planno when I was little, and at that time to Mother Doury, a big woman with dreadlocks so thick. She used to wash Planno's clothes, you know. This woman, she cooks for every bad man, he who go to prison and come out, she wash them clothes and cook for them if they have no money. She was blessed. She was the one who take care of Planno.

"Planno showed that there was a very important part for music to play as the message for the people, to uplift people. Not just singing alone about loving a girl. There are problems out there to sing about. Planno was the motivator for that. He motivated Bob Marley. He was the man that motivated us to tell the world the truth. Planno was the man for that. Another was Sam Brown. He just die here. He was a Rastaman and a teacher like Planno. A certain amount of us musicians go through these people's hands, you know, and get a certain motivation and teaching so we can take the right road, so we think about what we're doing.

"Planno recognised the music as a way to spread the word of the Almighty. That comes from Planno. All of Bob's inspiration come out of that, and Joe Higgs. I won't say that Joe Higgs taught Bob how to sing, but Joe Higgs lined him up. He groomed him and he groomed me, too. He groomed a lot of us. He was a great guy for us. He taught guitar and singing and the words to use, the message. Jamaicans don't talk about these things, about who do what to motivate them, but Joe Higgs, Sir Coxsone, Alton Ellis – they did a lot for us. Joe Higgs was a good man to us. I used to stop by and listen to them and learn. I loved singing, and I listened to them how to do harmony.

"And there were others, like the ice-cream man named Tattoo. Tattoo had a cream shack. We come up to the cream shack, and Tattoo, he wanted to hear us sing. Then, us boys in Trench Town didn't have any money. Tattoo said who sings the best gets a cream. He gave me two creams. He was a motivator."

At the Trench Town community centre, I met Magnus Steen. He was sweeping a room being converted into a restaurant as part of the yard's transformation into a tourist magnet. He had been born in that room. Winston "Pipe" Matthews of The Wailing Souls was born in the room next door, and the two grew up together.

"Yeah, I was here when Bob first came into the yard," Magnus said. "Pipe and I were little kids. We'd sit here on the step and listen to Tata and Bob rehearsing over there. I had a sardine-can guitar and an iron pipe I played as a fife. I copy what Bob and Tata were doing. I got good, and Bob would call over encouragement. Winston got jealous – he grabbed me iron pipe so he could play. He went around the yard shouting 'iron pipe, me want my pipe'. He said it enough that it became a song in the yard, so I started calling him 'Pipe'.

"When Bob came, we were doing the music here. He joined us. Those days, we loved music. Then we did ska, rock steady, and jazz. Bob said he was going to slow it down. Then he got experimenting and slowed it down to the one-chunk beat. That came right here, because

Bob was experimenting with the slower beat. That sound came from the feel how Bob feel it. That's what we did around this yard, create a sound we could make and the next man make his sound, and we join in the different instruments and sounds, and we find it. Simple.

"Us kids, we followed Bob to wherever he played. If our parents didn't find us in the yard, we'd be spanked. But we didn't care, we loved music so much. Sometimes I'd carry Bob's instruments when The Wailers played at the Queen."

The first gig that Marley, Peter Tosh and Bunny Wailer played was in a talent show at the Queen's Theater, about a mile from where they lived. The theatre is now a ruin, with only the façade still standing.

Delroy Lee, a community activist, joined Magnus and I to make the point that Trench Town wasn't a war zone. "This community has the reputation as a dangerous place, but it's not," he said. "This is a town of peace and war, but we have more peace than war. The people who cause the war are just a dot, a small, small minority. We don't have the political strife any more. Now gangs are our problem. If a coin drops on this side, the other side wants a share, so they fight over it. It's all about gun control.

"We need jobs. Not just jobs but jobs we can afford to live on. The average weekly pay here is $800 Jamaican [about $16 US]. Our dollar is pegged to the US dollar, so the prices are the same. Jamaica is not some cheap Third World country. You can't live on $800 a week. You have to borrow $500 just to get through, get food, get the kids to school, so you're always borrowing and never catch up. That's why youth today don't want to work. They'd rather sit on the corner firing off a gun and saying you can't pass unless you pay. The gun gives them power."

Delroy offered to guide me to the house where Marley lived with his mother. We walked down a narrow passage between a zinc fence and a building and emerged into the interior of the neighbourhood. The houses were one-storey grey cement boxes with single doors and windows, unadorned by paint or flower boxes. A single iron spigot in the yard provided water for several houses. There wasn't a blade of grass in the ground, which was littered with rusted tin cans, old mattress springs, dog shit, dead branches and rags.

We took a shortcut through the yards to where Marley lived at 19 Second Street. It was one of the few two-storey plaster four-units built in 1938 and still standing. The house was derelict, though, abandoned, its windows covered with sheets of zinc, its unpainted plaster walls peeling and shabby. Marley lived in the upper unit on the left. Nothing indicated that the site was of historical importance, not even a street number.

We exited onto Second Street and walked to the end of the block. At the corner, Delroy pointed to a building on the right. "That's where Marley, Tosh, Bunny and the others practised. Joe Higgs' yard was right over the fence."

The football field where Marley played was catercorner from the building. "I remember Bob playing here," Delroy said. "He was a very good player, very fast and rough. He loved playing the right wing or the forward."

Next to the football field was a bright-yellow building. "We want to put a recording studio in there," Delroy said. "There are so many good singer kids down here with nowhere to put their talent. We don't get any help from the music community. None. Rita Marley doesn't give us a dime. Now she pretends that she doesn't come from Trench Town because she lived in Upper Trench Town, the better section. All this improvement we are doing by ourselves. We are a community, and working as a community. It's safe to come down here. We need to bring cash and jobs here by developing tourism and a grocery store and a place for the kids to work on their music. People come year in and year out to see where Marley and Tosh and Bunny started, and we don't get anything from it but promises and promises, nothing but promises.

"I want you to put this in your book. We need contributions from individuals, corporations, foundations, whoever, to help us build this community. People can send contributions or inquiries to the Trench Town Development Association on 12B Collie Smith Drive. The mailing address is PO Box 118, Kingston 5. Address the letters to Mr Rainford Howell, treasurer. You put that in your book so people can help us."

The government has stated that it will redevelop the neighbourhood to make it a safe tourist attraction. The inhabitants, however, have little faith in the government's word.

Trench Town always has been delusional. At one time it thought of itself as a nice but poor community. Then there was the familial community phase. Then there was the era of Trench Town as a glorified battlefield for corrupt democracy, when politicians' gunmen shot up the meetings of the rival party. Now there is the Home Of Bob, Bunny, And Peter Family Entertainment Center. The residents have plans to spiff up the neighbourhood, but you can't plant colourful flowers and well-clipped grass in Marley's old yard. You can't even paint his old house. You have to leave the shabby disillusionment exactly as it is. This can never be Graceland. Marley's neighbourhood was one of, if not the poorest and most desperate sections of Kingston. Shy people don't live in Trench Town. To make it nice for tourists would be to destroy the fuel that gave Marley and the others their fire.

5 Babylon's Song

For weeks I had been like a bird dog trying to track a covey of quail, sniffing in confused circles to this studio or to that yard for the scent of the new authentic music. The ghettos, I thought. That's where to look, in the anguished heart that always threatens to spasm with rage. The deep bass notes of injustice made these slums a music box, more than the crime and poverty that pulsates in Trench Town and Rae Town and Grant's Pen and Denham and Tivoli.

Those places were breeding grounds for liberation reggae in the late '60s and early '70s. The economic and social conditions of 30 years ago still exist, only doubly bad now. Small money is a nail in the head but, as I discovered, worst is the knife in the heart that's shredding the family of bredren that nurtured the Trench Town boys.

I went to the ghetto yards looking for the kitchen-family atmosphere, a romantic recreation of nouveau Wailers *et al*, some budding group, harmonising righteous truth out of their pain, not only for themselves but for all of the oppressed, all of humanity. I believed that if I looked hard enough, risked my neck enough going into the ghettos where robbery is legitimate employment, if I persisted, I would find the next White Knights Of Reggae.

Yes, I was reassured over and over, the music still comes from the ghetto yards. You just have to know which yard and where to look. Who do I look for? I asked over and over. Don't know, came the reply over and over. I kept poking around the yards, with Jah Earl hanging tight on my shirttail so that I didn't stumble into a dangerous situation.

Then, one day, in a conversation with Homer Harris, I realised that I had been looking in the wrong places. I should be looking in Ethiopia.

To Luciano, Buju Banton, Sizzla and numerous other musicians, Homer Harris is for them what Joe Higgs and Mortimo Planno were to The Wailers. When Harris lived in England as a young man, his pals included Mick Jagger, Keith Richards, Chris Blackwell (founder of Island Records) and other leading lights in the music business. Harris and three other bredren ministered Marley when he came to England to recuperate after being shot in an attack on his studio in Kingston.

In England, Harris worked as an engineer for Saab and as a social worker, which was his main calling. He returned to Jamaica in 1988 to accept a job, which collapsed within a week of his return, so he founded a social centre, where youths, particularly young musicians, could socialise and learn. He put promising individuals through a self-devised 18-month programme designed to educate them in social and spiritual values. He taught them how to read music, the difference between a crotchet and a quaver, how to change the tempo and improvise a "ridim". He taught them how to enunciate Queen's English without losing the uniqueness of their Jamaican talk. Being understood is important if you want to break into the international market, he told his protégés. Most importantly, he schooled them in the spirit of creating conscious music. His centre at 2B Grove Road, in the building previously occupied by Blue Mountain Records, was the incubator for many young reggae performers now making their international mark. His full programme is now no longer in operation, although he still undertakes individual projects.

Harris worked with the third-form schoolboy Mark Anthony Myrie, who came from a middle-class suburb, and turned him into Buju Banton. Luciano, perhaps the most promising leader of this generation of reggae singers, came under Harris' tutelage as a fourth-form schoolboy.

"The family community of the 1970s is gone," Harris said. We were in the simple one-room office of Messenjah Productions, for which Harris is the co-ordinating administrator. When he's in Jamaica, Luciano climbs the 32 steps to this room every day for morning Bible reading and reasoning. "We had a family back then was because Marley, The Heptones, Alton Ellis, all those were singers, not DJs who think they only need themselves and a turntable. The older generation of musicians also has a responsibility for the deterioration of the community. They don't share with the younger musicians their technique and knowledge and spirit, or not as much as they should. The older musicians are not nourishing the young generation. Not that they don't put some time in, but you never hear a young musician say, 'I spent 40 hours or four weeks with Mr So-And-So, and I learned this or that.'"

Harris is a producer who, by choice, has never had his own studio. His most important work is done outside the studio. He spends most of his days walking the streets of Kingston's ghettos, with his eyes and ears open for promising talent that shows the discipline for the hard work required to be successful.

However, ghetto conditions aren't the main force behind the lasting music, he told me. Nor is the next wave of reggae to break out of Jamaica being fuelled by anger over economic injustice (although that is part of the message). Nor will the DJs, who continue on about guns and vanity and lewdness and their own egos, be enduring factors. "Those people and their music will not carry on for very long, because they don't educate. Their music doesn't carry any spiritual message. The Rastafari faith is a key source to the resurgence of the reggae soon to be heard outside of Jamaica. Reggae is an evangelical music. It's a music inspired directly from the King, His Imperial Majesty Haile Selassie. Haile Selassie said that players and singers are his temple. We don't need another Bob Marley to push the next wave of reggae. Bob was a repeater of His Imperial Majesty's message of love and justice. We can't wait for another Bob. We have to go directly to the King, His Imperial Majesty."

Harris is a Rasta of 30 years' standing, although he doesn't wear dreads. On the day that we met, he wore torn clothes, another old-time Rasta signature. Some early Rastas showed their contempt for vanity and materialism by purposefully wearing ragged clothes. Harris wore very clean jeans with shredded holes above both knees. His white shirt was buttoned at the neck. He drew attention to his jeans as a sign that he was "natural", without pretensions, and didn't consider himself better than or above his brothers.

"The record companies in Jamaica – Islands, Anchor, Mixing Lab, Black Scorpio, Penthouse, any of them – are not really doing anything to prompt the conscious music," he said. "The big record companies in the United States try to keep reggae down. They don't put money into it, and few radio stations play the music. They're more into the commercial aspects than educating with positive messages. We are coming to the United States to bash that down with Rastafari."

If that's so, then Rastafari had better start mending its own fence, according to Lincoln "Sugar" Minott, an internationally acclaimed reggae singer for some 30 years and also a producer. During a conversation at his studio on the edge of Trench Town, he told me that, "The Rastafarian movement is misleading the youth right now into believing in false illusions, because the movement has no rules. Rastafarian philosophy, as far as I'm concerned, is built up on the teachings of His Imperial Majesty Emperor Haile Selassie I. That's what I grow up to know. Now, a different thing is starting to happen. Now, Rastafarian doesn't follow nothing of the ways His Majesty said. You don't hear anybody saying what Selassie say or what Selassie preach. No sound. Maybe Mikey General and Luciano. Apart from that, everybody is glorifying them own selves.

"They say music is not religion, first of all. Music is music. If you want to bring religion to your music then that's all right, but in general music is just music. Now, these people are not dealing with music. They're dealing with religion. So let's say that this is a religious movement in the form of musical vibes. So that is a different thing. We have to examine it like that. It's a message they want to sing, so if you're not sending the message of Selassie then you're saying that Selassie is the heart of this thing. It's not going to work. These people are going to burn fire. No man can burn fire but the Almighty.

"There is a new breed of Rasta coming in with their own philosophy. They are working away from the old-time Rasta elders. The youth, they don't deal with the old ancient Rastaman. They don't accept their teachings. The teachings are there from His Majesty and the psalms and the proverbs. We grew up on that, and that was our teacher. Now they're lying about the good things that were said. This new breed of philosophy is almost forcing down the truth, and if you don't agree with it you get kicked or chopped.

"Forget about what colour is God. Go for the things that are good. Don't backbite your brother. Don't stop your brother from eating food. Don't sex your bredren's wife. We can't fight them natural good things. People burn away those things. They say we burn the Bible. Because white man write the Bible, we burn it. So what do you have to offer after you burn the Bible, that we was teaching from for thousands of years? And Selassie, which is the heart of your thing? And you're coming to tell you don't believe in Selassie?

"There are people who see that the dread thing is working, that singing about Jah and Rasta is working. There was a time when, if you had dreads, they lock you up and cut off your dreads with a knife. Now it's a bandwagon. Everybody wanta be dread, wanta be Rasta. It's a trend in the music. But they have to go right back to reggae. Toots And The Maytals, Culture, Burning Spear – that is cultural reggae. That is the reggae I know. I was part of that from the beginning.

"Rasta has to wake up, man. Rasta let down people. Rasta should come forward to the teachings of His Imperial Majesty Emperor Haile Selassie I. You don't fight against colour and race. Rasta still fights against colour and race. His Majesty said the colour of a man's skin and eyes is to be no significance to God. Now Rastas, some Rastas, say we hate white man, we hate Indians. You can't follow that if you want to teach the world love and unity."

Harris and Minott agree that the big record companies are afraid of reggae's core message: fighting against the Babylon system. "If those companies really sincerely got behind reggae music, they'd have to change the way they do business," Harris told me. "They would have to stop their greed and the injustices toward the musicians. They would have to stop sending the negative messages of killing people and mistreating women. Record companies, in Jamaica and everywhere, are the palaces of Babylon."

What is this Babylon that the Rastas and reggae singers groan on and on about? Buju, Michael Rose, Beenie Man, Third World, Lee "Scratch" Perry – all of them take a chop at Babylon. It's almost a cliché, this phrase "chant down Babylon", mouthed by any singer who wants the stamp of "right bredren".

"Chanting down Babylon" is an old Rasta catchword borrowed from Christian scriptures. "Come, we go chant down Babylon one more time," Bob Marley sang in 'Chant Down Babylon' on the *Confrontation Babylon* album. Count Ossie And The Mystic Revelation Of Rastafari sang 'Rasta Man Chant', popularised by The Wailers. Freddie McGregor has his own 'Chant Down Babylon'; Judy Mowatt adapts it as 'Sisters' Chant'; Lincoln "Sugar" Minott urges listeners to 'Chant Them Down'; and Bunny Wailer does his turn in 'Ready When You Ready'. In the song 'Babylon System', on his 1979 *Survival* album, Marley sings, "We've been treading on the/wine press much too long/Rebel/Babylon system is a vampire."

Some history. The 5,000-year-old city of Babylon, now a ruin, is located on the Euphrates River about 55 miles from Baghdad, Iraq, near Al Hillah. The city was one of a number of small city kingdoms of Babylonia dating from the third millennium BC. The Semitic Amorites captured the city at around the turn of the second millennium BC. Under the Amoritic line of kings (*circa* 2050-1750 BC), Babylon became the chief commercial city of the Tigris–Euphrates Valley of Mesopotamia. The city was the capital in the time of Hammurabi, the greatest of the Amoritic kings, who was responsible for the Code Of Hammurabi, the first written codified set of laws. Among other things, the code set out property rights and the logic that justice consists not of giving equal rights to men naturally made unequal but in giving every man his due.

Babylon was destroyed by the Assyrian King Sennacherib in 689 BC, and was later rebuilt. The city attained its greatest glory under Nebuchadnezzar II from 605-562 BC. The Persian king Cyrus The Great captured the city in 538 BC, and in 331 BC the Macedonian king Alexander The Great possessed the city. He died there in 323 BC.

Babylon is mentioned in 18 books of the Bible. In Revelation,

Babylon is portrayed as the final earthly city, a city of magnificence and glory, success, wealth and fame, and its power is matched only by God and the conquering lion of the tribe of Judah. In the Bible, the city epitomises everything that is evil and oppressive in the world. According to the Apocalypse of John, there will be an apocalyptic and dramatic collapse of Babylon, which is a constant theme of Rastafarians.

Babylon is the first city mentioned in Genesis. The city had a bad reputation, at least among Israelites-to-be, even back then. The prophet Jeremiah spoke of God's wrath against Babylon in 51:44: "And I will punish Bel [Ba'al, a fertility god] in Babylon, and I will bring forth out of his mouth that which he hath swallowed up; and the nations shall not flow together any more unto him, yea, the wall of Babylon shall fall." Jeremiah 51:7 describes Babylon's betrayal: "Babylon hath been a golden cup in the Lord's hand, that made all the earth drunken; the nations have drunken of her wine; therefore the nations are mad." The destruction by God's hand (or by shifting tectonic plates) is described in 51:37: "And Babylon shall become heaps, a dwelling place for dragons, an astonishment, and a hissing, without inhabitant."

For Jeremiah's God, the sins of Babylon included the worship of idols (statues of Ba'al in the temples) and licentiousness (phallic public statuary representative of Ba'al, and religious rituals featuring literal sexual union between priests and priestesses and between believers and temple prostitutes). Babylon according to Rastafari represents different sins than those.

Babylon was the first great beachhead of capitalism, and in that was emblematic of the fundamental change that permanently altered societies and cultures. Historically, it marked the shift from an agrarian society to a society of commerce, with all of the attendant re-alignments of values that dominate our way of life today. Since the rise of Babylon, humanistic values have gradually been mutated by the pursuit of profit. That has certainly been a chief complaint of many philosophers, social thinkers, economists, political leaders, poets and songwriters. Their common and justifiable gripe is that the poor, minorities, and those economically and politically powerless get the short end of the stick wielded by the exploitative upper classes.

The Rastas maintain that profiteering destroys any sense of community, a point made not exclusively by the Rastas. Marx formulated an entire economic theory as an antidote to exploitative capitalism. Jesus realised that high Roman taxes were destroying the agricultural base of his town, and that farmers were forced off the land and into the cities to find work in order to meet the demands of their Roman masters. The spirit of community and co-operation, a basis of agrarian life, was being destroyed. Much of Jesus' preaching concerns economic justice, and treating your brother or sister with justice. From the Rasta viewpoint, the economic Babylon system is a struggle for survival of the fittest, a Darwinian feature of the capitalist system. Stick a fork in your brother's ass and turn him over, because he's done and you're not. You're still cookin'.

In 'Babylon System', on the *Survival* album, Marley sings, "We refuse to be what you want us to be/We are what we are and that's the way it's gonna be." The song deals with workers spending their lives toiling in the capitalistic profit system. Rasta reggae lyrics speak to Babylon's realities: historical atrocities, economic rapacity, mental slavery and political trickery. The forces of evil Babylon are arrayed against God and the righteous (Haile Selassie, Rasta, the oppressed and poor everywhere in the world). These evil forces are not abstract metaphysical concepts, a never-seen Satan; they are the forces of human attitudes and activities out of touch with the divine natural order. Economic, political, religious and educational institutions and values that support these attitudes are manifestations of Babylon. Any countries or peoples who have benefited from colonialism or international capitalism are part of Babylon. Babylon, for the Rastas, embodies the cultural ethos of the forces that work against "the people of God".

Rastas see Babylon as a symbol of bondage for all people held in slavery and oppression, especially black people. Materialism is seen as bondage of the spirit. For Rastas, "steppin' outta Babylon" means creating an alternative culture that reflects a sense of their African heritage, of justice and of love. They use the term Babylon as the symbolic designation of the forces that seek to "downpress" and dehumanise them. Marley's song 'Pimper's Paradise' on *Uprising* (Island Records, 1980) speaks of this. 'Crazy Baldhead', on the *Rastaman Vibration* album (Island Records, 1980), addresses the Marxist concept that he who owns the means of production exploits the labourers in order to maximise profits. This is an accurate description of the Jamaican record industry dating back to the sound-system days of the '50s. In fact, it's a description of the record industry everywhere. In the song, Marley sings about "I and I" raising crops and constructing houses for the people, only to have profiteering capitalists take them over. The same applies to songs meant to nurture the people who are seized by marketers.

Kingston attorney, Rastafarian scholar and devotee Dennis Forsythe writes on the Babylon experience in his book *Rastafari: For The Healing Of The Nation*: "Babylon is the psychic image sustained by real-life experience, busted hopes, broken dreams, the blues of broken homes, and of disjointed drives of people trapped by history. It is an image of fire and blood, of being on the edge, in limbo, in the wilderness, in a concrete jungle… It is a desolation in which man feels disjointed and out of line with the plans of creation."

Kwame Dawes, reggae singer, professor of English, and author of *Natural Mysticism, A Critical Analysis Of Reggae's Cultural Influences*, said in one of our early-morning talks that, "The Babylon system is anything that presents itself as the god of all things but actually benefits an oppressive few. In that, it becomes the counter-god. Being against the Babylon system fundamentally attacks the very nature of commerce. This is why you get Burning Spear singing, 'Do you know social living is the best,' which is a great play on socialism. Marley said it takes a revolution for the solution. These guys were not unaware of the politics and economics. While they were advocating a theocratic sensibility, they were also recognising the social politics at work.

"In this they were, and are, warriors working in the cauldron of capitalism but advocating another value system counter to the tenets of capitalism. Pilfering Babylon is part of the ethics. That is the beauty and elaborate irony of Marley's 'Babylon By Bus' tour. He toured America, this ultimate beast of Babylon, but he was also doing some of his best money-making efforts on the tour. The tour was both an attempt to bring his message of peace and truth and love, but also a way to get money out of Babylon.

"In this sense, reggae was used as a weapon. Absolutely. The question is, who was wielding the weapon? Who was making the money? Reggae artists have always realised that, even in their own success and in articulating the statements against the oppressors, they were faced with producers and record companies that were bringing Babylon upon them. Reggae is defined largely by its popular commercial identity, despite what we say about its political intentions. Reggae is a music that musicians use to make a living. They need it to make money inasmuch as they have spiritual intention."

David Hinds, lead singer for Steel Pulse, had words on that subject during one of our conversations. "Reggae, as a revolutionary music, demands that people come to it on its own terms. 'Come to me and listen to me in my language, from my experience.' But it's also a music that needs to be sold to the world. To do that, the artist might have to take a few adaptations because of the whole infrastructure of the recording industry. Marley did this. For a long time you had a lot of musicians and a lot of music listeners who said he sold out because he took on a different way to expressing his views.

"Steel Pulse has taken on different ways of expressing our views. We tried revolutionary music – take it on our terms or else. Then we tried a format where we decided to mix the music, as far as having a politically orientated album along with two tracks that can sell the album. Then, when people hear the real deal, they say, 'Ah, that's what these guys are really about.' Then they realise there are more pro-political songs than just songs that say, 'Baby, I love you, let's have a dance.' We call those 'Baby, I love you, let's have a dance' type of tracks *bait music*. They're bait music to lure you in to the real deal. At the end of the day, no matter what, it's get the message and act accordingly. Do something about what that message is trying to relate to you."

6 Tuff Gong Journey

Three miles separate Trench Town from Bob Marley's museum, the shrine of success for many Jamaican singers. You go up Half Way Tree Road and take a right on Hope Road, and then it's straight on to the former Tuff Gong, once Marley's home and studio. The road from a ghetto nobody to an international celebrity is littered with visions cracked by the hard whacks of reality, egos flattened by the hammer of honesty, and burned-out hulks of talent still smouldering from arson exacted by record merchants. Yet every day aspiring musicians set out on that road, fully believing that they will march triumphant through Marley's pearly gates.

I met one of those aspirants at the gate of Mixing Lab Studios, one of Jamaica's premier studios where Sly Dunbar, the renowned drummer, records and produces. Twenty-five-year-old Mark Plummer, aka Mark Sparkling, is a small man, painfully thin, with beautiful liquid black eyes. On that day he wore clean but threadbare clothes, and his dreads fell over his eyes. He had come from the country nine years previously to put his name in lights, but realising that dream had been like slaking his thirst one raindrop at a time.

Mark spends his days hanging around the gates of various studios, hoping that a producer will invite him in for an audition. All that he needs is one chance to lay out the ridims of his songs, or a gig as a backup singer, or…hell, even to sit at the soundboard and hum to the engineer.

"It's very hard," he said to me, the tuft of a goatee bobbing on the end of his sharp, narrow chin as we talked. "I'm dry poor. I have to beg money for the bus fare or hitch a ride to the studios. Day and night I'm on the street. I don't have any money to make a tape, so I don't have any music to give people.

"I'm a DJ singer to defend the faith of Rastafari. I write and sing about how people come to know themselves, know about their blackness, the roots of themselves, and where they are going. I come to change the level of violence of the people. I don't do slack about oral sex, bashing batty boys [gays], degrading women, shooting people and general gansta violence. That leads the people astray and they lose their culture and heritage, the heritage of uplifting of people. People have to remember where I 'n' I come from. I write about every social condition to bring the music from the street, the same tradition of Bob Marley and Peter Tosh. My living models are Luciano and Buju."

"What's it going to take for you to get your chance?" I asked as we stood in the small shade of a tree.

Mark rolled a spliff. "The humbleness of the producer," he answered, firing up. "I have good music, ya, mon." He flashed a grin. "Ya, mon, you better believe it. The producers, they get to know you by persistence. So I'm here every day with my lyrics around upward work, singing and talking upward. These nine years have made my faith stronger."

Paul "Lymie" Murray took a different route. He, too, was a country boy, from the farm village of Royal Flats, near Mandeville. As a boy, Lymie, now 29, sang gospel and revival hymns in church. In high school he performed at barbecues, high-school concerts, and talent shows.

"I was the ballad singer of Mandeville, and my friend was the pop singer," he said when we talked in his "quiet corner" in his Kingston back yard.

After he left high school, he came to Kingston and worked for a year in the Ministry of Finance, "but I got tired of beeping on the computer. I left the ministry and got odd jobs. All the while I was doing my music, making tapes, trying to get producers to listen. I never did hang at the studio gates. I presented my tapes and said, 'You listen to it.' As professionally as I presented my music, I expected professional treatment."

Two years later he became the lead singer for the band School. "My first break came when I gave my tape to a gentleman, Desmond Lawson, a custom broker bredren of mine. He was just getting into the music business and I was his first project. We started the album *Happy Days*, but because of internal problems between me and Lawson – executive producer problems – the album wasn't released for four years. In 1993, I did a single, 'Raindrops Keep Falling On My Head', and that was popular all over the island, but I got no money on the record. When you're new to the business, you must pay your dues. I got along on the band money, and if I needed a piece of equipment or refrigerator or stove my custom bredren Lawson could get it cheap."

Lymie got his big break when School became the backing band for Freddie McGregor, one of reggae's long-lasting international stars. "There was a nice rapport between me and him. We gelled. When he was going on the road, he'd call me up to do backing vocals or to open the show. I've travelled to Japan and the US with him. Now I'm working on a new album in his studio. I'm coming through the ranks. I think I've paid enough dues. I think it's my time. Have no fear. Have no doubt. This year going into next year is Lymie time."

Another singer pushing his way forward is Zumjay, born Rohan Alphanso Stephens 20 years ago. The bow wave of his dinghy is now washing ashore in the business. He hasn't released an album yet, but his name is on the street as a comer, largely due to his song 'Courtney', a tribute to the famous Jamaican cricket player Courtney Walsh.

We met at Penthouse Studio, where Buju Banton made his hit album *Shiloh* with the producer Donovan Germain, who owns the studio. Zumjay is a fresh-faced kid working hard to give himself a distinct look. He wore a denim hat at a cocky angle over his braided cornrows and a big glittery zircon stud in his right earlobe.

"I started by writing a song and singing it for my friends in school," he said. "They liked it, so I did another. My name became popular at school, and people told me to go to the studios. I took a tape to lots of producers, but they just walked by me. Since 1994 I had been trying to break in. I came here and Germain said I had a lot of talent and gave me the job to learn engineering at his studio. I just finished recording my song 'Peace' with Marcia Griffiths... The song was inspired by the recent killings between the police and people in the Mountain View section of Kingston. All my songs are about reality, economic strain, and violence, not only in Jamaica but also in the world.

"I use DJ ridims, but I prefer the slower reggae line. I think there will be more of that in the coming music, the blending of dancehall and reggae tempo. That gives a grounding while keeping the music lively. I don't use derogatory music. The negative messages and slackness is also fading from dancehall.

"I'm not a Rasta. When I was young I'd hear 'oh, back to Africa, must go back', and all that. I really don't look at it that way. I'd like to visit Africa one day, because that's where my forefathers came from, but Jamaica is my home. Music comes from all over the world, but only the drums come from Africa, so we'll always have the African drumbeat in our music. I listen to a lot of Rasta songs and respect their music, but it's not part of my music. I don't sing from their point of view, although my music is about peace and love and living together. That's the foundation of reggae dancehall music."

We walked into the sound studio to play a tape of his music. Donovan Germain sat behind the console board sampling songs. Above the board was a 27-inch colour television tuned to the Pakistan–West Indies cricket match, an exciting game if you're a cricket fan. Germain is such a fan that he gave up on the music to concentrate on the game. Zumjay slipped his tape into the tape deck. He has a bigger, deeper voice than expected from someone so slim and light. His voice is less threatening than Shabba Ranks', and has a quirk of individualism that catches the ear.

For every Mark Sparkling or Lymie or Zumjay there are another 100 singers standing in line. Jamaica has enough good singers to fulfil the requirements of every North American men's glee club and still form a singing reggae football team with its own band.

Half Tree Road divides the Kingston studio scene. The well-heeled studios that produce most of the sounds on the radio are above Half Tree Road. Those artists below...well, you don't hear much from them.

"It's like crossing an ethnic border," Sugar Minott told me at his

Black Roots Production/Youth Promotion studio, which is below Half Tree Road. "Right now, behind us is Trench Town. This is not recognised by the uptown music business. They say there is no musical development on this side. My studio is the only studio on this side.

"There's lots of music happening in Trench Town, but who's going to deal with it? Youth Promotion here for the past five years has put out about 13 Jamaican artists who are top artists right now. I produced Garnett Silk, Tony Tuff, Junior Reid, Half Pint, Frankie Paul, Tony Rebel, Steely And Clivie. This is where they started. This is where they learned to hold the mic, learned to catch melodies, learned to touch the piano, to turn up a sound system.

"I'm not a record company. I'm a youth agency trying to help the youth at Black Roots Production. I don't have the money to sign all these artists. When I get them from Trench Town and promote them up to a level that they could be heard by the people up topside Half Tree Road, then those people come in with the $30,000 or $50,000. Now, a kid from the ghetto whose grandmother don't even have bread over there, it's hard for him to say, 'I don't want that $100,000 now because I know I'm going to be better later.' That's how every one of them leaves from here and becomes uptown.

"Now, if you're strong, you'll come back; but most of them are not so strong when they have the limousine, and girls, and that and that. It's a different lifestyle. They go away from the music that brought them out. Right now, 90 per cent of Jamaican music is foreign music overdubbed. Hip-hop rules Jamaica. There's no real reggae – maybe 20 per cent – but the Studio One sound is always there because everything is a piece of that sound. It's a foundation."

The Studio One sound is classic reggae. On leaving Penthouse Studio, I directed Jah Earl. "Marley's place. Let's see if it's an altar or a golden calf."

Jah Earl snaked through traffic to the Bob Marley museum, the house Chris Blackwell, founder and then president of Island Records, had given Bob. A white stucco fence, clean and pretty, had replaced the original wire fence, that and a wild tangle of plants used as a trellis. A long steel pole blocked the entrance. The guardian of the pole, dressed in a white shirt and black pants, approached Jah Earl's window. "You pay an entrance fee. $350 each." He raised the pole. "You pay there." He pointed to a wooden booth.

Jah Earl parked on what was once the dirt front yard where Bob and the crew played football. Now it's a paved parking lot. You've got to park the tour buses somewhere, I thought. I bought two tickets from the lady sitting in the wooden booth, who had three other ladies sitting behind her, making the booth as crowded as a toilet stall. "No picture-taking, except of the statue in front of the house and the façade of the fence," she sternly warned, twice, as strict as a schoolmarm giving a pre-admonishment to a known troublemaker.

We joined three others for a guided tour. The house was an old-fashioned two-storey wooden plantation house, with slat windows to catch the breeze. Our guide, a young woman, grouped us before the coarsely rendered statue of Marley, standing before the house in a circle of trees. She started her spiel with the flat enthusiasm of someone working by rote. She mechanically directed us to the herb garden, with three small marijuana plants. Over to the side was a big, gleaming white Ford pick-up that belonged to one of Bob's sons, the one lifting weights behind the truck. The family look was unmistakable – tall, lanky, long thin handsome face and *café au lait* skin colour. The smell of sweet ganja hung heavy in the air.

From the garden we went around the back of the house. "One day a swarm of bees came here," the guide said, pointing to the branches of a tree at the roofline, "so Bob built that beehive up there. In Ethiopia, a swarm of bees is a sign of good fortune, wealth, and a symbol of royalty. We know that Bob became wealthy, and that he is the king of reggae."

She then ushered us into a small back room. "This was Bob's personal rehearsal room." The room was 15 feet long and nine feet wide, with brick walls painted white. The outside wall was a bank of louvred windows. The floor was of dark-green tile. "This is where the gunman tried to kill Bob," the guide said, as if reading a photo caption. "That is one of the bullet holes." On one wall there was a hole the size of a quarter, showing the pale-rose brick beneath.

At that time, the room would have been the kitchen. What prompted the attack on Marley remains unclear. In *Catch A Fire*, Timothy White reports that the gunmen were thugs trying to shake down Marley for a horseracing debt. Another theory is that it was a political hit. Marley had agreed to perform at a JLP rally, so perhaps the PNP tried to stop the island's most popular entertainer from appearing for its rival.

Whatever the true story, two cars with at least seven gunmen invaded the compound at 9:12pm and opened fire. Rita ran from the house with the five Marley children. A bullet grazed her across the forehead, lifting her off her feet. None of the children were hit. A man with an automatic rifle burst into the kitchen pantry, where Marley was talking to his manager, Don Taylor. The gunman fired eight shots. Taylor was hit five times. A bullet creased Marley and lodged in his left arm. Later, a doctor warned him that to remove the bullet risked paralysis of the arm. Marley left the bullet in place.

The guide led us around the house to the front entrance and through the front door. The room on the left of the original Tuff Gong studios was closed off. The studios are now located at the Marcus Garvey Center. On the right was a room with eight gold records, nine silver records and other awards displayed on a wall. The wooden floors were covered with a dark stain and creaked. The place looked well used and in need of a few licks of paint, which gave it a more personal feel and made it seem less like a dead museum. Truth be told, though, the place is stuffed and hung on the wall.

We went up the stairs. At the top was Rita's private office. The first international room was off on the right, its walls plastered with yellowing newspaper clippings of Marley. Across the hall was the second international room, its walls plastered with more old clippings. Across the top of one wall were the original covers of Marley's 19 albums.

In the corner of the room was a replica of Marley's original record shop at 18a Greenwich Park Road. It was a wooden booth with a chickenwire front and a slot for passing records and money back and forth. Inside hung the bike that Marley and Rita rode around on, peddling his first 45s. On the adjoining enclosed porch were two Nyabinghi drums and the three-legged stool with a slat seat where Marley sat while playing.

"Here Bob did his morning rites," the guide said. In the corner hung a hammock of heavy braided cotton. "And here Bob smoked his spliffs and wrote songs." Next to the hammock was the bedroom, off limits in the best museum tradition. The room was simple: a queen mattress on a low platform was covered with a cotton spread, and at the foot of the bed there was a well-polished horn – goat or cow – that served as Marley's chalice. The tableau was completed by a pair of handmade slippers and an odd-looking guitar with a body as spiky as starlight.

On the other side of the bedroom was a kitchen, where Marley prepared big meals for the crowd around him, the guide informed us. There was just enough room for one person to turn around between the sink, the three-burner propane stove and the counter. On the counter sat a blender that Marley used to make the almost constant flow of fruit and vegetable drinks that he drank.

"And these are his plates, in his second-favourite colours, beige and brown," droned the guide. "His favourite colours were red, gold and green, the colours of the Ethiopian flag. Now follow me to the exhibition hall to view a short film. Please visit the souvenir shops when we've finished."

In the exhibition hall behind the house were photos of Marley playing football. He had thick, well-developed thighs. The film started with a staged children's party in London. Saccharine. Obviously staged. Bob sang to the tykes and danced with them, his locks bouncing like snakes in a hot skillet. The remaining film was of touring and rehearsal footage, interesting in that it showed Marley at work.

After the tour, Jah Earl leaned against his taxi and rolled a spliff. "You know the story about how Peter Tosh, one of the original Wailers, died? I knew Peter, in fact, visited his house a month before he was shot and killed."

The news reports claimed that burglars shot Tosh. Jah Earl had another story. "Peter was very aggressive. He was always talking 'bloodclot' this and 'clart' that, swearing about everything. He wanted to tear down Babylon with his bare hands. He would fight the police when they gave him trouble. One time the police broke his arm in a fight over him having a spliff. He was a tough, aggressive guy, but a good guy." Jah Earl smiled at the remembrance. "He was very erratic, and that made it difficult for him. Onstage, he would ride his unicycle.

"The story on the street about his getting shot was like this. He owed money to some men. They came to collect. Peter was living with a woman who was very aggressive and she started to make trouble. There was a fight and the men started shooting. Peter was killed. The woman was hit but she lived. The gunman, he's out of jail now."

Jah Earl fired up his spliff and inhaled. The story about Tosh's death put him in a thoughtful frame of mind.

"You know how Garnett Silk died about five years ago?"

"No."

"I use to take him around. He was just another singer, then suddenly he hit. People thought he might be the next Marley. He started getting money and wanted to fix up a place for his mother, who he was very close to, so he started expanding the house she lived in. But people would come in the night and steal the building materials, so Garnett called in some friends who knew how to deal with that situation. This guy came to the house to show Garnett how to load a pistol. The gun accidentally fired and hit a propane-cooking tank. Garnett died in the explosion, hugging his mother. She also died."

"Cheerful, Jah Earl. Let's go get a cold jelly."

Jah Earl pulled out into traffic. Am I the bullet or the propane tank? It's an inevitable question whenever risking Kingston traffic. The odds of smashing into something, or being blown up in a horrific accident, are in your favour.

Jah Earl stopped, blocking his lane, and edged the nose of the car into the oncoming traffic. I felt like I was the propane tank. Traffic turn lanes are as rare as full-time employment in Jamaica. When drivers want to cut across rushing traffic, they play chicken with the other drivers, just as Jah Earl did. He crept forward, gaining entry space inch by inch, looking for a gap to squirt through to the other side. We were poised crossways on the centreline. The odds were now two to one in our favour; we could get hit from behind or from the side. We were in the red zone; the oncoming cars had to either stop or collide with us. An approaching car flashed its lights and reduced speed marginally. Jah Earl waved his hand and seized the opportunity.

The split-second co-operation, and the comparatively low carnage, speaks optimistically of the Jamaican society. The unwritten rules of the road serve as a metaphor – if not examined too closely – for the Jamaican way of life. Jamaicans spontaneously take their pleasures when opportunities present themselves, but in doing so they are not careless with each other. Courtesy and good humour are part of the social contract. Cutthroat survival and good humour are equally part of Jamaican social behaviour. To trust in Jamaican traffic is to invite disaster. Not to trust people might mean that you'll be stuck forever trying to cut across lanes of oncoming traffic. The nation is stuck in traffic. The Jamaican music industry is stuck in traffic, not confident to cross the thoroughfare of commercial music and fearful of being rear-ended if it doesn't move forward.

We headed for Jah Earl's favourite jelly stand, run by his friend Josie. A motorcycle going at least twice the speed limit zoomed down the yellow centre stripe, like a bomb following its laser beam. Jah Earl whipped around traffic and fell in behind, drafting the motorcycle as we forced open a new centre lane down the middle of the street. We were now a honking bullet. If another driver imprudently strayed into our lane, we would do what all bullets do when they meet a target. Jah Earl, like a chess player, kept looking three moves ahead. If a car hinted that it might cut into our lane, he laid on the horn.

I had a sudden image of us as a furiously hissing gander warning all potential intruders to stay out of our territory.

We were approaching the jelly stand. Jah Earl deftly darted across two lanes of traffic without even a close scrape.

"Two cold jellies," Jah Earl called out, stepping out of the car triumphantly, as if he had just beaten the house in blackjack.

7 Kumina

There was one petrol station in Port Morant, on the eastern tip of Jamaica. Across the street from the petrol station there was a Rasta restaurant, a screened room with a dirt floor where men played dominoes. Attached to this room, like a carbuncle, was the kitchen – a propane two-burner with a skillet and a five-gallon stainless steel pot. Jah Earl and I sat eating plates of stewed fish with rice and beans while we waited for Ika Brown. The domino players violently slapped their plastic tiles onto the table – *smack!* – with a sound like pistol shots.

Ika Brown knew where to find Kumina drummers and dancers. Kumina is a fusion of two Ashanti Twi words, *akom* (to be possessed) and *ana* (by an ancestor). Here in St Thomas parish, the religious and psychic connection to Africa is stronger than anywhere else in Jamaica. Speaking in tongues, going into trances and flying back to Africa, conjuring up ancestors for advice, casting spells, communicating to plant and animal spirits and appeasing ghosts is normal behaviour here. Kumina is practised only in the Blue Mountains of St Thomas parish.

Ika Brown pulled up and flashed his lights to indicate we should follow. We headed up a snaky road into the Blue Mountains, which actually looked dusky lavender the higher we climbed, an effect caused by the haze dropping from the peaks over the deep green jungle. I glanced back towards the open sea out of an impulse to confirm the presence of an escape route. A mountain swooped around the curve of the road and closed out the horizon as firmly as a door slamming shut.

I'm entering another kingdom, I thought, as foolish and romantic as that sounded. We were in a cleft following an unseen stream back into the haze. A dense tapestry of palm fronds, vines and tree trunks scraggy with peeling thin flakes of red bark enfolded us. I could see only into this place, as if I were being dropped head-first down a hole.

We turned off the asphalt road onto a rough, rocky track. Down a hill, up a hill, past a loose grouping of houses, then a right turn onto a red dirt lane. Bushes brushed each side of the car. We stopped where a cluster of people stood before a house. A small wiry man with a stubble of white whiskers greeted us. "I'm Richard Campbell, the leader of the Airy Castle Katanga Kumina Group, one of four groups in the area who does the Kumina."

He led us to a small dirt-floor enclosure at the side of the yard. Under the tin roof was a table covered by a white cloth. On the table were two pints of white over-proof rum, a bottle of ginger and a vase containing a bouquet of silk glitter flowers. Two young men set their drums on the ground before the table. One of them straddled the *kbandu*, the bass. The other sat on the smaller "plain cast" facing his partner. (In Kumina, the cast drummer plays the harmony while the bass holds the beat.) A third man sat directly behind the bass so as to play his sticks on the wooden barrel.

The drumhead of the *kbandu* was ram goatskin because, the drummer explained to me, the ram's voice has "bottom". "The ram is not as vociferous as the ewe. The ram skin is best for a lower tone and slower beat."

"This drum," said the man on the higher-pitched cast, "has skin from a ewe. The ewe bleats sharp, so her voice is perfect for the soprano. Some like the pelican crop [stomach] more than the ewe. There are no pelicans in the mountains. Sheepskin or cowhide doesn't carry the quality for the music. Then you can't go along with the notes you want to sing out."

Richard Campbell, the "king" dancer and leader of the group, cleared his throat and, as if delivering a formal lecture, said, "Kumina begins in Jamaica from the ancestors from West Africa who were brought here as slaves. Many of them, to repatriate back to their homeland, they had to get the business to play this drum. The sounds of the drums communicate them from here right back to Africa to the rest of the people. The ancestors, the old-time people, they used the drums this way to fly back. The Kumina drum pattern is the basis for all other drum patterns in Jamaican music, including ska, rock steady, and reggae. Kumina led up to a lot of music. In drumming, all the drumming comes from this foundation. This drum is the drum of drums. All of Jamaica been talking about repatriation. Rasta this, Rasta that. If repatriation should come, I think that this is the drum. Our first and last music would declare that.

"Kumina is a fundamental source of the African's life. Is a fundamental source of the African's life," he repeated for emphasis. "It's like a Christian who believes in God. So the Africans believe in their life, and through that they can do anything they want to do in their human resource through their understanding with their original background that is life of the African people.

"The Christian churches offered God. Kumina offers man a number of spirits. So long as the spirits are not intimately drawn into human life, they can remain anonymous, like the Fairy Host in Ireland. They throng about the doors of houses, or follow humans at night. They can be propitiated, and even used in magic, without knowledge of their names. You have to know what you're doing in Kumina.

"Kumina is used for litigation, sickness and parties, like birth-night parties, for weddings, mourning, and other amenities of life. Sometimes, when the body is dead, the people come together until that deceased is buried. If you try to bury without the drums, people say, 'Where the drums?' If you play the drums, your yard is full and people come and dance and celebrate.

"There is a spiritual dimension to Kumina. It even depends on the type of Kumina dance you make. It works this way: if you can see, the ancestors will appear to you. They speak to you in tongues. They come to you and tell you exactly what's wrong. What caused this or what caused that. If it's something affects anybody, whether illness or so, and even litigation on a person supposed to go and face the judge. And, you make the right type of Kumina, the ancestors will tell you if you can get off or can't get off. If a person is sick, they will tell you if you'll recover or not. It has a deep background, a very deep background. It's more sensitive to those who know the life of the African dance, which is called Kumina.

"We were born in Jamaica so the little we know of Kumina comes from our ancestors. We really don't know the language to the roots, but we know a part of it that we can declare ourselves. So we do need, if we find a way, to develop more of the language. That will be better for us. What we do now, we know that the original Kumina setting came from Gold Coast Africa, which is called Ghana today. That's what we learned.

"Kumina is one of the greatest cultures that Jamaica had ever got. People have reggae, people have *dinki-minni* [Burru], but Kumina is only found in St Thomas. The other 14 parishes don't have this. I don't know why. They don't have the right understanding. They'll never go down to the roots of it because you have to have the right understanding about Kumina. Not whether they can talk the language or not, but you have to have the right noise to perform. This is passed on from generation to generation. My great-grandfather passed it down to his son, who passed it down to his son, my father, who passed it down to me. We are keeping alive the direct memory to Africa through the music. That's what I do."

Between 1841 and 1865, 8,000 Yoruba and Central African immigrants came to Jamaica as indentured labourers. They settled mostly in the St Thomas area. The most prominent cultural legacy of these direct African migrants is Kumina, an African ancestor-worship cult emphasising both singing and dancing.

The table was set back so that the dancers could circle the drummers. The *kbandu* sounded a couple of preparatory beats as the three men and five women dancers took their places. Mr Campbell sang a long note; the *kbandu* player thwacked his ram; the cast drummer struck fast sharp notes on his ewe; the dancers, picking up the song, began to dip and sway. Their shoulders rolled to the *kbandu* in slow, sweeping, steady circles. Their feet listened to the faster cast, doing a one-two forward and backstep, a heel-to-toe, a crossover step while twirling. The dancers' heads and shoulders responded to a different realm than their hips and feet, but in perfect syncretism. The dance and the music were simultaneously slow and fast. The heavy bass stroke seemed to come down on the dancers' shoulders to secure them to the ground. The staccato cast notes, as bright as rain on tin, seemed to push up through the ground, causing the dancers to jump and hop and twist from side to side, as if mini lightning bolts zapped their soles.

The drummers and dancers continued for 20 minutes, then three pronounced bass beats signalled the end. While they caught their breath, the drummers rubbed over-proof rum (110 per cent) on the drumheads. The evaporating alcohol tightened the skins, tuning the drums. The drummers splashed handfuls of rum over their sweating faces to cool off.

I asked Mr Campbell if there was a meaningful pattern to the dance steps. "It's just a style," he replied, mopping streams of perspiration from his face and neck, "but the beat can make you do things. You have some people, when this thing's ripe, you know, some people wash up the ground they get so in another state. You have to play the same music to take them out because you're dealing with unseen spirits that appear to them. But all that is for reasoning, not for entertainment. Entertainment is just entertainment. At a big stage show, you have to just entertain the crowd. Special Kumina is for special reason. That Kumina is still kept up in St Thomas. It never goes down. People keep it up at all times."

"Is it true that the Kumina ceremony is sometimes held to kill by magic a person disliked?"

Mr Campbell gave me the look of a teacher who had caught a student reading ahead in the textbook. "Kumina is powerful. It can do many things."

The drummers signalled another dance. The dancers circled, their feet chattering and their heads dreaming. Mr Campbell's head tilted back and his eyes didn't blink for a long time. The dancers sang harmony and counterpoint to the drums. The sound became a noisy sea of waves peaking and chest-butting one another, then crumbling in a glissando run as fast and light as foam. A swirl, a counter-eddy, a long low rumble of the sound waves building, the pulsating beat tumbling into the trough and flying off the crest. This music can drive all else from the mind. No thoughts, no dreams, no chat, no plans. All of that is vaporised by the relentless drumbeat. It's easy to understand how the tide of this music can carry a person out of sight of land.

At the next break, I asked Mr Campbell about the words of the songs. "Most of the time, how you get to the effect of the African language is when you are out there dancing and playing the drums. When we begin to dance, we start to get high, and then you start most of the language, which is not the words. Not all of them you really know the meaning, but we know how to say some things, like 'all the people keep singing', and 'a call to celebration'. We don't know all the language, but we can ask for our food. We can say, 'Morning, little girl.' The ram goat is 'billy *comba*'. The she one is '*comba*'.

"We Africans here fight for our rights, including our African cultural rights. These deep-down type of Africans, such as Nanny, Cudjoe, Bogle – they were heroes. They fight for justice. They need justice, and that's what they fight for. When the smaller people say, let it stay [injustice]. But the Bogles, they say no. They want justice and that is what they fight for. Because of justice, we lose Bogle, we lose Nanny, because they say they want freedom so they fight for freedom. St Thomas has always been a place of rebellion because the people here always go for their rights."

On the way back to Kingston, we stopped at Court House Square in Morant Bay, the administrative centre of St Thomas parish. On 11 October 1865, Paul Bogle launched a rebellion in the square against the plantation owners. A statue of a chained Bogle stands in front of the courthouse, behind which are buried many of those killed in the uprising. Bogle was a lay preacher and the spiritual leader of the free village of Stony Gut, six miles from Morant Bay. The Stony Gut land had been leased out to blacks after their apprenticeship on the surrounding plantations. A dispute arose when some of the occupants refused to pay rent, claiming that the land belonged to them by virtue of their settlement. The landowners wanted these small farmers evicted and went to court to get a magistrate's order.

Bogle knew that he and his people wouldn't get a fair hearing. The planters never gave the blacks a fair shake, so why should this be different? Black workers were subject to undue taxes, exploitative low wages and – salt on wound – some planters withheld money for work done. Thirty-one years after slavery was abolished, blacks were still being treated as slaves. Perhaps more than the economic issues, the indignity and injustice was an injury. Bogle decided that the only solution was to drive all of the whites and brown-skinned Indians from the country. He secretly drilled 200 of his men as the first-line force for his rebellion.

He also approached Major Sterling of the Windward Maroons and asked him to join the rebellion. The Maroons, Jamaica's original freedom fighters, were non-committal. They considered themselves a special group apart, who had enjoyed autonomy since settling their fight with the British nearly 100 years previously. Over time, the Maroons developed an inordinate sense of their own importance. They considered themselves superior to the blacks that had remained under the servitude of slavery. They did not have a strong sense of black solidarity, and in fact kept slaves themselves. As part of their deal with the British, the Maroons agreed to hunt down runaways and rebellious slaves. The Maroons were owned by the British.

On 7 October, Bogle marched into Morant Bay at the head of his "army", which was armed with fife and drum and an assortment of weapons. He entered the courthouse, where two of the land dispute cases were being heard. A minor scuffle broke out. Bogle and his men returned to Stony Gap with no injuries on either side. However, the law had been defied and the offenders had to be held accountable. Warrants were issued for Bogle, his brother and 25 other men charged with rioting and assaulting the police. Eight policemen were sent to apprehend the wanted men. The police were ambushed and beaten near Stony Gap and sent back.

The die was cast. Three days later, Bogle and his men attacked the courthouse to start their civil war for real. Eighteen people were killed, mostly whites, and 31 wounded. Bogle freed 51 prisoners from the jail and committed himself to a full-scale war. Two days later, on 12 October, his forces captured the small town of Bath (then and now known for its curative hot springs). On the following day, the British declared martial law, and the Maroons chose the British side. Within a week, Bogle's forces controlled territory within a 30-mile radius of Morant Bay, but this was eventually to prove to be a Pyrrhic victory.

The wanted posters for Bogle described him as "very black, shiney [sic] of skin; heavy marks of smallpox on face, especially on nose; good teeth, large mouth, red thick lips; about five feet eight inches, broad shoulders; carries himself indolently, with no whiskers".

The Maroons didn't need the description to find Bogle. On 22 October, Maroons captured him at Stony Gap and turned him over to the British. Two days later, he was hanged from the yardarm of the British warship HMS *Wolverine*, and the British then launched a scorched-earth counterattack. More than 100 blacks were rounded up and hanged. Another 400 were flogged and their houses burned.

Paul Bogle is now officially honoured as being Jamaica's First National Hero.

The Morant Bay courthouse was also the site of the trial of Leonard Howell and his compatriot Robert Hinds in 1933. There is no mention of this trial on the plaque outside the courthouse.

Howell started his preaching in St Thomas parish, a long-time hotbed of sedition and revolt. The people of St Thomas are a credulous lot, willing to rank emotional intelligence equal with rational logic. Perhaps that's why Jamaica's first prime minister, Alexander Bustamante, created his voter base in St Thomas rather than on the opposite end of the island, where he was born. Howell found fertile ground in St Thomas, where he lived for eight years in a rented house, travelling between St Thomas and Kingston, delivering his message of the living messiah in Haile Selassie and the need for the black race to step outside the white colonial world and return to Africa. Once the nucleus of his movement had been established, Howell decided to spread the word throughout the island. To raise money, he and his followers sold 5,000 postcards of Haile Selassie, for one shilling each, as passports to Ethiopia.

Howell was drawn to St Thomas by the work of the Reverend Charles F Goodridge and Grace Jenkins Garrison, who made St Thomas the base for their Hamatic Church to proselytise the teachings of the Holy Piby. The Holy Piby, known often as the Black Man's Bible, is considered a foundation book of Rastafari. Some early Rasta chants and songs, including Bob Marley's 'Rasta Man Chant', were taken from the Piby, according to Timothy White in his book *Catch A Fire, The Life Of Bob Marley*. The Piby purportedly pre-dated the Christian and Hebrew bibles, and was originally written in Amharic, the language of the Amhar tribe of Ethiopia. The book was compiled by Robert Athlyi Rogers of Anguilla between 1913 and 1917 and published in 1924.

Goodridge and Garrison arrived in Kingston in 1931. Fundamentalist, Christian and Revivalist preachers who considered the Piby an occult bible did not welcome them. The pair fled the hostile preachers and established their camps in St Thomas. They preached that the Amharic text had been deliberately distorted in translations to make God and His prophets caucasian instead of black. That fitted nicely with Howell's belief that Haile Selassie was the black messiah returned.

By 1933, Howell's meetings were attracting more than 800 people at the towns of Pear Tree Grove and Leith Hall. He wasn't the only one preaching dissatisfaction with white rule and promoting the self-esteem of the black race. Twenty years earlier, Marcus Garvey, a Jamaican from St Ann, had preached the same message to launch his international movement promoting black unity, pride and self-reliance. Alexander Bedward, Joseph Hibbert, Archibald Dunkley and Robert Hinds were also on the stump in Jamaica, delivering much the same message. Hibbert, Dunkley and Hinds met Howell in Kingston, and together they created the core of the Rastafarian movement.

According to a newspaper account, at a meeting in Trinity Ville on 16 December 1933, Howell told the crowd that, "The Lion of Judah has broken the chain, and we of the black race are now free. George the Fifth is no more our King. George the Fifth has sent his third son down to Africa in 1928 to bow down to our new king Ras Tafair [*sic*]. Ras Tafair is King of Kings and Lord of Lords. The Black people must not look to George the Fifth as their King any more – Ras Tafari is their King."

(Tafari is the family name of Haile Selassie, the former Emperor of Ethiopia. *Ras* is an Amharic word meaning "prince", or comparable to the English title "duke". When crowned Emperor of Ethiopia, Ras Tafari Makonnen – great grandson of King Saheka Selassie of Shoa, a province of Ethiopia – took the name Haile Selassie [Might Of The Trinity], to which he added "King Of Kings" and the "Lion Of The Tribe Of Judah" to confirm his place in the legendary line of King Solomon.)

Blacks cannot have two kings, Howell exhorted the crowd. Jamaicans cannot have an English white king and an African black king. Haile Selassie is the only true king of the black people.

Howell wasn't a church preacher in the normal sense, nor a spiritual teacher as you might think of a guru. He was more the Malcolm X of his day, an agitator for justice and equity and rightful living. His message wasn't that Haile Selassie, as God, would come down to save the black man, but rather that the black man should look to a black God instead of bowing heart, spirit and wallet to a God who sees the whites as His chosen people. Fair pay and working conditions were as much a focus of Howell's message as saving the soul. He was an agitator for human rights, including labour rights. Howell's message in St Thomas, seven years before he founded Pinnacle, was that the black man should fight for justice and equality. This message pervades the spirit of reggae.

Within three weeks of the Trinity Ville meeting, on 5 January 1934, Howell was arrested and charged with uttering seditious speech, intent to excite hatred, contempt for His Majesty The King and the government of Jamaica, creating dissatisfaction among the subjects of His Majesty, and disturbing the public peace and tranquillity...and fraud for selling the pictures of Haile Selassie as passports. Robert Hinds was also arrested on lesser charges. To the British authorities, Howell's message sounded like nationalism, specifically black nationalism. They saw Howell's anti-colonial preaching as a potential threat to the stability of their rule.

Howell pleaded not guilty to all charges. The jury found him guilty and sentenced him to two years in prison. Hinds received a sentence of one year. Soon after the trial, Archibald Dunkley and Joseph Hibbert were also arrested, in an attempt by the British to nip a potentially dangerous cult in the bud. Upon his release, Howell returned to St Thomas and continued his agitation against unfair labour practices, discrimination against blacks and the false religion of a white God.

There is no historical marker in Trinity Ville commemorating this history. After passing through Trinity Ville, a long string of houses and shops along the Negro River, we came to Serge Island. Today this is dairy country, the Wisconsin of Jamaica. Serge Island is not an island, or even a discernible village, but a huge dairy barn at a curve in the road. In the '30s, this was the land of sugar cane and labour unrest. Howell preached here, and in Sea Forth, a short walk down the road, he stirred up the workers' brewing resentment against the owners of the sugar plantations. The sugar planters regarded Howell's message as a threat to their profit margin. In January 1938, the cane workers went on strike. This sparked an island-wide uprising of spontaneous labour actions by workers in all industries and services, who were largely non-unionised. A violent strike by Kingston dockworkers nearly brought the country to a standstill.

Howell was again arrested. On 15 February, three weeks after the Serge Island labour action, he was committed to Kingston's Bellevue mental asylum in a blatant (and successful) move to get him out of the way. It was after his experience of mind-besotting drugs administered to him at the asylum that Howell decided to establish his own community of equality at Pinnacle.

My brief foray into the Blue Mountains had whetted my appetite to explore more. "Let's take this road," I told Jah Earl. On the map I traced a blue line leading from Morant Bay into the mountains and then looping back to the coast. Trinity Ville, Serge Island and Heartease were on that road, places important to visit in order to obtain some kind of understanding of the underlying motivation of Rastafari and some influences on reggae.

Beyond Serge Valley the road crested the first line of mountains at Cedar Valley. The nature and mood of the land changed dramatically as we dropped behind the front-range shield. I had the sensation of slipping behind a curtain and into a land of mystery, as I had when visiting the Kumina drummers. It was much quieter and cooler on this side of the mountains. Houses were hidden in nooks and crannies, so the land seemed almost devoid of people. An occasional cultivated field clung to the steep mountainsides at an impossibly raked angle. The farmers must stand as if crabbing up stairs, one foot always on the upper step and the other below for support.

Wild apples grew along the narrow and crumbling road of switchbacks. These fleshy red apples, shaped like pears, had a delicate fresh sweetness, like eating rainwater. The smaller golden globes of the rose apple smelled like perfume. They were hollow on the inside and tasted floral. As we stopped to pick apples from the trees, I began to have Edenistic fantasies of a Shangri-La, where the membrane between the homocentric mind and the natural spirit world dissolved. Why not talk to the spirits – plants, animals, and ancestors – in their own language? Think how enriched your living experience would be. Little wonder that Pocomania, Vodun, Shouter, Pentecostal, Revival, Revival Zion Convince and other Afro-Christian rites are popular in Jamaica, especially in St Thomas. They share the commonality of speaking in tongues, shouting, paroxysms of uncontrolled jerking, trance-like states, and being transported out of the rational mind.

Pocomania is Spanish for "little madness", although the word may also be a derivative of Pu-Kumina, or possibly even from Pucku, the possession god of rural blacks in Surinam. There, the Puckoo people dance the *puckamenna*, a state much like that achieved in Kumina. Mr Campbell had been careful to explain that there is no relationship between Poco and Kumina. "The Poco brought up under like a Christian thing," he said, "but when they begin it, they jump and sing hymns. They clap hands and rub their heads and talk in tongues, too, but those spirits are different from the African ancestor spirits. Quite different."

Pocomania incorporates the African-mystic belief that all spirits are powerful. There is no supreme good spirit, like God, and no supreme Satanic evil spirit. All spirits can possess you, and should be treated with respect, an attitude found in the Vodun (Voodoo) of Haiti and the Prias (Shango) of Cuba. Pocomania, a cousin to the Pentecostal, first emerged in Jamaica in the early months of 1861.

The central feature of Pocomania is possession. The mystical state is entered by dancing, during which the participant strongly inhales and exhales, making a coughing or barking sound. The effect of this hyperventilation is to reduce residual carbon dioxide in the lungs, which brings on light-headedness. The rhythmic grunting, inhaling and exhaling can also produce an auto-hypnotic effect, helping to induce a trance state.

The patterns of Poco sound can be heard in DJ ridims, especially in the beats produced by digital drum machines. Pocomania and Revival music helped to set the stage for the creation of a new style of dancehall music based on the traditional Revival rhythms. Lord Sassa Frass had a hit with 'Pocomania Jump' in 1984. "Poco jump, Poco jump, mek we do de Poco jump," he sang. The song ended with the heavy rhythmic breathing, or *trimping*, associated with the dancing and spiritual possession of the Poco and Revival religions.

Under the apple trees, the road dropped around blind curves. At Richmond Vale, we crossed over the chasm of the Yallahs River on a "quaint" one-way bridge. At Llandewey, we had a fine view of the 1,000-foot-high Judgment Cliff, created by the 1692 earthquake that destroyed Port Royal. According to local folklore, the collapsing mountain buried a venal slave owner, hence the name. When we reached Heartease, once again nearly at the coast, I asked Jah Earl to stop. I was bewitched by the name. Heart ease. I wanted that to be my new name, so that every time I heard "Heartease, come here" and "Heartease, help me out here" I'd be reminded of what I'm supposed to be doing in life. Ease the heart. My heart. Your heart. Strangers' hearts. Easing the heart comes with calmness and peace and compassion and love. Heart on the inhale. Ease on the exhale. A meditation on sensible living. I just loved that name.

Heartease is also known for its Revivalist spirit meetings. Revivalist influence on Jamaican popular music goes back to the early days of ska, when Revival-tinged recordings such as 'Six And Seven Books Of Moses' and 'Hallelujah' by the Toots And The Maytals, 'River Jordan' and 'Freedom' by Clancy Eccles, and 'River To The Bank' by Baba Brooks. Even The Wailers recorded a number of Revival-influenced spiritual songs before fully embracing the Rastafari. The hymn-like quality of much of '70s reggae was familiar to churchgoers all over rural Jamaica. The melodies and chord progressions of many Rasta reggae songs, as well as the biblical language and prophetic messages that typify the genre, owe much to Revivalism.

Toots and The Maytals (Jerry Mathias and Raleigh Gordon) were steeped in local Revivalism. Their first big hit, 'Bam Bam', owed much to the ridimic value and performance quality of Revivalism. Not only is there a strong Jamaican Revivalist feeling in The Maytals' many religious reggae songs – 'Loving Spirit', 'In The Dark' and 'Got To Be There', for example – but also some songs directly quote traditional Revival melodies. The appropriately named song 'Revival Reggae' sets the meaningless syllables of an old revival chorus – a type of chanting often associated, in the traditional context, with the onset of spiritual possession – to a driving reggae rhythm.

Many top studio musicians normally associated with reggae can also be heard on these Revivalist-influenced Christian recordings, such as Radcliffe "Dougie" Bryan (guitar), Barold Butler (keyboard), Ansel Collins (keyboard), Lowell "Sly" Dunbar (drums), and well-known reggae vocalists such as Larry Marshall (Bro Marshall), The Tamlins and Carlene Davis.

The hamlet of Heartease is only a few miles from Yallahs on the coast. After a day of natural mysticism, I was hungry. In the centre of Yallahs, next to the bus station, was a row of jerk stands with 50-gallon drums cut lengthways, serving as barbecue pits. We stopped at the first one, Watts, and ordered up chicken jerk with a hunk of white bread. Lots of people around Jamaica claim to make jerk, but good authentic jerk is hard to find. There's a big difference between chicken with jerk sauce and jerk chicken. I highly recommend the jerk stands at Yallahs for the real deal.

The two-hour looping drive that connects Yallahs with Morant Bay via Cedar Valley was also the real deal. If you want a quick hit of the spirit, mysticism and an essential history of modern-day Jamaica, you can't do better than follow that road.

8 Drumming

For Africans, the drum talks. For Jamaicans, the ridim talks. Ridim is a Rasta-created word that refers to the polyrhythmic drum and percussion patterns and tempo in reggae music. The man who created some of the classical drum ridims in ska and reggae is Lloyd Knibb, the original drummer for The Skatalites, the world's best-known ska band.

On a Sunday afternoon, Jah Earl and I sat in Lloyd Knibb's living room in the Harbour View section of Kingston, out near the airport. The room was crammed with two overstuffed armchairs, a sofa and a tall credenza full of knick-knacks. A knee-high carved wooden table sat between the chairs and the sofa, leaving no walking room. A colour television blasted out cartoons, which didn't stop the conversation and laughter. Lloyd and his wife, Enid, call this home when they are in Jamaica. Otherwise, they live in New York.

Lloyd wore only a pair of shorts in the humid heat. Still, his white goatee and glasses gave him a jazz professorial look. When he smiled, which was often, his gold-capped upper front teeth flashed brightly. Around his neck was a flat gold chain, from which hung a letter "L" in script, set in diamonds. He is 69 years old, and in the next six months will tour the United States, Europe and Japan with The Skatalites.

I sat next to him on the sofa as he rolled a spliff. Jah Earl, in an armchair opposite, rolled one for himself. Enid, recovering from major surgery four months earlier, lounged in the remaining armchair. Jamaicans don't share their joints, for sanitary reasons; they don't want to risk passing on germs. Also, if someone hands you a pre-rolled joint, you can't be sure what's in it. Ganja smokers usually carry enough herb wrapped in cellophane for one or two spliffs. Possession of marijuana is illegal in Jamaica.

"I don't smoke the chalice any more," Lloyd said. "Too much." He laughed and launched into an explanation of how to make a chalice from a long-necked bottle. "You break off the neck." He mimed smashing a bottle. "Then you put a ball of tin foil or a stone in there to keep the herb from falling out. When you pass it, you make sure that the other fellow has his hand down off the lip of the neck. You sip from the hand, not put your mouth on the chalice. Don't want to pass germs, you understand."

"The expert," said Enid good-naturedly. Lloyd laughed and she smiled her perfect teeth. She had a round, lovely face, and was just as lively as her husband. She said that Jah Earl's herb smelled better than Lloyd's. "Some of that homegrown stink up the whole place," she said.

Lloyd took a deep drag and started a diatribe on one of most musicians' favourite themes: getting ripped off. It seems that there was this lying producer who had changed a deal four times. Lloyd had had it with him, didn't trust him and refused to work for him any more. "And then this other fellow, I'm trying to track him down right now." He pulled out a piece of paper with a name and phone number. Enid punched out the numbers on a cell phone, but no answer. "This fellow, a musician, he asks if I'd sell him my old drum set. He says new drums are too expensive. I say me sell it, yes. So I do, for around $250 US. Then, later, these fellows in California, they want my drums for a museum on The Skatalites they're putting together. They have Jerry Hinds' guitar and Lloyd Brevett's bass and they want my drums. So I go back to this Bernard to get my drums and give him another set, but he wants a brand new set of Yamaha and $300 US to get my drums back. I don't see that's right, so I'm looking for him to get this set straight."

It's not surprising that Lloyd's drums will be in a museum. He's been at the core of Jamaican music for over 40 years and played behind all the greats – Duke Reid, Prince Buster, Dennis Brown, Justin Hinds, Bob Marley, and all the others you want to name. "I remember Rita, before she was Marley, crawling around on the floor of the studio, where I played with her dad, who was a sax player," he said.

"I used to change her diapers. I live up where Count Ossie first was, on 32 Adastra Road, and go by his place nearly every day to play. That's when he was back over the hill from where his centre is now. Musicians used to go there generally on Sunday nights. All the musicians. The jazz musicians would play the Burru beat. Everybody loved going there and playing."

The drumbeat pattern Lloyd invented is heard in some form in nearly every ska and reggae song. The ska beat, accentuated by the drums and the bass, a characteristic sound of reggae, was the creation of the two Lloyds, Knibb and his bass-playing partner, Lloyd Brevett.

"I's the man who changed the beat to ska," Lloyd confirmed. "I was with Clement 'Coxsone' Dobb, the record producer, and he wanted me to change the beat from the shuffle rhythm and from rock 'n' roll. He said his audience was getting older, so cut down the beat. I went into the studio and started fooling around. Burned into my brain is the Burru rhythm, mento, calypso, rumba, cha-cha, jazz, rock 'n' roll, the blues." He made drum sounds while his hands described complicated patterns in the air. He went on longer than a simple demonstration required, like he had put a foot in the tide of music and the current was threatening to pull him offshore. "When I play, you'll hear a little Burru, a little cha-cha, a little everything. That's where I get my style. So when I was fooling around, all those beats came together. I put in a dropped second and fourth, and the guitar played *chan*, *chan*, *chan*, that choppy beat. The term ska comes from the skat pattern of the guitar. There is no other bass player who can do ska like Lloyd Brevett, because he also has the same Burru feel, and no player can do Burru like Lloyd."

There are several explanations for the genesis of the term ska. Tommy McCook, a founding member and leader of The Skatalites, attributed the name to Cluet Johnson, the leader of The Blues Blasters. His nickname was Skavoovee. That's the way he would greet everyone – "What's happenin', Skavoovee?" Lloyd, however, dismissed that. "Ska was around before Cluet Johnson," he said.

"Then, later, we slowed the beat down by half again, and that was the rock steady beat. Then, later, we slowed the beat down by half again, and that is the reggae beat. We slowed it down for reggae to give the music a different sound from rock steady and ska. We were just doing what musicians do, making new music. Ska, rock steady and reggae are all second and fourth beats, only at a different pace."

At its beginning, in around 1956, ska was a rough and tough music that offended the official arbiters of good taste. "Decent people" regarded ska in much the same way that the bourgeois middle class regarded Elvis Presley and rock 'n' roll, as being dangerous to the well-being of youth and society in general. Outlaw music.

In its simplest form, ska is a bouncy sound full of horns on top of a mento ridim. Mento is based on calypso, a Caribbean folk music. Trombones, a holdover from the Don Drummond bluesbeat, were an indispensable part of early ska. It is a danceable party music that drew its influences from R&B, jazz and Jamaican folk music, with a faster tempo than reggae. Ska is a kind of jerky shuffle with the tremble turned up on the electric guitar and punchy brass accents. The emphasis falls on the upbeat rather than on the offbeat, as in R&B. Structurally, ska is a back-to-front version of R&B. The ska classic 'Oh Carolina', an old folk song, featured Count Ossie's drummers backing The Folkes Brothers. Another early ska hit was 'Carry Go, Bring Home' by Justin Hinds.

In 1962, ska got a big boost when Edward Seaga – record producer, authority on Jamaican folk music, then minister of development and welfare and later prime minister – pushed things Jamaican in all cultural expression. Seaga, who established one of the first record companies in Jamaica, West Indies Records, promoted ska as a respectable "native" form of music. He recruited Byron Lee And The Dragonaires, a class act playing the resorts of Jamaica's North Coast, as his show act. Lee, a polished performer, played a watered-down ska more acceptable to the general public. Straight ska was too rude.

Ken Khouri, who started Federal Studios, and Chris Blackwell, the most influential producer in Jamaican history as the founder of Island Records – and who launched Bob Marley And The Wailers – also jumped on the ska bandwagon. In fact, they put the wheels on the wagon. In 1964, Blackwell launched the first ska record to become an internationally popular hit, 16-year-old Millie Small's 'My Boy Lollipop'. The song was a remake of Marvin Gaye's 1954 hit of the same name.

The Wailers' first hit single in February 1964 was the ska song called 'Simmer Down'. The song had the sensibilities that would come forth in reggae, and came from the gut of the "sufferah" people who ordinarily had no voice in society's affluent economy.

In the summer of 1966, ska recognisably morphed into rock steady. Rock steady had the sassy tension of bossa nova and a little American soul to cool it down. In the late '60s, record producer Clement "Coxsone" Dobb and Jackie Mittoo, a composer of popular music, reduced the horn section and began to experiment with basic Rasta ridims with guitar, piano and voice. Ska's simple, repetitive two- or three-chord progression was retained. The walking bass became more flexible, and the overall beat slowed down to a bluesier beat. Out of this came rock steady, with hits like 'Get Ready Rock Steady' and 'Sound And Pressure' by Hopeton Lewis and 'Take It Easy' by Alton Ellis.

Rock steady, like ska, was dance party music, but with a subversive agenda. The easy ridim caught people's ear and put them in a relaxed, receptive mood. Then lyrics slid in about the poverty in the slums, the way the politicians sold them out, and the capitalist overlord class. Most of the musicians came out of the Kingston ghetto, and so knew about the conditions there first hand. They provided the music with a more menacing bass and lyrics with teeth.

The music took on an edge during the "rudie" period, the transition time between rock steady and reggae. Rudie lyrics were nihilistic, reflecting the criminals among the ghetto youth, whose goal was to live dangerously and die young. Not until reggae did the music speak to positive social goals, black pride, self-respect and standing up for what is right. Many reggae stars waded into the rudie waters, including Bob Marley And The Wailers, Desmond Dekker, Alton Ellis and Derrick Moron. Some of Marley's songs from that period included 'Rude Boy', 'Rule Them Ruddy', 'I'm The Toughest', and the rude-boy anthem 'Steppin' Razor'.

The rude boys had a self-assured, chip-on-the-shoulder attitude and a jive-ass walk, and they wore sharp, flashy clothes. The ranks of rude boys swelled as poor rural youngsters straight from the country poured into Kingston to make their mark and money. Rude boys earned (with good reason) the reputation of being small-time thugs, street hustlers, drug dealers, enforcers and aggressive domino players, guys with nothing to lose, and the music reflected their way of life operating beyond the pale of respectability. The ghetto and the music gave the rude boys a milieu in which they felt part of a culture, a culture that rewarded those who seized the opportunities they made, rather than the culture of institutional approval and promotion.

According to George "Fully" Fulwood of the group The Soul Syndicate, the rude boys protected singers and musicians as a sign of respect for what they did. "That respect, having them call out your name and tell others that you were a good musician, was a form of protection. When the rude boys called out 'Fully', that was my protection when we played in rough places. There were gunfights and killings right on the dance floor, but nobody messed with you if you were a well-known musician." Fully became well known because he could play popular bass lines, and he laid down some of the original bass lines still heard 30 years later in songs in Jamaica.

Fully had a Triumph car that his father had bought for him. Cars cost a good deal in Jamaica, and Fully's people were not rich, so the car was treasured. "It was very pretty, and I took pride in that car," recalled Fully. "I'd always be out there shining it. It was spotless. I used to be flashy about that car. It was white with two blue streaks painted on the side. Whenever you saw that car, you knew Fully was around. Nobody ever messed with my car because the rude boys gave me their protection as a musician."

Still, life in Trench Town required using your hands for something besides playing the guitar. Fully, Tosh, Marley, those Trench Town boys, they learned to fight early. "I knew Marley from the neighbourhood," Fully said. "Because he was mixed, white on his father's side, he was picked on by other darker boys in Trench Town. He'd be in fights over name calling, no matter that he was slight and stood no more than five feet eight inches."

Tony Chin, who formed the Soul Syndicate band with Fully, confirmed the account. "Marley was not a soft guy. He could defend himself. He learned to fight to protect himself, and he learned to sing as a way of protecting himself. As he became known as a singer, people wanted to be his friend."

The rude boys were a subculture of sound-system rivalries. Owners of huge sound systems – banks of speakers with a DJ playing on the turntables – were in furious competition for artists and the most up-to-date music to play daily on the street corners. Hired thugs would break up rivals' shows. Street fights, boxing matches, horse races, posturing tough and using and misusing women was the life in this subculture. Ganja, guns and macho, testosterone-fuelled competitiveness to be the "coolest Johnny Too Bad on Beeston Street" inevitably led to clashes with the police. The justice system acted predictably: the judges handed out longer and longer sentences to keep the troublemakers off the street. Prince Buster lampooned the judicial bench on a record about Judge Dread. On side one, the judge sentences weeping rude boys to 500 years and 10,000 lashes while admonishing, "Order! Order! Rude boys don't cry." On side two, the judge grants the rude boys a pardon and throws a party to celebrate their release.

Prince Buster, who was the main man during the rude boy period, urged his fans to moderate their behaviour, as in the song 'Free Love', in which he exhorts the listeners to "speak true", to "learn to love each other". He advises the rudies that "truth is our best weapon", and that "our unity will conquer". In these lyrics can be heard themes of reggae that emerged out of the rude boy phase.

The transition from rock steady to reggae, like the transition from ska to rock steady, was blending cream paint into white paint. The gradual change to the new sound went practically unnoticed. The music became more ethical and thoughtful, with Rastafari political and spiritual metaphors in the lyrics. The Wailers, Toots And The Maytals, Lee Perry And His Upsetters, The Melodians and The Lionaires shaped the emerging reggae. The violence and competitive individualism of the early '60s was channelled into a more focused and thoughtful protest of injustice against the "sufferers" by the perpetuators of the Babylon system.

Rock steady didn't have the hard edge, preferring to be largely romantic entertainment. Reggae put a downbeat on Africa, black deliverance and redemption. Reggae called on its listeners to have a consciousness and to put it into positive action. Reggae called on you to be a warrior, musician or not.

After we left Lloyd, Jah Earl and I set off to find Count Ossie's Mystic Revelation Of Rastafari (MRR) Community Center on Glasspole Avenue, in the Rockfort section of East Kingston.

"This is a rough area," Jah Earl said as we started up a hill of broken pavement. A group of young men sat on a table at a corner. Jah Earl stopped in the middle of the street, out of reach, and asked, "You know Count Ossie's place?"

"You go up the hill and right," one man directed.

"No, to the left," another man said. A shouting match broke out. Jah Earl drove off, made a right turn and followed the road higher up the hill. After a few blocks, he said, "I think we need to turn around."

I picked up a shade of worry in his voice, an unspoken request to get the hell out of the neighbourhood. He turned around and, instead of taking the most direct route out of there, flagged down a woman. "Count Ossie's around here?" he asked.

"Ya, mon. Up behind you."

"Still have drumming up there."

"Ya, mon." The women did not stop walking during the exchange, forcing Jah Earl to back up while talking to her.

He did a U-turn and tried to sniff out the woman's vague directions. We stopped again to ask a young Rasta, who told us exactly where to go on Glasspole. A couple of turns later we came to a cul-de-sac and Count Ossie's Mystic Revelation of Rastafari Community Center.

The three-storey building looked like a school, with louvred windows and a plain façade. Over the entrance was a mural showing Haile Selassie flanked by two dark-skinned angels dressed in flowing white robes. A cement bust of Marcus Garvey was atop the entry post.

Written on the wall was the words, "And God spake all these words, saying I am the Lord thy God which have come brought thee out of the land of Egypt…"

Here at his centre, Count Ossie and other drummers codified Nyabinghi drumming and introduced it to the secular world. As a boy, Oswald Williams (Count Ossie's birthname) had no drum of his own. He practised on empty up-ended paint cans down on Slip Dock Road in East Kingston, where he lived. He'd go up to the Salt Lane area, known as the Dungle, where a contingent of Rastas had settled. It was there that he was first introduced to the reasonings and the music of the Rastas. As a young man, Count Ossie sat in the yards for "groundation" sessions on Garveyism, Rastafari, black culture, the source of the music and redemption, and he learned Burru and Kumina drumming. By his account, he first learned the *fundeh* (the Burru bass drum) and graduated to the *repeater* (the harmonic drum), on which he became a solo virtuoso under the tutelage of Brother Job, a master drummer. When he could afford to, he ordered a set of custom drums from Watto King, a master drum maker.

Count Ossie based his drum set on the traditional Burru drums – the bass, fundeh and repeater, or *peta* – but to his specifications. The fundeh, which carries the steady ridim, or lifeline, was tuned to an alto pitch between the bass and the repeater. The fundeh was regarded as the "peace and love" drum. The balanced, regular, one-two one-two pattern of its "rational" head keeps the peace and holds the lifeline. The repeater is the colour drum. It supplies the melody line and the embellishments to the lifeline. The repeater protests. It defies the rigid bass patterns and cuts against the ridim. Much of the excitement of Rasta music comes from the repeater.

In Rasta music there is the *churchical* (religious music) and the *earthical* (music for entertainment). In chants and churchical songs, the accent of the lifeline ridim is on the first and third beat, while in earthical songs the accent is on the second and fourth beat, as Knibb had devised.

Count Ossie modified his drums because he wanted more freedom to work out his own ridims based on original Burru patterns. He teamed up with like-minded musicians and created a new style of African-derived music for Kingston's growing Rasta population. The bass downbeat in Rasta music symbolises the death of the oppressive society. The brighter, higher notes of the repeater represent the resurrection of the society through the power of Haile Selassie. "And that's how Rasta music was born," Count Ossie is reported to have said.

At first, Count Ossie performed only sacred music in Rasta camps. Other musicians soon heard about the new fantastic drumming in the Rasta camps and showed up to listen. During the '50s and early '60s, Count Ossie influenced some of Jamaica's leading non-Rasta musicians. The musicians invited Count Ossie And The Mystic Revelation Of Rastafari to play at their concerts. The drummers blended the line between the sacred and the secular. This was an important development in linking Rastafari to reggae. It wasn't a radical step. Among Africans and their New World descendants, few rigid dichotomies exist between the world of the spirit and the world of the living. As in Kumina, two realms meet in music and dance. The blending of the sacred and secular is common in contemporary African pop music, such as Zimbabwean *chimurenga* music pioneered by Thomas Mapfumo.

Count Ossie's 'Rasta Reggae' was the first reggae song to fully incorporate the Rasta drums into the popular music. By the '70s, Count Ossie's Rasta music began to dominate the reggae sound. The bass guitar and traps imitated the patterns of the Rasta bass drum, the patterns of which were based on the Burru bass drum. The lead guitar and the singer took over the repeater drum patterns, which are also played by the keyboard and horns.

When reggae hit its full stride in the early '70s, reggae lyrics initially reflected Rasta philosophy. Songs such as 'Mount Zion' – made popular by The Ethiopians and Cynthia Richards – and 'Satta Massa Gana' ('Give Thanks And Praise') were originally religious chants used at Rasta gatherings. 'Wings Of A Dove', 'Holy Mount' and 'Rivers Of Babylon' were Rasta chants that became popular dance numbers.

The music's impact continues to reverberate throughout Jamaica's society. Even people who do not accept the Rasta's redefinition of the society (African rather than European in outlook) accept reggae. The message of the music seeps into their consciousness. The Rastas created musical forms to strengthen the people and give them the confidence to beat down the violence of colonialism, which still lingers in Jamaica. The music was a warrior's cry to take on the thuggery of the Neo-Colonialism and transform the society on the basis of justice and equality. The music helped to create a popular culture based on the spirit of resistance. As globalisation spreads, people everywhere, even in the most capitalistic countries, feel that materialism warps their personalities. One of reggae's central messages is to resist the bribes that make people fools of a manipulative economic system.

Count Ossie doesn't play the drums any more. He died in an automobile accident on 18 October 1976, but Nyabinghi drummers and other musicians still gather every Sunday evening at the centre to rehearse. While Jah Earl and I sat before the centre in the late afternoon, I was just about to ask if he minded waiting for the evening session when he spoke first: "I don't want to be here when it gets dark. This is a dangerous place."

I wanted to give him a pep talk on warriorship, but I held my tongue. After all, it was cultural warriorship, not physical warriorship, on my mind.

Rastas regard themselves as the agents of Babylon's destruction, and reggae as their primary weapon for chanting down Babylon. They think of themselves as warriors. Bunny Rugs, lead singer for Third World, told me that, "Anybody who introduces change, who speaks against the system, who speaks against the colonialisation of our people, anyone who speaks about truth and right, who speaks against oppression, segregation and racism, that person is a warrior. Reggae music has been doing that for years now, speaking now in the voice of people, speaking out for truth and right.

"The biggest warrior we ever had in Jamaica was Peter Tosh. He was constantly hitting out on the system. Tosh wrote 'We Must Fight Against Apartheid'. He was arrested as a youth for demonstrating against Rhodesia's Ian Smith, who was on a visit to Jamaica. His albums *Equal Rights* and *Legalise It* had explicit political messages.

"The cultural warrior is more important than the political warrior. As a matter of fact, politics has no warrior. I don't see how you can make comparison. Okay, in this world you have a very few good politicians, but they all have to listen to the words of Bob Marley and of Peter Tosh and Bunny Wailer. You understand? Politicians cannot come out and speak the truth directly to the people. You understand?

"Nelson Mandela or Jomo Kenyatta are warriors, but I don't see politics and warriorship together. The warrior is always fighting against the politician. The politician deals with capitalism. The politicians don't deal with the people. Nelson Mandela is my hero. I named my son after Jomo Kenyatta. But they didn't complete their warriorship, partly because, in politics, you can't.

"Marcus Garvey wasn't a politician. That's what made the difference. When he started UNIA, he wasn't a politician. Once you get into politics, man, your warriorship becomes a warrior boat. The ship has been reduced to a boat. I've seen that happen in Jamaica, where individuals with great intentions to help the people went into politics and got so corrupted that they forgot what they went into there for. Politics always do that to you.

"Michael Manley, Jamaica's former prime minister [1972-80], was a true politician. Talked loud and said nothing. He was very charismatic. He was loved. But today Jamaica is even in a worst position. The people who get the work belong to whatever political party is in power, whether the People's National Party or the Jamaican Labour Party. The politicians didn't unite the folks. They introduced guns. So when Manley went upon the pulpit and spoke elegantly and beautifully, that meant nothing. It was just words.

"All politicians are corrupted, every single one of them. If they don't actually put their hand in the till, they know who is doing it and they won't come out and say. There is a code of silence. When the politicians hear some of the statements being made from music, I don't think they'll like it. To them, the music is a weapon because the music is speaking about them. People like Anthony B and Sizzla, you think the politicians in Jamaica feel comfortable about what they sing?

"Musicians are loved by the people, but there are responsibilities. Once people have accepted you and decided to give you the keys to continue then you are responsible for being a helpful person. You are representing the people."

Most Jamaican musicians, especially the roots reggae performers that I spoke to, consider themselves cultural warriors. Here's a sample from some of them:

Bread, of The Wailing Souls: "I definitely think of myself, and other Jamaican musicians, as warriors. We're cultural soldiers. It's just life. You have a work to do, so you keep soldiering on. The musicians have to do the soldiering, but reggae lacks a lot of support from the structure that controls music.

"You'll notice that reggae doesn't have no big multinational record company promoting it. Every now and then a reggae artist will get a little break with a record company. Basically, it's just Jah and the love of the music and the people out there that are keeping reggae going. The music can only get bigger, 'cause the people love this music so much and support this music so much. We have to search the radio dial to find reggae and people keep finding us.

"We need to get a step up in the marketing. We need to market the music. We need to get this music to the widest possible audience we can. It keeps marketing to do that. This is a business world. You have to go through the system. As long as we're not tying up or compromising your creative ability, you know what I mean? We need to put our foot more in the door to push it open."

Marcia Griffiths, who received the award for Best Female Vocalist at the 19th Annual International Reggae And World Music Award in 2000, was one of the original Wailer's I-tal backup singers, with Rita Marley and Judy Mowatt. "The Wailers were three strong revolutionary brothers who believed in standing up for what they believed in. They were three ardent brothers who wanted to defend the rights of the people. They just put whatever they wanted to express in the music. To be part of The Wailers, I also have that warrior attitude. I send a lot of messages through my music, particularly to the sisters because we are always seen as the weaker sex and always put on the back burner. I try to strengthen the sisters as much as I can and speak out for truth and right.

"Even when I was touring the world with Bob Marley, we were seen as missionaries, trotting through the Earth, preaching the gospel through the medium of reggae music. We saw ourselves as preachers, philosophers, and going through Earth appealing to people trying to save souls, because a lot of times, when I'm out there with Bob, when we walk on stage, over 100,000 people out there, I always pray that even one from the congregation receives the word and the message, and their souls are filled, and you can do something positive for them, to bring them to a certain consciousness and for the music to unite the world.

"I was 12 years old when I started with the music, in 1964. I didn't have vision of what the music is today. Bob Marley is one of the persons who really opened my eyes to it at this level. He taught me from his action toward what he was doing and the conviction that he did, that the music was serious business. It was his life. You can always enjoy what you are doing, but he knew – I don't know that he was even aware – that he had a purpose. He was like a prophet sent to do a work and to deliver. He knew that what he was saying was serious, and he was prepared. He was very much prepared for, one would say, death before dishonour. He was serious about it.

"I saw him exercise that warrior quality at the Independence Day concert in Zimbabwe, when we were on stage performing. There was a sudden uproar and tear gas came floating up to the stage. Bob was ready and willing to go down with his people. The rest of us ran for our lives except Bob. I always quote the words he said to the three of us – me, Judy, and Rita – when he finally found us after we ran away from him out off the stage. He said, 'Now we know who are the real revolutionaries,' quoting a line from one of his songs. I know that he really practised what he preached. He really stood for what he believed in.

"I've carried on the work because he wanted to see us carry the work, taking it through. We are fortunate that we still have his message and his music to guide us. We find that, since his passing, more people are listening more keenly to what he is saying, rather than just dance at the beat. Those words are like words we'd read in the Bible. Everything is being manifested in this time today. We have been begging the people over years to listen to the words. It's not just fun and dance and entertainment. The message is there."

David Hinds, lead singer for the Grammy Award-winning band Steel Pulse: "I most definitely consider myself a warrior. A warrior, as far as I'm concerned, is anybody who is not supportive of all the wrongdoings of a system. As a warrior, I use reggae as one of my weapons. I'd like to know that I could branch out with books and take part in movies that show the cultural aspects, the positive side, of us as a people. There are too many movies, too many documentaries, where we are shown in a negative light. I don't mind reality kicking in. I like those movies that show the warfare in the ghettos, like South Central LA. I like them a heck of a lot because that's reality kickin' in. That does happen.

"But there are so many programmes where Africa is shown in such a negative light. When people see that, even people of my age or my father's who have been in the Western society since two, three hundred years ago, they think the whole continent of Africa is like that. Or if they see a coup happening, they think every African country has lawlessness and anarchy. There is such a negative light painted about Africa, especially by the Western world media, that I'd like to play a part in changing all that.

"Unfortunately, I don't have such a project. That's the story of our life. Since we, Steel Pulse, have taken such a stance within our music, a lot of doors have been closed for us to go out there and make things happen in a big way. Every time a door gets opened, it's by a black American. For example, we've been dreadlocks and talking about exploitation for quite some time. Back in 1985, you had Live Aid to raise funds for the starving Ethiopians and there was not one single reggae band on it. We had been talking about the situation in Ethiopia for God knows how long, and there was no reggae band at the event for something that reggae's always been all about. For me, that was absurd.

"These are things that show we haven't had a chance to have our views aired because people are still pulling the strings and still closing the door and not making it happen. That's why it's been very difficult for me to get other projects going."

Kwame Dawes, an eminent thinker on the aesthetics of reggae and a reggae performer, added this: "The musicians are cultural warriors. The cultural warrior is the person who is suddenly aware that their sense of place and their sense of identity are under attack and is being denigrated. Their quest is to restore a certain pride and a sense of connection and value in their identity and place.

"At first, the artist warriors are reactionary, and then proactive. Their job begins in reacting, as in Peter Tosh's song 'You Can't Blame The Youth', where he says we no longer want to hear about the very great man Christopher Columbus or the pirates Hawkins or Morgan. That song says we don't want any more of that history. We want a new kind of history. The artists are fighting against the myopic all-consuming notion of history that is white and Eurocentric and destroys any notion of history outside of that self-serving version of history.

"History is rarely about truth; it's about telling and who tells it. Reggae is definitely a retelling of history. The way that history was taught at the colonial level excluded the narrative of people who were oppressed or defeated. It was a history that literally made people invisible. Took them out of the equation. Reconstruct that history and you start telling the same history but from another perspective. Suddenly the history begins to take on a new dimension. It has a different psyche and political implication.

"Reggae retells the history and brings another angle to the way we view history, so when Peter Tosh does his historical story in the song 'You Can't Blame The Youth', he says, if you tell the youth that the pirate Hawkins was a very great man, and if the youth become pirates and criminals, don't blame them. Tosh is reshaping the way we approach that history. That's very important.

"The question of truth and who holds truth are not the same. Truth is a fact of time. How we tell that truth becomes the fundamental way history has an impact on our present.

"As reggae has evolved in time, we hear the same thing over and over: fight against oppression. The only way that message stays fresh is that the oppression keeps being fresh. If oppression continues, then reggae will continue being lyrically interesting. Bob Marley, Peter Tosh, Bunny Wailer, Burning Spear wrote – and write – lyrics that make you go, 'Wow.' It wasn't just because they are better artists; the truth is they are gladiators doing their songs.

"There are tons of other people singing, 'Blood, blood, blood, in the Babylon,' singing against Babylon. Babylon has become such an easy phrase. There are lots of dancehall singers who say, 'I'm going to go roots and culture now,' and all they're saying is the old cliché of Babylon must fall. They have no lyrical strength, just badly written lyrics. When you see somebody who comes with lyrical strength, you say, 'Yeah. There is a moment.' That moment is someone who is a gifted artist finding a way to articulate and freshen in a new way.

"As long as oppression continues to exist, as long as the artist sees himself or herself as fundamentally a kind of prophet in the midst of that oppression and that oppression remains true in Jamaican society, the artist will be a warrior.

"I go back to a more African notion of warrior as prophet, king, poet, the *griot* figure, and part of being a warrior is to have an artistic credibility and a prophetic voice. Artists achieve or do not achieve this position depending on who they are. The warrior becomes someone who is at once fighting for his or her own survival but also perceives his or her own self as speaking to a larger community. The warriors must come on beyond themselves, in spite of themselves, in their quest to speak about their experience in preserving a culture and language, or generating a language. They must have force enough to face the culture on its own terms, even if their agenda is merely to make some money. The motivation of warriorship is important. If warriorship is rooted in the idea of community, then generosity, compassion and tenderness become part of it, too.

"The reggae warrior uses the music as a weapon. Absolutely. The question is, who's wielding the weapon? Who's making the money? Reggae artists have always realised that, even in their own success and in articulating statements against the oppressors, they are faced with producers and with record companies that bring Babylon upon them."

9 Reggae Culture

Frederick "Toots" Hibbert, who formed Toots And The Maytals with Jerry Mathias and Raleigh Gordon in 1961, asked me to meet him at the Aquarius Studio. "Just come to Halfway Tree and look for the chicken place," he said on his cell phone. That was about as precise as directions get in Jamaica.

Halfway Tree, one of Kingston's commercial hubs, was a busy square. On one side, buses lined up to take on and drop off passengers. The snarl of traffic, the infamous Kingston chaos. People swarmed about, as numerous and as busy as maggots at a ripe feast. Vendors' tables piled with a mish-mash of cheap goods forced pedestrians off the pavements to squeeze between the kerb and the honking metal rushing past.

What kind of chicken place was I looking for? I circled the square and saw no sign for a recording studio.

"Where's Aquarius Studio?" I asked one of the street vendors. He took me by the hand and led me to a locked iron gate between Popeye's Chicken And Seafood and Olive's Hotpot. Behind the gate, at the end of a narrow passage between the restaurants, was a varnished door. There was no sign, no indication whatsoever, that a recording studio was behind the door. The helpful vendor reached between the bars of the gate and pressed a hidden buzzer. After a couple of minutes, a large man wearing a huge knitted black tam opened the door and came to the gate.

"Is Toots here?" I asked.

"Ya." The man unlocked the gate. I thanked the vendor and promised to buy a pair of sunglasses from him when I left.

The industrial kitchen fans blasted me with smells of hot oil and cooking chicken as I walked down the passage. Once inside the varnished door, I was hermetically sealed from city noises and smells. In the small studio, Toots, wearing a Kangol cap, sat next to his grown son, Hopeton, who was playing a bass guitar. They were patiently laying down the bass tracks for the song 'Proud Mary', which Toots was preparing to record. Toots waved with a big smile and kept on working.

Satisfied with the bass line, Toots and the sound engineer fiddled and fiddled and fiddled with the drum machine, searching for the right rim shot. It took a good half hour to hit upon the exact *crack! crack!* The bass line and the drum are the foundation upon which the song would be built. If those ridims were mislaid or misaligned, the whole song would be askew. It might make the difference between a well-crafted song or an also-ran, a hit or a miss.

Then Toots turned his attention to the keyboard player, who had been patiently sitting at his synthesiser. A tape of the bass and drum tracks was played. The pianist listened intently, then played a steady, pounding rhythm, like a second drum line. Toots stood at his side and listened and listened. On the eighth time through, he reached over the pianist's shoulder and played three notes, once in major and once in minor. It sounded like a three-tone birdcall, a statement with a seductive echo.

He demonstrated again what he wanted, the little trill that alerted the ear to expect the unexpected. The keyboard player had difficulty in getting the timing right. Toots demonstrated again. The keyboardist practised a couple times, then nodded that he had it. The song started from the top...and started from the top four more times. The guy obviously wasn't hearing the same ridim and timing as Toots, who had every nuance of the arrangement in his head. They worked for another hour getting the pianist's fingers inside Toots' head.

Think of a waitress who transforms herself into a Las Vegas showgirl. That is the contrast between the Toots in the studio crafting a song and the Toots who performs the song on stage. In the studio, Toots was plain, calm, deliberate, doing the job of setting the table and getting the food down. When I had previously watched him perform live, he wore stage glitter and worked like a one-man chorus line performing a routine based on a tent-preacher's act. He ran back and forth across the stage exhorting the audience to "Rise up! Rise up!" to the good times. Using the old call-and-response warhorse, he had the audience verbally sign up and fall in as he marched them into songs. Sweat poured off him as he pranced across the stage, leading his reggae crusade in the name of Jah. He sang for two hours non-stop. Young women reached up their hands, begging to get on stage with this short 60-year-old man with a paunch. He pulled them onstage until there was no more room, and all the while he never stopped performing with the fervour of a man saving souls.

In the late '60s, the two most popular reggae bands in Jamaica were Toots And The Maytals and The Wailers. Toots is credited with giving the music its name, in his 1968 dance single 'Do The Reggay'.

There are numerous explanations for the origin of the word *reggae*: that it came from a rough street dance that was very sexually suggestive; that it came from Rega, the name of a Bantu-speaking tribe on Lake Tanganyika; that it's a corruption of *streggae*, Kingston street slang for a prostitute; that it's a derivative of a Jamaican sweet made from sugar cane and crushed fruit, the sweetness likened to the music.

When Toots took a break from the studio, I asked him about the word. "It comes from the beat of the music," he said. "That ragged rhythm and good body feel. It was a fun word for a fun music. But it had more than that. The beat was fun, but the message was about regular people in the ghetto who don't have what they want, like food. I put the *R* in the music with 'Do The Reggay'. A lot of people know I named the music, but in Jamaica people don't talk about live people, who made the music, while you're alive. But if you die, people can give you all sorts of awards. In Jamaica, they don't give you what you deserve."

"Did you deliberately set out with the music to redefine the identity of Jamaicans?"

"I don't know if reggae in the late '60s was a turning point in redefining the Jamaica identity with regard to their African heritage. Reggae culture is words to make people be aware of what's happening, or singing about what happens to you or other people. Conscious words is reggae culture. Wisdom, knowledge, and understanding are the culture of reggae.

"All my songs are love songs. I didn't even sing about what's happening in Jamaica because it's not spiritual. I don't like to help to put the physical thing on the first page of *The People*. I just leave it alone. It's not really cultural. It's against the Father. What's happening in Jamaica is against God. I won't even talk about those things because, I tell you, if I say those things, not everything from my heart, it will not be fair. But it's no secret that the whole world is turning upside down. The whole world, including Jamaica."

He then launched into a 20-minute tirade against the Pope, and a speech about the God Almighty Rastafari. "It's important to know what to sing about, who to pray to, know who creates and who gives life, and then start to pray to that God Almighty," he said as the lead guitar player, a tall, slender Rasta in dreads, arrived to lay down his tracks. Toots, who grew up a Rasta, is a "plainclothes" Rasta who has never worn locks. "Time back to work," Toots said.

I followed them into the recording studio. Toots stood in front of the guitar player and sounded out the ridims he wanted. The guitarist, very competent and a quick study, picked up and ran some riffs. Toots coached him on the beat, at one time actually placing the man's fingers on the chords Toots heard in his head. Two hours later, with the studio hazy with spliff smoke, they were still at it.

While I listened, I thought about Toots' term *reggae culture*. There are national cultures, ethnic cultures, tribal cultures, corporate cultures and country-club cultures, but does reggae have its own culture? If so, what are its characteristics? How does reggae culture affect people's points of reference? What are the values of reggae culture?

I had spent hours mulling such questions with Kwame Dawes, my mentor on the subject of reggae. Kwame is the lead singer of Ujamaa (which means "togetherness" in Swahili), and is also the author of *Natural Mysticism, Towards A New Reggae Aesthetic In Caribbean Writing* and an associate professor of English at the University Of South Carolina. When he's not in the classroom, he performs, writes songs and prepares new books on reggae.

Snatches of our conversations drifted by as I sat, stoned on secondary smoke, listening to Toots at work. A main purpose of reggae, Kwame ventured, is a sense of mythic for a social purpose. "I'm speaking of the classic roots reggae of the 1970s," he cautioned. "Reggae's primary intention is to bring knowledge and wisdom and an awareness of the suffering of the black and poor people. Reggae also brings an awareness of a larger scheme in the way that we see the world. Rather than trying to win Rastas, in that everyone should become Rasta and grow their locks, reggae tries to suggest that there is a larger cosmology, a construction of the world where there is a godhead and consequences for action.

"Reggae incorporates the very humanistic principle of caring for human beings," Kwame continued. "That is the core of reggae. It's presenting a world view that can be applied to many cultures and ideas, as opposed to the evangelical hard sell that attempts to make you become something, rather than opening you up to something. In that, I think, reggae's agenda is not as daunting as other agendas. That's part of why reggae has such a broad international appeal."

What does this sense of mythic do? It makes white kids jump up and down at reggae concerts and shout "Jah". These same kids would not be caught dead shouting out in praise of God at a rock concert. When David Hinds of Steel Pulse sings, "Am I black enough?", these white kids shout back, without irony, "Am I black enough?" The message of the music transports these kids beyond their race, beyond their economic class and into a universal association with poor black people. The music says that this is bigger than all of us. Only Jah is greater, so let us praise this mythic father figure of Jah. If we align ourselves with Jah then, in His reflected glory and power, we will rise against oppression and suffering.

That message is a common characteristic of reggae. It imparts humanistic values. The effect is to uplift the consciousness in realisation that we are all one, brothers and sisters, and that we should stand by one another. Let's say that this is an attribute of the reggae culture, okay, professor?

For Jamaica, and other former colonial countries, the message of reggae has helped to create a new sense of identity. Reggae urges you to be proud of who you are and where you came from. Fight for the right to know yourself and to express that self. Reggae artists write songs that use images out of their own society. 'Start Up' is a song about love, but what was the image? A cooking pot left out in the yard.

The reggae artist tells the world "You need to access what I have to say from my experience if you are going to make sense of this music. You need to come listen to my language, to what I say in the language that I speak, in the idiom that I speak, and then maybe it will make sense to you. If it does, we're talking."

Self-esteem is part of the reggae culture. If we all become strong links, there will be no weakness in the chain, and brothers and sisters we are all linked together. There is nothing mythic about the fact that the world drinks Coca-Cola. There is nothing mythic in the television pictures of people massacred by dictators. We must all stand up for the rights of each other, for our rights, and you must be strong within yourself in order to do that. The reggae culture expounds equality, respect and individual effort for the common good.

The creation of a sense of personal identity and a sense of place, of nation, begins in the telling of one's idea and the claiming of one's own space. For people coming from a colonial environment, or any oppressive situation, this is a radical concept. Reggae has established an African identity within the colonial mindset that lingers in the Jamaican identity. This has been reggae's most profound impact on the Jamaican culture. Reggae has delineated a cultural image within the dominant culture, and this new image is causing a shift in values within Jamaica. In this respect, reggae is revolutionary. Reggae is winning the cultural war.

Reggae music creates its own sense of arrogance and place. It says, "This is what I am, what I stand for, and I don't apologise." Kwame once commented that this is a style of music that came out of his street and his ghetto. And yet this is the kind of music that I think you should listen to. There is something very arrogant about it. There is no victim situation in it. The very act against victimhood makes reggae stand out. Reggae is arrogant, defiant. More importantly, it just presumes its presence. It says, "You've got to listen to me!"

Part of the reggae revolution is the striking out against the victim perception of woe, poor me, this abject subject of slavery (or at least the slavery of ancestors), now I can't do anything for myself. Lyrics of Marley or Burning Spear or Peter Tosh or Capleton (the DJ who currently rules Jamaica) aren't written from a victimised position. Get up, stand up. Stand up for your rights. There is nothing victim-driven in it.

Reggae lyrics, especially those of early reggae, come from the working-class culture, and as such are deeply political and social. "Forget your troubles, forget sickness and dance," says the music. If dance is understood as a kind of protest, and if jumping to the music is a violent act, Kwame pointed out, then reggae promotes the acting out of a social consciousness, and the reference points are working class. Is reggae a conduit through which to create unionised action? Not in the same way that Woody Guthrie wrote a song for the union; but reggae got some of its authenticity and intention from the working class. Part of that working-class sensibility is a distrust of politicians.

Bob Marley said that you should never trust a politician because they will try to control you forever. He wasn't speaking about a hypothetical situation but from his own experience of being taken around by politicians to speak on behalf of the politicians. Many reggae songs were written during the '70s primarily for political purposes, and the artists were exploited and abused by the politicians in a number of ways. Marley questioned that. This questioning is a case in which reggae music articulates both its role as a tool of working-class political activism and at the same time becomes a tool of questioning those politicians.

"Reggae became the soundtrack for what was going on in the 1970s," Kwame said, "which was essentially, in Jamaica, a revolution. In 1972, Manley came to power, and by 1973 it became clear that he was embarking on a socialist agenda. He began to develop relationships with Castro in Cuba and other socialist leaders, including those in Africa. Jamaica became a socialistic country. Part of the way in which the socialism of Jamaica was being sorted was through this music. Reggae music reflected the sustenance of the revolution. Now, this is important. This is not part of a larger political plan. People weren't responding to a political plan. All musicians didn't support Michael Manley. But there was a spirit of revolution that privileged the working-class experience. Reggae spoke to and endorsed that experience. Suddenly, black people came to understand themselves as having value. The music shored up that notion. In that sense, it is a real revolution that reggae is speaking to.

"Reggae music is a curious fusion of Rastafarian peace and love and a fire and brimstone that will destroy Babylon, both the economic system that sows injustice and the mental outlook that perpetuates all injustice and oppression. In this, it shares a political consciousness with the Black Power movement through Garveyism. You have an amalgamation in reggae music where all these things are taking place. Prince Buster was a clear Black Power movement man. His lyrics, his 'Judge Dread', speaks to that. I don't see any music anywhere that was political and popular at the same time like this music."

Universal and international revolution, which is a kind of socialist revolution, spoke through reggae. Burning Spear sang, "Do you know that socialism is the best?" He knew that he was punning on socialism. Bob Marley would sing that it takes a revolution to make a solution. He knew what he was talking about.

At the same time, there is another kind of social revolution taking place, which is the relationship between the people and the state or government. The protest against the state that does not work for all of its citizens equally and resistance to the police are very much part of Jamaican culture.

"The state becomes the object of oppression and the music begins to speak at it and towards it," Kwame once said. "My point is that whatever political action is in the lyrics of reggae songs is not hypothetical. It is growing out of everyday existence, and what people are trying to do to survive in the world that they live in. In a sense, reggae and Rasta is reactive in that it is acting against oppression. Therefore, the presence of oppression is pre-requisite to the articulation of reggae. It's pro-active, in the sense that it no longer begins with the premise of a colonial order. It begins with the premise of a new order, a reconstructive order. That is why it is different from the blackening of a belief system. It comes out of an experience that goes back beyond colonialism."

Spirituality is very much part of the reggae culture. The dichotomy between the secular and the spiritual, between the sensual and the pure – which is part of the culture of Western societies – does not exist in reggae, with its antenna tuned to African-based belief systems. In those beliefs, a sacrosanct line separating the white hats and the black hats doesn't happen. Wherever people make their living with the land there is a more holistic sense of walking hand in hand with the sensuality of mysticism. Reggae offers this duality of experience, the spiritual and the sensual.

Your body dances when you listen to 'Get Up, Stand Up For Your Rights', a deeply political song. You dance in a sexual way, shoulders and hips rolling and thrusting to the round, fat bass line that is melodic and sweet and sensual. It's good music to make love to. At the same time, the music cries out for freedom and for the struggle against injustice.

Is it a cultural influence of reggae to have people lay down for the right reason? Do not lay down at the feet of oppressors; only lay down for your lover. Never stop the struggle for everyone's freedom, but learn the skill of gentle aggressiveness. Humour makes a good rubber knife with which to flay the Babylon masters.

Reggae's political message gave the music an international appeal. It is the successor to Black Power without the aggressive edge of that black liberation movement. Instead, reggae emphasises peace, love and brotherhood. It calls for the unity of subjugated people around the world to fight oppression. Materialism is a form of that oppression, as is white domination and discrimination. The music calls for solidarity among the poor and powerless. It is a quest for freedom, justice and righteousness that can be translated into the experiences and aspirations of downtrodden people everywhere.

Reggae culture's call for pride in African heritage and identity strikes a major chord with Africans. There are long-standing and sizeable Rasta populations in West Africa – particularly Ghana, Senegal and Gambia – that mirror their Jamaican counterparts. African Rasta also has ritual and secular use of marijuana. Reggae is the music of choice. One of reggae's international stars is Alpha Blondy, a Dimbokro-born Seydou Kone on the Ivory Coast. African Rastas wear dreadlocks and the Rasta colours of red, green and yellow, and also have an outspoken commitment to social, political and religious ideologies promoting pan-Africanism. They believe in a black God, and use biblical allusions and allegories to support that belief. Jamaican Rastas look to Africa; African Rastas look to Jamaica.

Sizeable Rasta populations also live in Canada, mostly around Toronto, and in urban centres in the United States, primarily on the East Coast. Central and South America, the Caribbean basin, Europe, Japan, Australia and New Zealand also have Rasta populations.

In England, Rastafari and its attendant reggae culture came out of the disappointment of many Jamaican immigrants who came to the mother country to find social acceptance and equal opportunities, finding instead only bitter disillusionment. The values of reggae culture as a means to counter those injustices appealed to David Hinds, who became the lead singer for Steel Pulse.

"I always loved reggae music, but when it started to say things that I wanted to hear, that's when I decided that I'm going full swing to being part of being the messenger, instead of being on the receiving end of the message," he said from his home in Birmingham, England. "I choose reggae over other musical forms because it is part of our cultural heritage, our background, the music that was fed to us during our childhood, with our brothers and sisters coming from the Caribbean. My attraction was because of the music of Bob Marley and Burning Spear more than anyone else.

"Reggae does help create a communal memory and history among oppressed people everywhere, no matter their colour. And, more specially, the music has very much created that community between the Caribbean and Africa. I find that reggae music has played a big part – which was the initial idea – to unify Africans at home or abroad, whether they lived in Zimbabwe, England, Jamaica, St Lucia or Brazil. All of us with African heritage have come out of a psychic trauma, which has been slavery and all kinds of institutions, whether physical or mental. Then you've got fine guys like Burning Spear talking about Marcus Garvey. Marcus Garvey stood for Africans at home and abroad uniting into a united front, where there was a respect as a people. He was always saying that a nation without authority was a nation without respect. You can say that Garvey was all pro-black in every sense of the word.

"But at the same time, when it comes to humanity, he was helping mankind. I don't think that mankind can survive if one side of mankind is down. You find in the Western world society, which is of the caucasian race, when it comes to technology, the military forces, that society is very high, so to speak; but at the same time, we can't have that balance of harmony among mankind if another is down, regardless of colour or creed. This is where Rastafari comes into it. We're saying, 'Yeah, this has happened to us. Let's try to better ourselves so that we can be respected and we can go on and continue with whatever love or business there is to be negotiated to make this world a better place.'

"A lot of people can misinterpret Rasta as being pro-black and pro-African, as to appear to be anti-white, but it's not that, you know? Like in the case of Louis Farrakhan as being anti-white. But Louis Farrakhan is very well versed as to what historically happened with his people. He knew, and we know, that we need to establish mankind on a better level than what it is right now. We, as all people, are in a predicament, and we need to sort ourselves out. A lot of people can misinterpret that as being anti-white or being pro-black on the point of superiority. It's not that at all.

"Reggae is a revolutionary music. Music, especially from a Western world viewpoint, has always been viewed as a safe way of expressing yourself outside other pressures around you, whether you can't pay the bills or political problems or whatever. Music has always been viewed, initially, where one goes out and says, 'Baby, I love you. Let's dance.' That's how Western world society has been portraying music, especially of the last and this [20th] century. Reggae comes out and says, 'Hey, we're not satisfied with this. We're tired of that. We want freedom now.' Western world music wasn't saying anything like that. I can't think of any, apart from Bob Dylan, that airs views in that way.

"Reggae music has been a revolutionary vehicle where [people have] expressed themselves for liberation. I think the music played a very big part in liberating most of Africa. It played a part in liberating Zimbabwe. Bob Marley was invited there 20 years ago at their independence celebration because of what his music said. Reggae played a part in the liberation of Mozambique and South Africa. I don't recall any pop music helping to liberate a country, you know, from any struggles. It's rebel music, reggae music."

10 Negril

Forecasters predicted that a record number of hurricanes (11) will whiplash the Caribbean from June to November in this year (2000). A sky with a belly full of rain accompanied by a 110mph rage straight from a bellicose Neptune, that's what we're to expect. Hurricanes usually hit Jamaica from the eastern end. On one day before the season officially began, I shifted to the island's western tip to ride out the raging tempests on the infamously hedonistic beaches of Negril. Normally, the bus ride from Kingston to Negril via Savanna-La-Mar on the south coast takes from four to five hours. By choice, my trip took nearly two days.

An hour out of Kingston, we were in the highlands of Manchester, the bread and fruit basket of Jamaica. This is a really sweet country of broad valleys and steep mountains. Just past Mandeville – the main town, which sits on the edge of the uplift – the road began its descent towards the coastal plain. The view of lush, broad valleys below was worthy of a travel magazine. At East Lacovia, I took my first detour deeper into the mountains to find the source of the Frontend Loader. A beautiful woman in Kingston had told me that the Frontend Loader "can do for a man what no money cannot". I loved the twinkle in her eye when she said that. My destination was the Appleton distillery, which processes 90 per cent of the over-proof white rum in Jamaica. I figured that the bartender at the distillery, which gives public tours, probably makes the best Frontend Loader on the island.

At Maggotty, the jitney bus took the road further up the Black River Valley and into the Nassau Mountains, gorgeous country of frothy mountains and fields of sugar cane. The people there walked slowly, and they smiled a lot.

At the distillery, the manager offered me a tour to explain the arcane details of the pot still versus the column still methods. I thanked him, but Ponce De Leon didn't search out the Fountain Of Youth just to take a drink of water. "The Frontend Loader," I said. "A woman told me to seek out the best Frontend Loader on the island. She said I'd learn something about Jamaica."

The manager laughed. "Come, I'll introduce you to the bartender."

The Frontend Loader is two ounces of white rum blended with pimento liqueur, molasses and clear syrup, and poured over ice. "It gives great strength," the bartender said with a wink as he set the drink before me.

Later, I discovered that there is a herbal Frontend Loader called Long Journey, made with blood root, nerves root, red root, lily root, star root, genital root, red clover, cock stiff, strong back, goldenseal, black jointer, lavender, median, raw moon, ginseng and sarsaparilla. I figured that anything containing ingredients called cock stiff, strong back, black jointer and raw moon must be a potent concoction.

"White over-proof rum is used for many things in Jamaica," the manager said as I cautiously sipped. "We use it mixed with herbs to cure colds, sore throats, headaches, fevers, and the spirit when it's not well. It's used as a disinfectant in medical clinics. Insecure men use it to be better lovers. Sometime newborns are washed with over-proof to cleanse them. Father's bless their baby with it."

Over-proof rum is a traditional part of the Nine Nights ritual, the manager said. Nine Nights is a wake to prepare a dead person's spirit for its final departure. The deceased is laid out for nine nights to allow friends to visit. On the ninth night, over-proof rum is liberally sprinkled about and drunk to chase away the *duppies* (harmful spirits). The death party was probably borrowed from the Irish, who were brought to Jamaica as indentured servants by the colonial British.

"On the ninth night, the turnin' out ceremony, everyone stays awake with the coffin until dawn," the manager continued. "We're not just sitting there but putting our energy, our thoughts, our intentions to welcome and entertain the duppy of the dead person. We sing and play games to prepare the deceased to leave the house and not come back as a spirit. At midnight the house is swept clean, the furniture rearranged and the belongings of the dead person removed. We don't want the person's duppy to feel at home if it should return. The body is always carried out feet first because duppies never travel backwards, so the duppy can't walk back in to haunt the house. After a person is buried for three days, you may see smoke, a vapour, rising off the grave. That's the duppy."

My Frontend Loader, a seductively sweet and spicy drink, was replaced with a second.

"Actually, there is a firm reason why over-proof rum is used in the death ceremony," the manager continued. "In older times, the body would rot quick, especially in this heat. The 110 per cent over-proof killed germs."

I slowed down on the second Frontend Loader or the only thing I'd load would be my soggy self.

"Over-proof was once the drink of the labour class," the manager said, "but now the middle class has adopted the rum. But the real over-proof culture is in the roadside rum shops."

I promised to hit every rum shop along the coast to Negril, like a boxer going for a knockout.

"You'll be knocked out," laughed the manager.

A promise is a promise. In the countryside, rum shops can be the corner grocery store or a local social club. After I left the distillery, I kept an eye peeled as the jitney barrelled through hamlets. Nothing looked promising. Not until Whitehouse, on the coast, did I find a typical one-room rum shop. The advertisement on the front wall for Wray And Nephew, the island's leading rum brand, was faded and peeling. Two women in very short skirts sat on stools beside the open door, obviously awaiting the trucker trade. They nodded pleasantly as I entered. Inside, the bar was a Las Vegas of colourful Christmas lights, busty pin-ups, and an out-sized mural of a naked woman spread across one wall. A cityscape of bottles stood before a huge mirror with twinkling mini lights snaked around the edges. The bartender, a hefty woman wearing a Florida State sweatshirt, smiled a broad welcome. Three men at the bar edged aside to give me elbow room.

"A Frontend Loader." I felt as if I was ordering condoms from a fresh-faced drugstore clerk.

"You don't care if the sun not go down yet?" the bartender laughed. "Any time is a good time, ya, mon."

The men laughed at her double entendre.

She set the drink before me and the men raised their glasses in salute.

"The over-proof, she's good for you," said the man wearing a yellow hard hat. "I'm a builder. I sprinkle over-proof on the foundation of every building I put up, ya, mon. The rum is a sacrifice to the spirits of the land. All things have spirits. I offer the rum to the spirits for protection and blessing of the house. If I don't, maybe the house doesn't stand true. The duppies can disturb the relationship between the foundation and the structure."

"Be careful around duppies," cautioned the second man. "They can control your mind and body, and your thinking, what you do. A duppy can be good or evil, but whatever, you should fear them."

"How do I know a duppy when I see one?" I asked.

"They roam only at night," the builder replied, "but they can fool you. They act just like a human, sing and whistle and smoke and do human things, like cook. You can always tell a duppy when it rides a donkey. They ride with their head pointing backwards and hold on to the tail. But they can take the shape of animals, too, so the donkey may be the duppy. Duppies are very tricky."

"So to reveal a duppy I need to get the suspect to ride a donkey." After the Frontend Loader, anything seems possible, even getting an evil ghost to ride a donkey while singing and smoking a spliff.

"Yes, but that be difficult." The builder was perfectly serious.

"They never touch the ground when they walk," the second man added. "They float like a breeze. And they go back to their graves before sunrise, like vampires."

"They talk funny through their nose." The builder pinched his nose shut to demonstrate. "And their laugh is like a witch's." He gave a high-pitched cackle.

The second man leaned close and whispered, "If a duppy is after you, strike a match and throw it. Then strike another match and throw it. Then strike a third match so the duppy can see but stuff it out quick. The duppy will search all night for the third match. Duppies love to count, but they can only count to three. While the duppy searches for the third match to count, you escape."

"No," countered the builder. "A duppy can count to ten. If a duppy stalks you, make an X in the soil quick. The duppy will be detained at that spot trying to count to ten. He'll stay there until wind or rain washes the X away."

"Duppies count in Roman numerals?" I asked.

The third man, a Rasta in dread, joined in. "You have to drive out these odious superstitions and replace them with the revelations of Jah Rastafari, His Imperial Majesty Haile Selassie The First. The superstitions keep your mind occupied so you don't think about real things. While you're chasing duppies, the Babylon man is chasing your power. He makes you a dope. You have to be duppy conqueror, someone tough and courageous, a person who can defeat evil in all its supernatural forms. You must be a true mystic to battle even the devil himself."

Bob Marley was considered to be a duppy conqueror. He titled an album *Duppy Conqueror* in case anyone missed the point.

"A duppy can be Jah," the builder said.

"Maybe a white god but not the true Jah," countered the Rasta.

"A duppy is a duppy." The builder spilled some rum from his glass onto the floor as an appeasement.

Before this theological discussion got to the how-many-duppies-can-stand-on-the-head-of-a-pin stage, I announced that I needed a hotel for the night.

"I have a friend," the builder said. "I built his hotel." He polished off his over-proof and drove me to a modest hotel on the shore a short way out of town.

Yes, we have a room, said the owner, Norman Anderson, in perfect American English. It turns out that he had a degree in hotel management from Cornell University. His dream was to open a chain of small Hospitality Inns along the south coast as an alternative to the big tourist hotels. "There is a battle for the south coast shaping up," Anderson told me over coffee, which I requested to counteract the Frontend Loaders. It seems like the hotel conglomerates at Negril see a new market on the south coast. Ground has been broken for a new Sandals all-inclusive resort near Whitehouse. A 400-villa residential complex is also moving off the drawing board. However, according to Anderson, the local people didn't want another Negril or Montego Bay in their back yard.

"We need economic development along the south coast, but without destroying the nature of the place," Anderson said. "I want to create employment for the local people in order to keep a sense of community, which is very deep in the Jamaican make-up. We are always laughing and talking and playing music together. Most Jamaicans, especially the rural people, suffer great material poverty, yet they have a happy nature, in part because of their sense of belonging to a family and to a community."

The coast itself may discourage large-scale development of tropical paradise resorts. The shore is mostly rocky, rather than fronted by postcard sand beaches. On the other hand, the few sand beaches – most notably Bluefields, and Parrottee Beach – look like cash machines to developers. The people of Bluefield regard Negril tourism as a threat rather than a blessing. They fear that farmers will be forced from their land by rising real estate prices. Fishermen are already economically suffering from the dwindling fish stock resulting from mangrove destruction and overfishing, a condition they fear will be exacerbated by more stress on the environment.

British sugar cane planters who drained marshlands and harvested the hardwood forest began the environmental desecration 300 years ago. Jamaica has managed to protect 22 per cent of its 2,667 square miles of forest cover, more than any other Greater Antillean island. Most of this is mangroves and upper montane forest. However, the island is losing its forest cover to coffee plantations, agriculture and new development at a rate of five per cent a year, making Jamaica's rate of deforestation the highest of any country in the world.

"The Bluefields Project was formed in 1988 to promote small business and establish links between environmental and economic sustainability," Anderson said. One such project is the Bluefields Beach

Zumjay, a 20-year-old DJ singer who is seen as being one of the most promising emerging reggae artists

Paul "Lymie" Murray, one of the rising performers within Jamaica, who is starting to break into the international scene

Yami Bolo (bottom right) with other reggae artists, giving the Rasta symbol, which is part of the Star Of David

Jesus Afari, one of Jamaica's best-known dub poets and an influence in revolutionising language in the music

The 2000 Boys, reggae performers in Ocho Rios who are trying to make their mark on Jamaican music without going the Kingston studio route

Prezident Brown, an international reggae performer who finances the Music Avenue Studio in Ocho Rios to support young Jamaican musicians

Sugar Minott at his studio on the edge of Trench Town, warming up for a studio session

Freddie McGregor and his daughter, Shema. He received the Jamaican Living Legends Award in 2000, while Shema is considered to be one of the up-and-coming female singers in Jamaica

Ken Booth, one of the original reggae singers who came out of Trench Town. He received the Jamaican Living Legends Award in 1999

Kumina drummers and dancers of St Thomas keep the African cultural and musical connection alive

The Reverend Danny Dread, a long-time DJ who is part of the movement to lead the music away from computer ridims and back to singers and acoustic drums

Nyabinghi drummers joining with Maroon drummers at Accompong for an afternoon session. Bongo Cutty, sitting alone, plays bass while Zaccheus, dressed in white, plays the fundue

Mortimo Planno, Jamaica's honoured philosopher and the man who chose Bob Marley to carry the message of reggae to the world

Trench Town – where Marley, Tosh, Bunny Wailer and other roots reggae artists started – is attempting to become a tourist attraction

Bob Marley's childhood home at Nine Mile, the "one room with a single bed" made famous by his song.

Marley's tomb, with the two angels, is next to the house

Arnold Howell, son of Leonard Howell, who founded the first organised Rasta commune of Pinnacle. He points over the land where the Rasta movement started

Jah Earl, a friend of Bob Marley and other roots reggae singers from Trench Town. He knows the ins and outs of Kingston

Park, the site of a small mausoleum honouring Peter Tosh, who was born down the coast at Belmont. Tosh was murdered in 1987. Each mid-October a reggae festival is held there on Tosh's birthday.

Developers also face the formidable obstacle of environmentalists, who have launched a campaign to preserve the south coast for low-impact tourism. Nearly half of the south coast shoreline has been proposed to be designated as national parks. The 3,150-acre Font Hill Wildlife Sanctuary, one of the least-disturbed natural ecosystems in Jamaica, stretches along two miles of shore, while the Great Morass – a 125-square-mile wetland that extends inland from the mouth of the Black River – is the premier ecotourism attraction. The Great Morass is Jamaica's most significant refuge for saltwater crocodiles. About 300 live in the swamp, and can be seen easily on a boat safari into the swamp. The tours can be booked in Black River.

"You should go to YS Falls," Anderson advised, "to see how ecotourism stopped the destruction of a beautiful river."

In the morning, leaving my gear at the hotel, I hitched to the falls, which were not far from the Appleton Rum Estate. The road was a lane of crushed white rock wrapped in dense, dark-green foliage. Large trees with long, snake-like branches sprouting clusters of pink blossoms arched over the lane. They are locally known as *quickstick*, because they grow so fast. The lane stopped at a general store-cum-gift-shop-cum-snack-bar, where Massey-Ferguson tractors attached to wagons waited to pull visitors up to the falls.

A Captain Scott and his partner, Mr Yates, operated the original YS Estate as a sugar cane plantation on land granted to Scott's ancestors in 1655 by Oliver Cromwell for services performed. The present owner, Tony Browne, raises racehorses in the surrounding pastures and intends to keep the falls in their natural state.

I climbed onto a wagon of blue padded seats with other tourists. The tractor pulled us along a farm lane through rough pastures. A 12-minute ride delivered us to the 120-foot-high cascade. Browne has made parkland at the falls, with trimmed grass and colourful flowers around the centrepiece of a huge tree. Small wooden steps implanted in the ground lead up the sides of the falls, the three tiers separated by perfect swimming pools. A vine dangling over the lower pool made a convenient Tarzan rope for swinging out over the water and dropping for a refreshing plunge.

For years the government wanted to build an electric hydro dam on the YS River above the falls. That would have dried up the falls. The established tourist trade, which provides local jobs and income, has proven an effective defence against the dam.

By early afternoon I was in Savanna-La-Mar (Spanish for "The Plain By The Sea"), waiting to catch a jitney to Negril. When the van stopped, I could see no room for another passenger. The conductor directed me to a rear seat. I looked at him, like, are you crazy? There's no place to sit there. Yes, yes, he urged. I squirmed between bodies, being as polite as possible, to the seat. I looked dubiously at the non-space between a grandmother and her teenage granddaughter. The old lady smiled and shifted slightly. I wiggled my hips into the offered sliver. It was like pushing down through wet cement. I rode the 18 miles to Negril with the grandmother's and granddaughter's shoulders up under my armpits and my butt barely touching the seat.

Negril is a strip town along the seven-mile Long Bay. Actually, the town – post office, bank, police station, grocery store – is huddled around a mini shopping mall, and the hotels are along the sand, discreetly tucked back among palms. I found a hotel in the middle of the beach but on the "garden side", across the road from the beach. At "garden hotels", the rates are half of those at the sand-and-surf properties.

I came to search out music. In truth, I came to search out an erotic encounter. Everything I'd heard about Negril put my expectations on tiptoes, eager to topple into whatever cream pie invited the fall. Sun. Sea. Drugs. Exotic location. Women on vacation out of sight of familiar eyes. Women eager to shake booty more vigorously than at an office party. Hotels are in on the complicity. When I checked in, the lady behind the counter said that if I had overnight guests they had to sign in, as if this was expected.

I walked out onto the beach. The flat blue Caribbean rolled gently at my feet. Cloud galleons moved across the horizon with towering sails, billowing, as if running before a full gale. Yup. A postcard. To my right, on a promontory at the far end of Long Bay, were Hedonism II, Sandals and other all-inclusive hotels. You never have to leave the premises to have all of your wants and desires fulfilled. That's the marketing promise. Hedonism II is infamous for its lingerie dinners, where the women wear their most revealing attire. A glutton's all-you-can-eat pie-in-the-sky pig heaven was the marketing promise. These are places of safe adventures. You never risk meeting a Jamaican who must sell something that day in order to eat dinner. You never need to find the skill of rejecting the sales pitch without being dismissive. I found that the beach entrepreneurs just wanted to be recognised as hardworking people doing an honest day's work. They wanted acknowledgement for the hours spent and the skill needed to make the woven bracelets and hand-carved pipes and beaded necklaces. They wanted – needed – to make a sale, yes; but equally important, they wanted an appreciative word about the good job done. When you walk away without a purchase, they thank you for looking, for talking with them, for being friendly, rather than treating them like a used car salesman with AIDS.

It must be noted, though, that these high-end hotels have more substance than being merely playpens. Sandals has adopted a local school to assist, and on Labour Day the employees started construction on a two-bedroomed house for an 82-year-old woman.

At the end of the beach to my left were the cliffs of West Negril. On the top of the cliffs were Rick's Café, the Pickled Parrot and the Negril Yacht Club, hot spots, hot, hot, hot, catering to tourists who promised themselves a holiday where you hide the pictures from the children. That's where I started my search for an erotic encounter.

The road up the backside of the cliffs was narrow and windy with no shoulder. On the right were the walls and façades of hotels. On the left was a neighbourhood. Behind Negril Below is the Great Morass, a swamp inhospitable to human habitation, so most local people live on the high ground of the cliffs. The neighbourhood of banana and mango trees had an easy swing feel. There was no reason to jitterbug here, moving so fast to have a good time that you don't listen to the music. Small wooden houses were barely seen in the greenery, giving a feeling of spaciousness, of the land not being used greedily. Along the road, the juice bars and jerk stands and "ital" vegetarian eateries and handicraft stalls, painted in the heraldic Rasta colours of red, yellow and green, invoked hippie idealism rather than crass commercialism.

It was a $6 US taxi ride to Rick's Café, the most famous bar on the cliff. Tourist buses from the various hotels charge $20 for a ride. The normal taxi fare for anywhere along the beach is $200-$400 JA ($4-$8 US).

Rick's was set back behind a low stone wall. Tourist buses parked on the concrete apron. Back in the early '70s, before the beach became Hotel Row, Rick's Café was the hangout particularly favoured by North Americans, who flew small planes to secret landing strips in the nearby hills. To "catch the sunset" from Rick's was a nightly ritual of drinking and jumping off the cliff into the sea 40 feet below. That tradition continues.

I walked into Rick's and found a pleasant upscale restaurant bar. The only thing Jamaican about it was the waiters and waitresses. Americans, with a smattering of Europeans and Jamaicans, drank and chatted and ate, while a few brave souls jumped off the diving platform. I settled at the polished concrete bar and tried to order. You need a token, the helpful young man informed me. Tokens are purchased at the entrance. This only enforced the feeling of being in an automat, despite the upscale décor and million-dollar view. And the drinks and food were, by Jamaican standards, overpriced. I might as well have been in Miami.

The in-house band plugged in. Well, if not an erotic encounter, at least I would get reggae. If I squeezed my eyes shut tight, it could be almost the same. The third song was a cover of 'Wish You Were Here.' I fled.

I landed at the Pickled Parrot further down the road. A water slide replaced the cliff jump, but little else changed. The scene was another tropical holiday joy in sunburst shirts. I felt that I had stumbled into a travel agent's package tour. Everyone was having such a determinedly good time, as if they knew that they had an allocated number of breaths before – bus for the airport leaves at nine – they sank below the surface of their at-home lives. Everyone was part of a couple, or too young, or too like me, so I moved on down the road to the Negril Yacht Club.

The catamarans anchored below the cliff had ferried in a throng, clad in bikinis, T-shirts, shorts and sunburn. I was determined that this would be a fun place. However, the scene was that of a floating cocktail party that had drifted down from North America, cruised over from the Mediterranean, and never changed accent. There was a live band. I squeezed my eyes as tight as a hatch on a submarine to invoke a reggae rush, and got a headache. The beach, I decided, would be my land of opportunity.

On the following day I discovered the opportunities: para-sailing, glass-bottom boat rides, jet skis, SCUBA diving, and rent-a-rastas. I'd heard about these guys, the fabled Nimrods sought by female sex tourists. The song 'The Big Bamboo', by The Mighty Skipper, was their theme: "I give my woman some coconut/Some like it cold, some like it hot/The only thing she said to me/What good is the nuts without the tree/She like the big bamboo."

Lyrics boasting of sexual prowess are a staple ingredient of DJ songs. Shabba Ranks' 'Stamina Daddy', Lady Saw's 'Life Without Dick' and Little Lenny's 'Nine Inches Long And Coming' give the idea. Terry McMillian wrote of her experience with romantic, sensitive, considerate and passionate Jamaican men in her novel *How Stella Got Her Groove Back*. She married her man, in the film. She was lucky, though, because Jamaican men are not known for their commitment to the home fire. Single mothers are the norm in Jamaica. Philandering husbands contribute to the continuing rise of AIDS and HIV infection among women in Jamaica.

On my second day at the beach, I saw him. He rippled. His walk was carefree, with lazy hips and swinging shoulders, the whole motion an easy-going rock and roll. With him was Delicious, perhaps 19, in a bright-blue bikini. They were hand in hand, puppies pinching each other's butts, staggering with laughter, and flirting so hard it made my balls ache. I wanted to run up and tell her that Caribbean men were lousy lovers. The West Indian academic Everold Hosein had conducted a survey and the women said that their men tolerated few deviations from the straight missionary position. Cunnilingus was as rare as a snowcone in hell, despite Shabba Ranks' song about the "poom-

poom". Foreplay was perfunctory, a clearing of the throat before the solo, in which the woman was only a backing singer. The women complained that their men usually rushed through self-indulgence with little interest in, or knowledge of, female sexuality.

But I couldn't be a spoilsport. Nimrod and Delicious were having too much fun being young and sexy and at Negril.

They were the biggest thrill of my day, that and the old lady beneath the coconut tree who sold me, for $2 US, a quart of freshly squeezed orange juice in an old vodka bottle.

Where's my exotic erotic? I asked on the third day of trolling. Maybe I should pal around with a rent-a-rasta and learn the tricks of the trade. I hadn't seen Nimrod, but why would he come out of the dark? But I knew, in my heart of hearts, that I didn't have what it takes to be a rent-a-me. Jamaicans, both men and women, have a natural way of saying hello and making it sound like they're inviting you – the most desirable, funny, good-looking person on the planet – to their beds. My North European charm was monosyllabic compared to the poetry of their smiles. All I had was pretty blue eyes, and the blue eyes that I saw on the beach weren't looking for their own kind. I tell you, after seeing a few dozen breasts parboiling in the sun, they all started to look like sunny side up fried in too much oil.

A sign at De Bus, a beachside stage, announced that Admiral Tibet would be performing that night. So my exotic erotic would be reggae. I accepted that. That evening, on my way to a beachside restaurant before the show, I was given another opportunity.

"You want brain food, man? Smoke? Coke? Hash?"

The only thing more plentiful than sunshine at Negril was drugs. Whenever I strolled down the beach at any time of the day or night (some of the eateries stay open 24 hours), I was offered a cornucopia of drugs.

"Come. I'll buy a beer," I told the hustler. "But you have to tell me things."

After the beer was delivered, I asked, "What's the preferred drug by the tourists?"

"Coke. People want more cocaine than ganja."

"Where does the coke come from?"

"Colombia. Straight to here. No Miami or New York middleman to jack the price, and no baby powder mixed in. We give good stuff at a good deal."

"Where does the ganja come from?"

"Over the hill. Westmoreland herb is some of the best."

"Are you afraid that the Kingston drug gangs might move in on your territory?"

"They would not live," he replied with serious heat. "We can take care of that."

"Gango-a-gango?" He looked at me blankly. "Gang to gang," I clarified. "You have gangs in Negril?"

"No. Not organised, like Kingston. We all know each other here and help out."

He sipped his beer, casually scanning the beach. "The police, they watch us close. You can't smoke on the beach or the police will grab you, too. They want a bribe." He finished the beer. "You want something for tonight?" He was actually a nice young man, polite, no tough-guy attitude. "It's hard to make a living here. We do what we can to help you people have a good time."

"No thanks. I'm just looking for music."

"Admiral Tibet is the big show tonight."

"When does it start?"

"The sign says nine but maybe 11."

At 11:30 I walked down the beach to De Bus. Ten-foot-high sheets of zinc closed off a section of sand. Christmas lights were strung around a stage. The only action was a small knot of gullible tourists milling about waiting for the show to begin. An hour later, still no performer had appeared on the stage. Hell with it. I went to bed.

On the fourth day, I wished for a hurricane. Anything to break the monotony of lying on the beach. I'm not a beach person. Beaches are high-tech holding cells and the ocean the jailer keeping me landlocked. The only way to break out across the ocean is by commandeering a ship or a plane. I knew where to find the bus, so I grabbed it and headed around the island, past Montego Bay, to a country house that a friend had arranged for me.

11 Marcus Garvey Reggae

Yesterday I went looking for Winston Rodney, aka Burning Spear, the reggae icon. He keeps a house in his home town, St Ann's Bay. Burning Spear was Jomo Kenyatta's *nom de guerre* when he headed the Mau Maus' successful war, waged to free Kenya from British rule. Kenyatta, a British-trained sociologist, was Kenya's first president. Rodney is St Ann's Bay's first son. In 1974, he had a hit song, 'Marcus Garvey'. His newest album, *Calling Rastafari*, won a Grammy in 2000. A folk historian, sociologist and poet, Burning Spear always urges Jamaicans to look to their African heritage, and yet he doesn't turn his back on Jamaica. He tells his countrymen to constantly strive to make their country better: "Mek it sweet."

Burning Spear is revered in Jamaica, although his music is not often played on the radio. When he gives concerts in his home country, the youth wait out his set and call for the DJ Bounty Killer.

The battle against the colonial version of history is Burning Spear's warriorship. His songs laud a kindred warrior, Marcus Garvey. In one song, he says that Garvey was a great man and a married man – that is, a man like any other man, with ordinary concerns; but Garvey added to his "common man" a political and social activism, like a bass guitar and keyboard playing over the heart drum. His life has taken on sensuality, if you will, a sweaty love. Garvey became reggae, sings Burning Spear, because he lived a love song for the oppressed.

Burning Spear sings of Martin Luther King Jr in the same context. King understood the complexities of reggae: politics, sensuality, love, and having a fun time even when doing the hard work of political and social activism. Martin Luther King didn't even know what reggae was, but nevertheless he was reggae.

In St Ann's central square, I asked if Rodney Winston – the name most people here know him by – was in town. "Ya, he was here, but left Friday. Back to New York for a concert."

Reggae sings of a trinity: Jah, Rastafari (Haile Selassie) and Marcus Garvey. In any ten-song set played on Irie FM, the proudly "non-aligned" radio station that is the voice of reggae in Jamaica, eight of the ten songs mention Jah, Rastafari or Marcus Garvey. But Garvey was a critic of Haile Selassie and of Rastafari, so why is he revered in the music? Why is he given a place in the pantheon of Rasta and reggae heroes? To understand why Garvey has been placed at the right-hand side of the throne, some history in necessary.

Marcus Mosiah Garvey, St Ann's most famous son, was born on 17 August 1887. His middle name can be read as a combination of *Moses* and *Messiah*, given the Jamaicans' fondness for word play. His childhood nickname was Moses. He was one of 11 children of a prosperous printer and his wife.

Garvey grew up with other black and white boys and made them "respect the strength of his arm". He wrote of his childhood: "At home, in my early days, there was no difference between white and black… We romped and were happy children, playmates together. The little girl whom I liked most knew no better than I did myself. We were two innocent fools who never dreamed of a race feeling the problem." But at the age of 14, adults forced the playmates apart. The rules of the day dictated that blacks and whites had to be consigned to separate worlds.

Garvey developed into a short, powerfully built man. He moved to Kingston in his late teens, where at the age of 20 he took part in a major printers' strike in 1907 and gained experience as an organiser and orator. He went to England while still a young man, and lived in London from around 1912-14. While in London, he read Casely Hayford's novel *Ethiopia Unbound – Studies In Race Emancipation*. Published in London in 1911, the book was all the rage among the small black intellectual community in London, and it greatly influenced Garvey's thinking.

In July 1914, at the outbreak of World War I, Garvey returned to Jamaica. He was in Kingston less than a week when he founded the Universal Negro Improvement And Conservation Association (UNIA) and the African Communities League. The organisation's chief goal was to institute a separate, but equal, collegiate educational system for Jamaican blacks, modelled on Booker T Washington's Tuskegee Institute.

In 1916, Garvey travelled the United States to expand his organisation. UNIA flourished throughout the '20s. Chapters were established in 35 states and branches opened in Lesotho, Ghana, Nigeria, Liberia, Sierra Leone, Namibia and South Africa. At its peak, UNIA claimed a membership of two million people. UNIA organised spectacular parades and held rallies in Madison Square Garden, where Garvey delivered speeches such as "Ethiopia, Land Of Our Fathers". He was a prominent public figure, perhaps the most visible and important black man at the time. At the end of World War I, he sent a commission to the League Of Nations' conference in Geneva to request that certain captured German territories should be given to American blacks as a reward for their service in the war.

Garvey and the leaders of UNIA advocated an end to colonialism in Africa and the Caribbean. They envisioned the eventual development of the African continent into a modern network of nations, much like a United States of Africa. Garvey taught that the black man would always suffer as long as he was separated from his African homeland. In his song 'African Bound', Burning Spear keeps this "homeward bound" yearning alive as a real goal for Jamaicans.

However, Garvey didn't envision a mass exodus back to Africa: "We do not want all negroes in Africa," he said. "Some are no good here, and naturally will be no good there." He dreamed of the creation of a black nation, spearheaded by UNIA, that would be strong enough to defend the interests of its black citizens and to gain the respect of the rest of the world.

He became the leading proponent of pan-Africanism. In this, he owed much to United States black nationalists David Walker, Alexander Crummel and others. Their ideological lineage reached back to the African-American church leaders of the 1700s and 1800s, such as Daniel Coker, Martin Delany and Bishop James E Wood, who popularised the biblical statement "But the promise is that princes shall come out of Egypt, Ethiopia and shall stretch out her hands [the lands] unto God." In his 1898 speech "God Is A Negro", Bishop Henry McNeal Turner was the first theologian to declare that God is black.

Garvey also owed much to fellow Jamaican Dr Robert Love, whose journal *Jamaican Advocate* promoted pan-African unity, anti-colonial ideas, and race consciousness during its existence from 1894 to 1905. Love's motto was "Africa for the Africans". In 1901, Love and H Sylvester-Williams of Trinidad launched the Pan-African Association. Their mission was twofold: to secure Africans and their descendants throughout the world their civil and political rights; and to ameliorate the condition of their oppressed brethren in Africa, America and other parts of the world.

Garvey settled in Harlem and promoted his UNIA as a fraternal organisation for local politicians, business leaders and civic-minded blacks. He also sponsored a newspaper, *The Negro World*, whose slogan was "One Aim, One God, One Destiny", and a monthly magazine, *The Black Man*. His most ambitious plan was the shipping company the Black Star Line, which later proved to be his downfall. The Black Star Line, established in 1919, was designed to "link the coloured peoples of the world in commercial and industrial discourse", and trade runs were initiated between Jamaica and the United States. The shipping line was not established to transport blacks back to Africa, as rumours had it, but that rumour prompted the Ku Klux Klan to offer their assistance to Garvey in shipping blacks back to Africa.

The Black Star Line went bankrupt in 1922, and Garvey and three associates were indicted on several counts of tax evasion and mail fraud stemming from the sales campaign for the company's shares. Garvey maintained that he had been framed. He was indicted for mail fraud in 1923 and found guilty. He remained free on bond until 1925, when the conviction was upheld and he went on to serve two years in the federal penitentiary in Atlanta until President Calvin Coolidge commuted his sentence. He was then deported back to Jamaica.

Garvey's slogan was "Africa for the Africans at home and abroad; settlement movement". He believed that the dignity and equality of blacks was linked to their ability to claim land they could call their own, a land in which they could be their own masters. Unity. Equality. Self-respect. Pride in a liberated Africa. Those were the foundations of Garveyism. It is therefore no surprise that the Jamaican Rastas were attracted to the man and his message. Next to Haile Selassie, Garvey is the most important figure in the Rastafarian cosmology. It's a commonly held belief among Rastafarians that Garvey was the forerunner to Haile Selassie, like John the Baptist was the forerunner to Jesus, and Garvey's birth date is a major holiday on the Rasta calendar. The Rasta colours – red, yellow (or gold), green and black – combined the original colours of the Garvey movement – red, black and green – with yellow borrowed from the Ethiopian flag (red, yellow and green).

Rastafari and Garveyism share many similarities: both movements are committed to an ideology of nationalism that supports political and economic independence for blacks; they both strongly advocate the respect, beauty, and dignity of Africa and of people of African ancestry; and both show great respect for the Bible and distance themselves from the Eurocentric interpretations of scripture that contribute to the oppression of black people.

However, Garvey was not an admirer of the Rastas. He treated them with scorn and disavowed any association with them. Garvey refused Rastafarian leader Leonard Howell permission to distribute pictures of Haile Selassie in Garvey's headquarters at Edelweiss Park, Kingston. He was also highly critical of Haile Selassie's conduct of Ethiopia's war with Italy, when Mussolini invaded in the mid 1930s. (In truth, the Ethiopians put up a stiff, valiant resistance, but their antiquated rifles were no match for Mussolini's modern mechanised army.) Garvey regarded Selassie as a ruler, a political being. Howell taught that Selassie was the Messiah, the Black God.

When a Rasta delegation led by Robert Hinds, Leonard Howell's lieutenant, attended a UNIA convention in 1934 at Garvey's Kingston headquarters, they were kept at a distance. Hinds wrote, "We the Rasses march, and when we went to Edelweiss Park [Garvey] said he welcome everybody but the Rasses. Because he ignorant, of course, for him never know that Ras Tafari was God; him only say that God was black. And he made a junction between us. Him deh ya so, and we deh ya so. And him have a crowd at the back so that we couldn't come near to him."

The early Rastas were drawn predominantly from Jamaica's African underclasses, and the African rites and beliefs of the Jamaican peasants influenced Rastafari practices. Garvey's movement had the stamp of the emergent black *petite bourgeoisie* – intellectuals with middle-class aspirations.

The Rastas challenged the colonialism of the British monarchy but justified the feudal monarchy of Ethiopia. Garvey attacked both monarchies equally. The Rastas regarded ganja as a sacrament, a holy weed that could put the user in touch with divinity, while Garvey called ganja a "dangerous weed... The smoking of it does a great deal of harm or injury to the smoker; we understand it has the same effect on the subject as opium has."

Still, the Rastas regard Garveyism as one of the ideological cornerstones of Rastafari. Garvey never considered himself as part of Rastafari. He was brought up a Methodist, and regarded himself throughout his life as a Christian, although one without a denomination.

The Rastas regard Garvey as a prophet because of his "Image Of God" speech given in 1922: "We, as Negroes, have found a new ideal. Whilst our God has no colour, yet it is human to see everything through one's own spectacles. We have only now started out – late though it be – to see our God through our own spectacles, the God of Isaac and the God of Jacob. Let Him exist for the race that believes in the God of Isaac and the God of Jacob. We negroes believe in the God of Ethiopia, the everlasting God – God the father, God the son, God the holy ghost, the one God of all ages. That is the God in whom we believe, but we shall worship Him through the spectacles of Ethiopia."

Dissatisfied with Jamaica, Garvey left for England in 1935, where he died in 1940 and was buried. He was later re-interred at St Ann's, his birthplace.

Before I left the town of Burning Spear and Marcus Garvey, I took a long look at St Ann's Bay, the site of Columbus' humiliation. On 5 May 1494, Columbus first stumbled upon Santa Jago, the original name for Jamaica, and anchored at St Ann's Bay. He named the bay Bahia Santa Gloria, "on account of the extreme beauty of the country", as he noted in his log. There he met the Arawaks, whose original name was Taina, an Amerindian group that over centuries had migrated up the Caribbean archipelago from the Guianas in northern South America. They arrived on the island, which they named Xaymaca ("land of wood and water"), in around AD700. There are about 120 rivers on Jamaica now, although nearly all are dry for most of the year. The island was originally rich with forest and marshlands.

The Arawaks were short and slightly built, averaging about five feet tall, with bronze skin, broad faces and shiny black hair. They wore their hair in a topknot to emphasis a prized beauty mark – a pointed skull – an effect that they achieved by pressing the still-malleable heads of babies between two slats of wood. They lived mainly at the mouths of rivers along the coast, and were principally farmers who grew sweet potatoes, beans, cassava, maize, spices and tobacco. The word *tobacco* is derived from the Arawak word for the two-pronged nostril pipes they used. Other Arawak words now in the English language include canoe, cannibal, hammock and hurricane.

The Arawaks were skilled potters, carvers and boat-builders. Their ocean-going canoes, hewn from silk cotton trees, were up to 100 feet long and could carry 50 people. They also were skilled weavers, adept at spinning cotton and making clothes, which they traded with neighbouring islands, and they also wove hammocks (an Amerindian invention), rope, carpets and watertight roofs from the stringy bark of the calabash tree. When the Spanish dominated the island and enslaved the Arawaks, the Indians were forced to weave sailcloth for the Spanish ships.

The Arawaks were also musicians. They fashioned drums and tambourines from the trunks and stumps of trumpet trees. For drumheads, they used the supple skin of aquatic mammals, like the manatee. Primitive woodwind instruments were carved out of tree limbs and animal bones. Tribal chieftains played the instruments at ceremonies celebrating a good harvest or bemoaning the burial of slain warriors.

Religion played a central role in Arawak life. They believed in a glorious afterlife and worshipped one supreme god, Yocahu, the sun god, who also was the "giver of cassava". They also had lesser gods, who were thought to control wind, rain, sun and hurricanes. These gods were represented by *zemes* (idols of humans or animals). More than 230 Arawak sites have been discovered on Jamaica.

The Arawak were largely a peaceful people who had fled from the warlike Caribs, after whom the Caribbean basin is named. The Caribs, also from northern South America, swept up the island chain, killing and enslaving the Arawaks, although the Caribs never made it to Jamaica. Perhaps because of this experience, the Arawaks did not welcome Columbus and his men with open arms.

When Columbus' ships appeared in St Ann's Bay, the Arawaks lined the shore and shook their spears to drive the intruders away. After the hostile reception, the next morning Columbus sailed to Discovery Bay, a short distance up the coast. There, another group of Arawaks stood on shore warning the strange people not to come ashore. Columbus ordered his crossbowmen to fire on the group, and killed several. After this military "victory", Columbus claimed the island for Spain and christened it Santo Jago.

But Columbus paid dearly for his rash act. Nine years later, on his last trip to the Caribbean, still seeking a passage to Asia, a storm forced him to shelter in St Ann's Bay. His two worm-ridden, barely seaworthy ships began to take on water. Columbus and his crew of 120 salvaged what they could before the rotten ships sank into the bay.

The coastal road where I stood imagining this scene was sea-covered when Columbus watched as his only way home slipped beneath the waves before his eyes. Columbus' dismay must have been compounded because his son Ferdinand and his brother Bartholomew were part of the crew. The great admiral had failed his family, his men and his king and queen. There was no way to keep this disaster a secret.

Columbus and his crew built temporary shelters and settled in, waiting to be rescued by a passing ship. The Arawaks, watching from the safety of the wooded hills that still surround St Ann's Bay, offered no assistance. They hadn't forgotten Columbus' murderous ways. Columbus and his men weren't threatened with starvation in the land, where mangos, pineapples (the progenitor of the Hawaiian pineapple), avocados, cassava and pawpaws – a tree melon that Columbus called the "fruit of angels" – grew wild. Nevertheless, they still suffered from malnutrition, since the Arawaks refused to share their agricultural knowledge. Melancholy, homesickness and infections, made more virulent by the foetid tropical heat, also beset the hapless Europeans.

Columbus and his men waited for nearly a year to be rescued. No one came looking for them. No sail appeared on the horizon. Finally, in desperation, two officers paddled a canoe 150 miles to Hispaniola to seek help from the Spanish governor. The governor promptly threw them in jail. Reportedly jealous of Columbus' fame, the governor sent a captain to check if Columbus was dead. The captain found Columbus, but he didn't land at St Ann's Bay. He sent a message ashore advising Columbus that a vessel couldn't be spared to rescue him, and sailed back to Hispaniola.

Eventually, the jailed officers were released and chartered a boat to rescue their captain and crewmates. On 29 June 1504, Columbus sailed from the New World back to the Old World, where he was disgraced and sank into obscurity. He died on 20 May 1506 at Valladolid, an inland town in northern Spain.

An historical footnote: where is Columbus buried? This is something of a mystery. His passing was barely noted at the time, and he was humbly interred at a Franciscan monastery in Valladolid. The body was reburied at some time between 1506 and 1514 at the Carthusian monastery of Las Cuevas in Seville. The explorer stated that he wished to be buried in Hispaniola, and his heirs pushed the Crown to grant that wish. In 1537, 1539 and again in 1540, the Crown ordered that Columbus' bones should be sent back to the New World. The records at Las Cuevas show that the body was sent to Santo Domingo in 1536. He was reburied in the Cathedral of Santo Domingo in 1541.

In 1795, the eastern part of Hispaniola was ceded by treaty to the French. The Spanish didn't want Columbus' bones to fall into French hands, and so his supposed tomb was opened and some bones were gathered into a gilded casket, transported to Cuba and reburied in the cathedral of Havana. However, in 1877, workmen opened two burial vaults in the Santo Domingo cathedral and discovered a secret chamber behind the place from which Columbus' bones had been removed. In the hidden chamber was found a leaden casket with the inscription, "Illustrious and renowned man, Christopher Columbus." The initials CCA on the side of the box presumably stood for Cristobal Colon, Almirante (Christopher Columbus, Admiral). A silver plate found in the chamber was inscribed with the words, "A part of the remains of the first Admiral, Don Christopher Columbus."

So who is buried in the cathedral in Havana? Historians speculate the bones are most likely those of Don Diego, Columbus' son, who had been buried in the sanctuary near his father. Columbus' brother, Bartholomew, and his grandson, Christopher II, were buried in the cathedral as well, and are also possible candidates. For 21 years, Santo Domingo and Havana debated as to who had Columbus' remains. Then, in 1898, when Cuba gained independence from Spain, the Spanish authorities removed the disputed relics to Seville, where they are now displayed in the cathedral. As a goodwill gesture, the Spanish government sent some of Columbus' dust to his home town, Genoa. Four different cities – Santo Domingo, Seville, Havana and Genoa – all have claims on Columbus' remains.

I left St Ann's Bay for Ocho Rios, a charmless cruise ship pit-stop and tourist town ten miles further down the coast. I was looking for Music Avenue, a small studio set up for local musicians by Fitz Cotterell, aka Prezident Brown, a painter and reggae performer. He is one of a small group of Jamaican musicians who put their money where their mouths are in supporting and cultivating unknown musicians. Sugar Minott, in Kingston, is another such benefactor.

"You know where to find Prezident Brown's?" I asked the first man I met after getting off the jitney.

"Keep up the street past the market. Cross at the Almond Tree and ask the shops."

At the Almond Tree Restaurant, I crossed the street to the shops and approached four young men who were lounging under the shade of a large almond tree. "I'm looking for Prezident Brown's studio."

"Right here," one of the men replied.

I looked around in puzzlement.

"Follow me." The group led me to a narrow passage behind a tailor's shop. One man held the door open and gestured for me to enter. The space was smaller than a small bathroom with no room for a tub. At one end was a console and tape decks. Two steps away was a recording cubicle. "This is where we work," said a man who introduced himself as Albert Harrison, aka Braveheart, sound engineer and singer. "All the best talent isn't in Kingston." His tone challenged me to contradict him.

"Right. Bob Marley, Justin Hinds, Burning Spear all came from the north coast," I confirmed.

"St Ann's parish. Right here," Braveheart replied.

"And the Century 2000 boys," said Michael "Richie Richie" Reed, another singer. "That's us. Bob Marley was the real thing. Peter Tosh was the real thing. We're the real thing."

"You want to hear?" Braveheart put on a tape. From the speakers came the reggae sound, faster than the classical but not quite hip-hop. Hip without hop. A richer texture than early reggae was built on the original bass and ridim structure. I checked the immediate impulse to dance.

"It's not finished," Braveheart explained. "We have to put in the Nyabinghi drum track."

Over the music, the musicians told me their disappointments and difficulties and hopes in struggling to carve a career from the hardwood of the music business. "The system is a fraud. If you don't pay, you don't get played on the radio."

"Producers are looking for fast money. Money comes before music. So we get same machine ridims over and over. Cheap to do."

"Producers have to come to the country to find the talent."

"Lot of us won't go to Kingston. They just steal what you have for them. They're not interested in building up champions."

"Kingston give you quick money. Countryman has time to think. Listen to the birds and plants. The countryman give you clean."

"We give you real live music. Cut out the computers."

"No creativity is killing music."

Prezident Brown eased his way into the studio and introductions were made. He was a soft-spoken, handsome man who wore his dreads under a small tam.

"Why do you finance this studio?" I asked.

"I personally know what it is to be on the street as an artist. I grew up really poor. I know of waking up with music going in you and having no place to go with it. In my day, I had the sound system. I started out in that and dancehall. With the sound system, the producers were looking for new singers every week, so new artists could get a shot. Now that's not there. So I decided to put this together to give these artists a place. It's nice to have a place to go play, express music – at least talk about it with other musicians. This little studio is what I can do to keep young fellows in tune."

Prezident Brown grew up in the rural hills of Clarendon, on Jamaica's south side, and developed his art on the north coast, which has a long history for producing Jamaica's best singers. He is much better known in Europe than in his own country. His song 'Faith', on the *To Jah Only* album, was a 1998 hit and still gets airplay. He was about to return to Germany to release a new single. "I was trained by Jack Ruby, who produced Burning Spear, all his albums, including *Marcus Garvey*. I was a DJ and Ruby taught me to keep the crowd in the groove. I went to Kingston to record and lived there for one month, and left. I couldn't live there. The producers said my conscious music wouldn't sell. It wasn't about girls and guns, so I had to retreat."

Many musicians maintain that dancehall in whatever form is reggae, which is like claiming whales and men sing alike because they're both mammals. Prezident Brown made a distinction between reggae and dancehall. "Dancehall has one beat, a sort of mento, semi-calypso without chord structures. It uses computers and a few instruments to produce a synthesised sound. Dancehall uses sound instead of music. Before, people played music – it had real vibes – but now dancehall is just recycling. Producers put ten artists on one ridim track. DJ music will drive you nuts. It gives you no place to go. The

DJs seem stuck in the aggressive mood, and don't lead people to a new place in their music. Now you don't have a Jamaican sound. A Kingston DJ sounds like a New York DJ sounds like a London DJ, who sounds like a Tokyo DJ.

"Whenever there's an oldies dance – always sold out, people dancing, always full of music. Why do the producers and promoters keep missing the point?

"I've reached the stage where Marley was in the 1970s. He was more famous out of Jamaica. I'm more famous and get more respect music-wise in Europe. That gives me a platform not Jamaican based, so I can work independently of what Jamaica is producing. Personally, I'm back to instruments and singing, acoustic vibes, more drumming. I'm a Nyabinghi drummer, too. I'm going to come forward with contemporary Nyabinghi put on the now-familiar sound. Put the new on the root. That's what Bob did. His roots were Nyabinghi. Even to survive doing this is like going to war. I'm a warrior. I want to be a warrior who makes sense."

Braveheart put Prezident Brown's CD on the sound system. "We're trying to build back to the roots," he said. "More bass and drums, real drums, so you get the feeling from the individual. We're making the music come back and forth. You understand? We're going forward by going back to the roots."

That was Marcus Garvey's strategy: go back to the authentic roots in order to build a foundation for the future.

12 Rise, Rastafari

As a singer, songwriter and producer, Yami Bolo is in a prime position to influence Jamaican music. He constantly writes new songs for his own CDs, produces other artists and tours the island performing. He works a good deal with producer Stephen Marley, Bob Marley's son, most recently on the single 'Vanity' and on the record 'Still Searching'.

Yami is a very engaging, handsome man with a bright smile. He is the father of three young children and is a dedicated Rastafarian, and he has a quick and agile mind, and articulates clearly what he thinks almost as fast as he thinks it. I immediately liked him when we met at Sugar Minott's studio yard.

The first thing he said after we shook hands was, "Bob Marley sang about greetings in the name of His Imperial Majesty Haile Selassie The Almighty and said, 'This is our King,' and the people looked to the King and rise. The King had the vision, and people without a vision shall fall. Bob Marley was the greatest artist in the history of reggae, and all he told the people was 'Greetings in name of His Imperial Majesty Emperor Haile Selassie I, Jah Rastafari.' That is what he told the world."

Now warming to his subject, Yami went on non-stop. "It's not our lyrics, our words; it's God's words telling the oppressors, whosoever they may be – in the Congress, in Buckingham Palace – telling them that this is people, life, the Almighty response. If you don't listen to the urge of their cry and their call, we'll be sending fire and typhoons, brimstone and lightning, earthquakes and thunder, like everything you see happening in America. That is the accuracy of [Haile Selassie's] judgement. If they don't listen, it's going to be more a terrible catastrophe that not even the darkness of wars of Babylon shall no one escape his judgement.

"The man who came to save the world, they crucified him already, so no more can man come to save the world. It's only Haile Selassie I. Just listen to this man, the Almighty. Listen to him. He is the man who governed the nation, and if you don't listen to the man who governed the nation, who else can you listen to?

"Where Rastafari is revolutionary is that Rastafari overthrew God, the white god. The black race gave birth to all races, including the white race. You can't instruct the Father, Haile Selassie, about the history of the Father. The white people must be made humble enough to accept the fact that, contrary to what your ego and history teaches you, I 'n' I are your parents. The first thing Rasta dub out is the first god. Overthrow that. Expel that. Reject that and install the God that is in harmony with the concept of love. We don't see any love in the colonialism and its brutality. We love in people coming together, working together to overcome our weaknesses and share our strengths.

"We don't owe any allegiance to a Jamaican flag. They have to take down the X flag [the Jamaican flag has a big yellow X from corner to corner] and put up the red crown with the lion. Then this would be a more beautiful country. Remove all policemen in their red, green and black suits [a uniform based on the British design] and blessed my Lord, no more guns, blessed unto the Lord, and give respect unto the people. The symbol [the Jamaican flag] represents the brutality and injustice. So you have to put up the right symbols. The X flag in Jamaica represents that the people are X'd out. The people are red, gold and green [the colours of the Ethiopian flag] as they are rainbow country people. We are all nations from black, white, China, India – all nations contribute to the colour of the rainbow. We owe our allegiance to humanity. Too much people die over flags and little images and awards and rewards and nothing really change. Someone still have to pay for all the injustice.

"It's not for us to say when the next wave of reggae will come out of Jamaica. Haile Selassie is the wave master. He created the whole foundation, the whole house. Whenever time the wave is going to come, he's the one that is going to really do that. We as singers know something great is happening, and we want to be part of it. Jah is the man really who do things. You don't jump into Jah's face, because Jah has his work.

"There's no struggle getting this message out because this message is already out. The music is a remembrance, a reminder. You can't hold down this message now. It has no borders, no boundaries. It transcends all empires. It's fire, man. It's eternal. That's why they say music shall always live. It comes from the most high creator. The music of Bob Marley, Peter Tosh, Jimmy Cliff, Burning Spear, Culture, Steel Pulse and the other musicians who give the idea of love and upliftment and hope and betterment and self-assertion and a new cultural identity. We don't think this music is too familiar, that no one hears it any more. We don't care about familiarity and unfamiliarity. We care about the deep understanding and accepting and applying these values and teachings into your life so that we can make you a better person.

"The Father used music to talk to his people from ancient time and even now. That's why the artists are so important. They are the edge carrying the word. Music is a God-given thing. No man on the face of the Earth has the power to conquer this music, like you lock a man in prison. You cannot lock up music. It will bust out in a billion other people in the world, the same message, regardless of race, colour or creed.

"Did you know that the brightest man on the face of Earth planet was Emperor Haile Selassie I? And the first man should come as the doctor of laws of all degrees. The heads of government embraced that within our time. Why did 72 nations bow unto this man at his coronation? Why did they call him king of all kings and lord of all lords? Because there is only one man who was so worthy. It is coming from the god lineage.

"The artists are writing a new Bible. That's the reality. We're not saying we're done with the old Bible, because we'll never remove an old corner stone. If a man do that, judgement will come upon him. However, the Father is saying new things every day, and if the people are listening, they get the knowledge and teach their children.

"God come white. God come black. God come China, too. So God has no colour. Yet still Him come black, still Him come white, still have no colour. Father lives in every man. But one was found worthy who was the King of Kings, who was the conquering lion of the tribe of Judah, elect of God, light of Himself, light of the universe. Light of the universe. And the world see it but never listened to him. If they had listened to Haile Selassie then World War II would never start. From that war we get all these little wars happening now, so they should heed him.

"What shall we do with evil persons? Leave all vengeance unto Haile Selassie I. Let him judge. It is good to leave all judgement unto Jah. Jah is the rightful judgement. As people, we can judge wrongful. Even I as a judge, I judge upon the precepts of Haile I. I have asked for the rightful judgement, so when I speak I speak as a judge. But when Babylon owns the judge, they judge different. They judge to partiality. But there is no partiality in Jah's kingdom. There is no level higher than Haile Selassie I level."

Yami stopped to take a breath. I nodded dumbly. I couldn't respond until I knew where this "Jah" comes from. And who is Haile Selassie of the highest level?

The Old Testament gives many different names for God: Elohim, Jehovah, Adonai, El Shaddai, El Gibbor and Yahweh, or Jahweh. The name Jah is derived from the Tetragrammaton, the Hebrew name of God written in four letters, YHWH, articulated as Yahweh. The Hebrew Bible reads, "Sing unto God, sing praise to his name; extol him that rideth upon the heavens by his name JAH, and rejoice before him." (Psalms 68:4.)

The nature of the Rasta's Jah is rooted in the Old Testament God. Jah is a brimstone character that can strike you down, as Peter Tosh and other reggae singers have pointed out. However, Jah's acts of justice do not come from "believe in Me or you shall die". Rather, if you are wicked, Jah will smite the evil with a terrible sword of justice.

In his early song 'Adam And Eve', Marley stated that Eve committed the original sin, and that that is why white women are the root of all evil. The song came from his pre-Rasta days. Rasta music deals with sin, but never sin in reference to an individual person. Falling into sin and asking God for repentance is not a theme in Rasta music. Reggae lyrics do not dwell on sin located inside the individual. Rather, sin is part of the Babylon system. Rastafarians do not approach the Bible with an unbiased mind. They interpret the Bible to support their point of view and prejudices. A multitude of believers use and abuse the Bible to support their beliefs, often in the condemnation of other belief systems. Part of the Bible's popularity is that the holy book can be twisted and distorted by anyone to justify all sorts of stupidity and ignorance.

Rastas regard the Bible as essentially false, even though they constantly quote it for evidence to support their positions. Rastas maintain that the Bible is false because whites purposefully misinterpreted the original scriptures of the Hebrew Bible in order to support their self-appointed position of being superior over blacks. The Rastas understand the Bible as a history and a prophecy rather than as a religious text. Rastafarians use the Bible to address their specific historical, economic, political and social situation. They move freely between the figurative and literal senses of the Bible and search for texts that they believe speak to contemporary events and issues. They see clear parallels between ancient biblical and modern times.

Rastafarians regard Revelations 5:3-5 as the most important text in the New Testament, with special interest on the King James version's rendering of verse 5: "Then one of the elders said to me, 'Weep not; lo, the Lion of the tribe of Judah, the Root of David, has conquered, so that he can open the scroll and its seven seals." Rastas apply this to Haile Selassie's life and his death – or his "disappearance", as Rastas prefer to term his absence from this Earth. When the Ethiopian royalist group the Emperor Selassie I Foundation planned to hold an official funeral for Haile Selassie on 2 November 2000, a quarter of a century after his reported death, Ras Sydney DaSilva, president of the Rastafari Centralisation Organisation (sic) in Kingston, called the event a fake and strongly objected. Ras Sydney maintained that Haile Selassie wasn't dead but that he resided in Teman, Africa, preparing a place for his sons and daughters.

Rastafarians find biblical support for the blackness of God in the King James version of Jeremiah 8:21: "For the hurt of the daughter of my people am I hurt; I am black; astonishment hath taken hold of me." Rastafari is fraught with apparent contradictions and deeply troubling problems, as is any religion, be it Christianity, Hinduism, Buddhism or Islam. It draws on a multiplicity of belief systems, including Judaism, elements of the occult, African belief systems, Christianity and Hinduism. In this, the Rastafari belief system is a New World phenomenon, just as jazz is a New World phenomenon, constructed of various threads of history and experience. Reggae is also such a construction of various threads, forming something completely new.

Rastafari is neither a Christian nor an African traditional religion but is instead one that is distinctly Caribbean. Like its antecedents within the African Diaspora – Voodoo (Voudon) in Haiti; Santeria in Cuba; Yoruba, Kaballah and Orisha in Trinidad and Tobago; Shango in Grenada; and Candomble in Brazil – Rastafari is a modern Afro-Caribbean cultural phenomenon. It combines concepts from African culture and social, historical, religious and economic Caribbean realities.

Rastafari can lay claim to being the only indigenous Caribbean-Creole phenomenon of its kind, apart from Garveyism. All other "total systems" that have served Jamaica and the Caribbean have been imported: Christianity, political nationalism, militant trade unionism, various constructs of socialism, and the present market-force-driven social economics. These are not magic bullets to solve all problems in Jamaica, or anywhere in the world. At best, the various approaches help in one area at the expense of another area of human wellbeing and quality of life and spirit.

So why can't Rastafari serve just as well as the imported systems in addressing human needs and nourishing the spirit, and perhaps even better?

Social, economic and political forces drive the rise of Rastafari and its ethos. Rastafari is more than a spiritual way of life; it's a cultural movement, "a system of beliefs and a state of consciousness…that advances a view of the economic survival and political organisation and structure that challenges the dominant cultural political ideology in the politics of Babylon", as Barry Chevannes, dean of the social sciences department at the University of the West Indies, wrote in *Rastafari: A New Approach* (1990).

In Rastafari, the divinity of all black people – in fact, of all human beings – becomes the basis for equality, liberty, dignity, mutual respect and equity, in terms of access to economic resources – all of the values claimed by civil or democratic society. Since the early '70s, Rastafari has been recognised as the most popular Afro-Caribbean religion of the late 20th century, gaining more popularity than Voodoo. It is also one of the leading cultural trends in the world. The Rastafari Centralisation Organisation (RCO) in Kingston claims that there are 8.4 million Rastafarians globally, and nearly a million in Jamaica. If those figures are accurate, nearly a third of Jamaica's population are Rastas, an unsupported number.

The message of Rastafari, as with other spiritual paths, is liberation. Specifically, Rastafari sets out to alter the social construction that whites are superior to blacks. The message not only counters the negativity of the background of African slavery but also reinforces that being black is good and worthy. In that, Rastafari gives liberation to the spirit.

But Rastafari is a monotheistic construction. Theism can be seen as colonialism, both metaphorically and in practice. God has power over us unworthy, undeserving lowlifes. Our happiness, substance and goodness depends on the goodwill of the overlord. God is the master and He can crack the whip across our mortal flesh. Feudal societies were built upon this model stolen directly from the Church, which perpetuated and encouraged the system for its own benefit. The overlord – the slavemaster, the plantation owner, the corporation, the King or Queen and their ruling minions – is simply an extension of the theistic structure.

In the theistic set-up, individuals want individual salvation. Lord, have mercy on me. Sweet Jesus, get my sorry ass out of this jam and I promise never to be human again. I'll be a saint. I'll be like You to the best of my ability; but, please, O Lord, save me. I'll do my part.

I'll have faith in Your goodness and forgiveness. There. Do we have a deal?

Well, not quite, according to my reggae mentor Kwame Dawes. "The issue is about mental colonialism, about how colonialism appropriates the good and the bad," he said in one of our wide-ranging conversations. "Colonialism didn't originate the notion of a higher deity functioning on a people. That colonial theistic point of view can be ameliorated by the African belief systems that the ancestors overlook our activities and in many ways are our overlords.

"In Rastafari, the liberation figure is presented as the epitome of justice and what is positive. This is a fundamental difference to the kind of theism that colonialism brought with it, the Christian theism, and a very dubious Christian theism, which was an oppressive construction. Built into that construction was somebody saying to somebody else 'I know what is best for you, and I'm going to make you believe that, too.'

"I think reggae is perhaps the most evangelical music in the world; but reggae's agenda is not the typical gospel agenda in converting others. Reggae doesn't plan to make everyone Rastafarian. Its primary intention is to bring knowledge and wisdom and awareness both of the suffering of the black and the poor people, but also to bring an awareness of a large scheme in the way that we see the world. Rather than trying to win Rastas, in that everyone should become Rasta and grow their locks, reggae tries to suggest that there is a larger cosmology, a construction of the world where there is a godhead and a consequence for action. There is a very humanistic principle about care for other human beings. That is the core of reggae.

"In a sense, reggae is not a hard sell. It's presenting a worldview that can be applied to many cultures and ideas, as opposed to other evangelical hard sells that attempt to make you become something, rather than opening you to something. In that, I think reggae's agenda is not as daunting as other's agendas. Reggae becomes successful because of that. The very basic notion of human rights and justice, and the need for human rights and justice, is elemental to reggae."

I countered, "But reggae does not offer any understanding of the suffering or oppression – other than the rubric of 'they' are doing it to us. Reggae doesn't offer any effective resolution to the suffering, other than stand up and fight. But what does that mean? Reggae doesn't have a militant message. There is no call to arms and murder your enemies. Just the opposite – reggae's message is love. Reggae offers hope, and escape into a divine mercy, as the weapon against the suffering and oppression of the Babylon system. And yet reggae is an integral part of the Babylon system as surely as money and power is integral to the capitalistic system. So why all this bleeping about being oppressed, being the sufferers, being still under the colonial thumb?"

"Listen to Pablo Moses' 'Will Power', on the lead track of his 1995 *Mission* album," Kwame advised. "'Close yuh kip, stop yuh chatter/Pull in yuh gut, get up off yuh butt...' This approach says not only to have faith alone but also to have faith in individual existence. You alone, being individuals as you are, actually can achieve salvation without joining some kind of basic lineage.

"We have to appreciate that Rastafari is a fairly remarkable phenomenon of the 20th century worldwide. There are very few religious systems that have so thoroughly defined and constructed, within such a short space of time, such a belief system. It is a very distinctive and unique thing.

"The other element, which is most telling, is that Rastafari emergence was not in the sense of a cultist emergence. It's become such a pervasive cultural phenomenon that affects the language, the worldview and whole cosmology of the Jamaican people and Caribbean people in general. For the first 20 years of its conception, Rastafari may have been a kind of isolated cult movement, but through the music, and through the way it captured the imagination of the young people in the '60s and '70s, it has deeply influenced the behaviour of the fabric of Jamaican society.

"Rastafari has introduced a new complexity of myths and reconstructed the myths. That was ripe to happen. Rastafari is a movement that speaks to the cultural and colonial history and the history of religious imperialism in Jamaica, where Christianity was treated not as something that emerges out of a culture but something that is a goal. In that kind of environment, and in an environment where there is a strong sense of Africa in the working class and peasant people, that Rastafari would take root is, in retrospect, not surprising.

"I don't think you're going to find any 20th-century religious movements that have done the same. The Mormons of the 1800s certainly never had that kind of impact on the imagination of American society. They remain kind of an isolated cult, even though they are huge and growing in numbers. They remain isolated, but that is not true about Rastafarianism and its emergence.

"Most religions will create their own myths. That's how they become religions. The process of myth-making is not in the sense of making up stories. It's a sense of creating a cosmology that becomes the way to explain one's existence. The veracity of the stories is immaterial. The story could just as well be true historically, but it doesn't have to be historically valid. It becomes a construction of beliefs and a cosmology that rationalises and gives meaning to current experience. Religions create myths. They make myths of history and experience. Religion makes myths out of the imagination. Rastafari does that."

13 Who Is HIM?

Haile Selassie is by far the most prominent name in reggae. He is honoured in the majority of reggae songs and exalted by the Rastas as Jah. Why is His Imperial Majesty Haile Selassie I, former Emperor of Ethiopia, given the status of God?

First, some background. In ancient literature, including the Bible, the name Ethiopia applies to the whole of the African continent, or to the territories south-southeast of Egypt. "The biblical 'Cush' is a vague term connoting the entire Nile Valley, south of Egypt, including Nubia (Sudan) and Abyssinia (Ethiopia)," according to biblical scholar and archaeologist Edward Ullendorff.

In classical writings, the term Cush referred to that part of Africa south of Egypt as far as Zanzibar, dominated by Egypt from the 11th dynasty until it became independent during the 23rd dynasty. The biblical land of Cush was part of the Sabaean kingdom of Axum. The Queen of Sheba and her son Menelik were of the Axum dynasty, which is very important to the Rasta line of reasoning. Menelik I allegedly abducted the Jewish Ark of the Covenant and took it to Ethiopia. This belief is of critical importance to claims made concerning the lineage of Ethiopian rulers and Ethiopia as the new Zion.

The Hebrew word Cush was redacted, in the third and second centuries BC, as *aethiops* (Ethiop) in the Septuagint, the Greek version of the Hebrew Bible. The Septuagint was created when the Ptolemys – Ptolemy I, Soter – and his heirs, who created the Great Library in Alexandria, summoned 72 Jewish scholars to translate the Torah, creating the ancient Greek Old Testament. "Ethiopia" is a Greek translation for the Hebrew word for blacks. In Greek, *ethiop* meant "burnt" or "black". In Hebrew, *Cush* is the word for "black". *Cushite* is used to refer to people of black Africa.

In the Bible, Cush (Kush), is the oldest son of Ham. He was seen as representing the black people of the world. He fathers the world's first mighty man, Nimrod. In Jamaica, a particularly mightily endowed man – especially sexually – is called Nimrod.

The Rastas cited numerous biblical passages – including Revelations 19:16 and 5:5 – as being prophecies of Haile Selassie as the messiah. Two psalms in the King James version are favourites: "I will make mention of Rahab and Babylon to them that know me; behold Philistia, and Tyre, with Ethiopia; this man was born there" (Psalm 87:4); and "Princes shall come out of Egypt; Ethiopia shall soon stretch out her hands unto God" (Psalm 68:31). Rastas interpret this to mean Haile Selassie.

Haile Selassie was born Tafari Makonnen on 23 July 1892. He was the son of Ras Makonnen, governor of Harar, a province in southern Ethiopia. As a child, he was automatically granted the court title Lij, meaning "child of an important nobleman". His father was the first cousin to Emperor Menelik II, and it was this family connection – bolstered by the fact that he was the great-grandson of King Saheka Selassie of Shoa – that would be the basis for Tafari Makonnen's claim to the crown.

In 1909, Menelik II suffered a stroke, and later died in 1913. Before then, he appointed his grandson Lij Yasu as heir and successor, but Lij Yasu was a Muslim in the Coptic Christian country, and the Council Of State deposed him in 1916. Menelik's daughter, Zauditu, became the successor. Tafari Makonnen was one of several princes and cousins who had a claim to the throne, but he proved to be politically astute and a master of manipulation. From 1916 to 1928, he held the high military title of Ras ("head of an army"), corresponding to a British duke or prince. In 1928, he became Negus (King) Tafari.

On 2 November 1930, at the age of 38, he was crowned Negusa Nagast (king of kings) at his coronation as Emperor, to which he added his baptismal name, Haile Selassie (power of the trinity). His complete title was Emperor Haile Selassie I, Power Of The Holy Trinity, 225th Emperor Of The Solomonic Dynasty, Elect Of God, Lord Of Lords, King Of Kings, Conquering Lion Of The Tribe Of Judah. This was the culmination of a career marked by political shrewdness, intrigue and deft manoeuvring through the ranks of nobility.

None of these titles were unique to Haile Selassie. The title King Of Kings Of Ethiopia (shortened to Kings Of Kings) was used by many emperors, and indicated simply the most powerful ruler in Ethiopia. Regional leaders, who fought and schemed for national supremacy and the title Negusa Nagast (King Of Kings), ruled Ethiopia for centuries.

"Lord Of Lords" was never an imperial title in Ethiopia. Imperial titles were either assumed by a ruler or conferred by the Abun (the head of the Ethiopian Orthodox Church). The Ethiopian Orthodox Church doesn't recognise the divinity of Haile Selassie but sees him as the earthly defender of the faith and head of the Coptic Church, in the same way that the British monarch is head of the Church Of England.

"Conquering Lion Of The Tribe of Judah" – the motto "the Lion of the tribe of Juda hath prevailed", culled from Revelation 5:5 – was used by Ethiopian emperors on their seals to indicate the Christian nature of the empire. This tradition goes back to the 16th century, under Lebna Dengel. Meanwhile, "Elect Of God", meaning appointed by God, is approximately equivalent to "one nation under God".

The names Haile, Selassie, Tafari and Ras were not unique to Tafari Makonnen. One of his cousins was named Imeru Haile Selassie, who later became Ras, and Tafari Belaw.

The principal source of information supporting the lineage of Ethiopian emperors is the Kebra Nagast, the Ethiopian national saga, compiled during the late 13th or early 14th century CE. The Kebra Nagast has two basic themes: the descent of Ethiopian kings from Solomon and Sheba, and the transfer of the Jewish Ark of the Covenant to Ethiopia by Menelik I.

Historians cite political, patriotic and religious motives behind the compilation of Kebra Nagast. One of the compilers wrote at the end of the work, "for I have laboured much for the glory of the land of

Ethiopia, for the going out of the heavenly Zion, and for the King of Ethiopia". This king was Yekunno Amlak, founder of the so-called Solomonic dynasty, whose regency was between 1270 and 1285.

The Kebra Nagast was seemingly written to justify the claims of the Solomonid dynasty over the Zagwe family, which ruled Ethiopia for approximately 150 years from the 12th century to the late 13th century. The Zagwe family, from the Agau people and perceived by ancient Ethiopians as being of Hamitic (not Semitic) stock, fought long wars of resistance against the kings of Axum. The Agau defeated the Axumite kings and ruled Ethiopia as the Zagwe dynasty.

The Kebra Nagast, written with a pro-Semitic bias, implicitly denounces the Hamitic Zagwe dynasty: "for, by the will of God, every kingdom in the world was given to the seed of Shem [Semites] and slavery to the seed of Ham [Hamites]".

In the Kebra Nagast, the Queen of Sheba, "Queen of Egypt and Ethiopia", had a child, Menelik I, by King Solomon. Solomon, one of the most notorious womanisers in the Bible – both Old and New Testaments – accomplished this deed through trickery.

According to the Kebra Nagast, "And Solomon sent meats to her chamber which would make her thirsty. And drinks mingled with vinegar and other dishes spiced with pepper. After the meal, the King rose up and went to the Queen and they were alone together. He said to her, 'Take your ease here for love's sake until daybreak.' And she said to him, 'Swear to the God of Israel that you will not take me by force.' And Solomon answered, 'I swear that I will not, but you must swear to me that you will not take, by force, any of my possessions.'

"The Queen laughed and so swore, for she needed nothing from Solomon, being very wealthy in her own right. The King went to his bed on one side of the chamber and Sheba to her bed on the other side. The King instructed a manservant, 'Wash out the bowl and set in it a vessel of water while the Queen is looking on, then shut the door and leave us in peace.'"

The food made the Queen very thirsty, and this woke her up. When she went to get a drink of water from the vessel, the King "seized her hand before she could drink, and said, 'Why have you already broken your oath that you would not take, by force, anything in my house?'

"'Is the oath broken by my drinking water?' replied the Queen.

"'Is there anything under heaven richer than water?' countered Solomon.

"'Then I have sinned against myself, and you are free of your oath,' she told him.

"'I am free from the oath which you made me swear?'

"'Yes, but please let me drink your water.'"

So Solomon permitted her to drink, and after she had drunk her fill they made love and then slept together. Haile Selassie later emerged as a branch of the dynastic tree planted on that fateful night.

In 1955, Haile Selassie gave 500 acres of royal land for "the people of the West" – that is, Jamaicans. The land, called Shashamane, was in Shoa province, Haile Selassie's home turf, 160 miles from Addis Ababa in the rolling country between the Malcoda and the Shashamane Rivers. The local farmers did not look kindly on the land grant. They were not overtly hostile to the settlers who arrived from Jamaica, but they didn't welcome them as their own either. The royal land grant associated the Rastafarians with being favoured retainers of the Emperor. The Rasta emigrants were given tractors, fertiliser and other assistance that the local farmers had never received. From the beginning, the settlement was linked to the royal family and not to the local community.

In the late '70s, at its peak, Shashamane had between 40 and 50 Rastas and Afro-Americans, a pharmacy, school, clinic, store and modest dwellings. It was not an easy life for the settlers. They eked out an existence without the amenities – running water, electricity – of a more developed place.

On 21 April 1966, Haile Selassie paid a state visit to Jamaica. The Rasta community was ecstatic. Thousands upon thousands poured into Kingston to welcome their king, the messiah. His Ethiopian airliner, with the Lion of Judah insignia emblazoned on its tail, landed at Palisadoes Airport at 1:30pm on that warm Thursday. More than 100,000 Rastas broke through police barricades and swarmed around the plane. They were smoking spliffs, and the airport authorities feared that the fumes of jet fuel might be ignited, and tried to move the crowd away from the plane. They may as well have been trying to empty the ocean one cup at a time.

Haile Selassie came to the plane's door, took one look at the chanting crowd and retreated back into the plane. When he failed to reappear, the Rasta elder Mortimo Planno – the same man who schooled Marley in Rastafari, and who was the silent hand behind reggae – was called to the plane.

Let Planno tell what happened next. "That was mystical again," he said during my visit. "His Majesty wanted to show the Ethiopian people me, so the mystical thing happened that I was called to come up so that the camera could show me. What had happened before was that, in 1963, at the brutal massacre in Coral Gardens, in Montego Bay, a lot of Rastafarians were killed and Ethiopians were sad that I was reported killed, so His Majesty wanted to show them that I 'n' I was alive.

"He was not afraid to get off the plane, as was so often reported. His Majesty is the one who creates all these things. A state visitor was being marooned by love, threatened with love. He was in the plane and the plane was surrounded. The officials thought there was no way for him to get through the crowd. Then the brigadier general called out over the loudspeaker, 'Calling Mr Planno. Calling Mr Planno. The Emperor calls you.' So I say, 'Call me?' 'Yes, call you.' I went up to the plane and was introduced to His Majesty. The general man asked if I could get the bredren to move from around the plane. I say, 'Yes, if you give me the mic,' but the general objected. He say *no*. He was afraid I'd give a prayer or preach or something like that.

"I was recovering from having a goitre removed from my throat. The place where they put the tracheotomy in my throat was seeping blood. I couldn't talk loud. The Emperor said, 'Talk.' He held my hand, and my voice came out in a lion's roar. That was an example of the Emperor's healing.

"His Imperial Majesty has emerged in a projectory [*sic*] that was anticipated. His dawn, his coming, even to now, has manifested ideas and concepts that are within the foundation of this civilisation, the

Western ethos. Just as Christ fulfilled certain prophesied signs, so has His Imperial Majesty. To talk about comparison between Jesus and Haile Selassie is to deny the evidence of the moment. His Majesty's history speaks for himself.

"My understanding of a messiah is that of an anointed one. He is a saviour by virtue of his knowledge and his example. The significance of His Majesty is undeniable. There is a global movement now that bears his name. Rastafarian presence is in all the African Diaspora and the non-African diaspora of all nations. My generation is not as absorbed in the compensation of the significance of His Majesty. History has proven his worth. A messiah is one who fulfils and is the fulfilment of actualising.

"If you go back into the notion of kingdom, and an Ethiopian kingdom, then His Majesty signifies the central leadership of a kingdom. There is a real sense of honour that he is worthy of. His work within the United Nations and OAU (Organisation Of African Unity), and in general toward the cause of oppression, and in particularly the oppression of Ethiopia and Africa, placed him in a category that is more than any world leader has been able to attain."

Haile Selassie and Planno emerged from the plane after half an hour and descended the stairs to the ground. Haile Selassie promptly ducked into a car and was whisked into the city to meet with government officials.

On 12 September 1974, Ethiopian junior army officers – led by 38-year-old Mengistu Maile-Mariam – executed a successful coup, ending the 43-year reign of Haile Selassie. The officers, who formed the ruling Co-ordinating Committee Of The Armed Forces, known as the Derg (meaning "conclave"), were fed up with the Emperor for many reasons. Rebels in the northern province of Eritrea had been waging a 20-year war of liberation, and winning. The army was tired of the embarrassment. The army officers had finally had enough of the corruption, inefficiency and disinterest in the people's wellbeing exhibited by the government, controlled by entrenched nobles. In the previous year, a famine had swept through central-east Ethiopia, claiming between 100,000 and 200,000 lives. Unwilling to admit before the world its inability to care for its people, the government tried to cover up the disaster. The loss of life was horrific before Haile Selassie finally asked for assistance from the world community.

In the early '70s, the vast majority of Ethiopians languished in poverty while the noble class lived in splendour. The average annual per capita income for the masses was $90 and the literacy rate was seven per cent. In the countryside, peasant farmers worked under a feudal system – many virtually as slaves – on land owned by the nobility.

On the day of the coup, Haile Selassie was arrested and held prisoner in his palace, and many of the nobility were executed. Selassie's wife, daughters and sons and their families fled to London, where many live today. The Emperor was held in a small, plain apartment in the palace and kept incommunicado. He died under mysterious conditions in August 1975. Rumours have circulated for years that the old, frail man was smothered with a pillow in his sleep and surreptitiously buried in an unmarked grave in the palace grounds.

Rastafarianism has spread since Haile Selassie's death. Christianity spread after Christ's death. Why should the historical process be restricted to Christianity?

After Haile Selassie's overthrow in 1975, the local people took Shashamane from the Rastas as part of the new government's land reform, which nationalised all rural land, abolished tenancy and set up peasant associations. The poor Galla farmers seized Shashamane's tractors and all of the Rastas' assets. After negotiations with the Provisional Military Administrative Council, 44 hectares were returned to the Rastas who wanted to stay.

14 Nyabinghi In The Bush

Zaccheus Thompson has been a truck driver, keyboard player, bass guitarist and sound engineer. Now he is a Nyabinghi drummer, drum-maker and right-hand man to Bongo Cutty, a Rasta country preacher. Bongo signifies priest or spiritually learned man. Bongo Cutty is the leader of The Mount Equal Nyabinghi Chanters.

Nyabinghi drumming has been part of reggae since Count Ossie took the sacred drumming secular in the late '60s. There is now renewed interest in re-introducing Nyabinghi drumming more prominently in reggae music, according to various recording artists in Kingston. Count Ossie's Nyabinghi drumming group, The Mystic Revelation Of Rastafari, made its first United States appearance in 25 years in July 2000.

"Bongo Cutty will meet us today," Zaccheus said. Bongo Cutty is the high priest of Trelawney parish, he explained. There are 14 Nyabinghi mansions in Jamaica, each with its own priest or priests. The hierarchy of priests is based on their level of spiritual understanding and mystical knowing.

From my country retreat, Zaccheus and I caught a ride in the back of a pick-up to the main road, where we flagged down a collectivo taxi for the ten-mile ride down the coast to the nearest town. Then we took another collectivo for the 20-mile ride back into the hills to the edge of the Cockpit Mountains. The road followed the Martha Brae River, a mild flow that supports a tourist-rafting cottage industry. The rafts are 14-foot-long bamboo logs lashed together and fitted with a bench to seat passengers, and are poled by a raftsman down the gentle river.

According to local legend, Martha Brae was the name of an Arawak priestess who knew the location of a secret gold mine in a cave near the river and lured Spanish gold seekers to the cave. She then diverted the course of the river, sealing the cave and drowning the Spanish. The river comes from a lake under the Cockpit Mountains, gushes through a hole in the back of the Windsor Caves and flows to the sea.

I tried to image an Arawak king and queen looking lovingly at their newborn: "What shall we call her, dear?"

"I rather like Arawi, or Kerry. What do you think?"

"Well, I was thinking of a soft sound because our little darling is so soft and cuddly. Something like Martha. The name just breathes, don't you think so?"

"Mar-tha. Yes, Mar-tha. Mar-tha. And Brae, because I heard a donkey the moment she was born. That must have been a sign."

I couldn't stretch my imagination that far.

The road ran through a verdurous tunnel of bamboo until we climbed out of the river valley to open fields of sugar cane. We passed Perth Town and went on to Reserve, a non-descript junction, where Zaccheus told the driver to stop. I followed him on foot along a lane around the back of a hill, past the last houses and a couple of hundred yards further on, until we reached a set of steps hewn into the rock. The steps led to a shack perched 20 feet up on the hillside.

The shack's façade was pale yellow and wasn't completely painted. Climbing the three deep-red-painted cement steps to the shack proper, I saw that the place was a single-room bar containing a counter, bottles of beer and sodas on shelves, a refrigerator, a cell phone recharger and a television. To the right was a bamboo wall with a doorway which led to an open yard. A trellis with ripening passion fruit partially covered the 10' x 10' yard.

Zaccheus gently lifted a passion blossom and interpreted the symbolism. The stamen had the shapes of three fish tails when seen from one angle and three loaves when viewed from the top. Around the stamen, on the flower itself, was a purple ring that represented the masses waiting for the fishes and loaves. Around the purple was white, representing the truth. Under the blossom were ten segments, signifying the ten commandments. In the centre were three segments that supported the stamen, representing the mother, father and child.

Mystical symbolism is an integral part of Rastafarian. For example, the number nine is considered the highest number. After nine comes one again, as in ten. Then you get to 90, then back to one, as in 100. The number one signifies unity, one indivisible, as in Haile Selassie I. The triangle's three sides multiplied together equal nine.

The symbol of life can be depicted by a zero bisected by the number one. If you split the zero circle and move each half in opposite directions, one half up and the other down from the centreline of the number one, you have the dollar sign, a trick of life played by Babylon.

Here is another example of Rastafari symbolism. Black absorbs and white reflects, so the black man absorbs wisdom, absorbs from nature, takes things in, instead of reflecting them back out. The implication is that the white race is shallow.

Bongo Cutty stood at the bar's doorway but did not greet me. He was 5' 7" with honey-tan eyes, a round face, a grey goatee and isolated curls of a beard on his cheeks. He was bald on top and wore his locks wrapped around his head, like a bird's nest. When he let down the dreads, they fell to his heels. Bongo Cutty had been a Kingston bus driver, a telephone installer and a waiter at the Sheraton Hotel, and had also worked on a cruise ship before retiring to the country to await a vision of his calling. He waited for 17 years before the vision appeared to him.

Three Nyabinghi drums were removed from black plastic bags – a large bass, a smaller *fundue*, and the smaller-still repeater, and herb and a chalice were then prepared. The chalice had three parts: the base was a small wooden bowl that held water to cool the smoke, and a short plastic hose, yellowed with smoke, was inserted into a hole in the side of the bowl, while a wooden funnel that was shaped like the smokestack of a steam train was firmly wedged onto the bowl. A pebble was then dropped down the funnel to prevent herb from falling out the bottom.

Before lighting up, Bongo Cutty led a formula prayer along the lines of "Thank you, Lord, for our daily bread," and gave thanks and praise to Haile Selassie. Great billows of smoke enveloped Bongo Cutty's and Zaccheus' heads as they stoked the chalice. Bongo Cutty buried his face in the smoke, as if snuggling into the pillow of his loved one.

A third man, Kirby, arrived. Bongo Cutty nestled the three-foot-wide bass drum between his knees. Zaccheus put the fundue – the "heartbeat" drum – between his knees. Kirby sat with the repeater.

"The bass is a dangerous drum," Bongo Cutty warned. "It can destroy you, even kill. So is its power, if you are not pure when playing it. It cuts through. A weak or evil person cannot survive the bass drum."

With that, he thumped the drum powerfully with a cloth-covered mallet and looked at me meaningfully, as if to say, *See? I am strong and pure enough to play this drum.* The three drummers performed a Rasta chant with a melody clearly borrowed from a Methodist hymn.

"I know 145 militant Rasta songs, and new Rasta chants are continually being written," Bongo Cutty said. He meant "militant" as in *bad equals good*. "But I won't play any of the secret chants for you," implying that I wasn't qualified to hear their mystical significance.

He then launched into the meaning of drumming. The drummer must keep his spine straight to aid breathing. Steady, deep breathing is very important, as it is in any practice of meditation. The drums are held between the knees so that the vibration goes into the body. You are not playing the drum so much as surrendering to the drum. The drum becomes an inner consciousness cruiser, transporting the drummer into himself so far that he pops out – as if through an hour glass – into another realm of sensibility which cannot be described or explained by the finite nature of rational understanding. The Sufis do the same with dance; Buddhist monks do it through the mind-numbing repetitions of sutras; Christian monks do it with chanting. The mind is overwhelmed, filled to overflowing, with the harmonics of the sound. All thought, fear, panic, hope, dreams and desires are floated out of the mind like twigs over a dam.

The bass was the downbeat – "down" chasing the oppressor, said Bongo Cutty. It is the power drum, the chastiser. The fundue is the heartbeat, one-two, one-two, as steady as life. The repeater sings the song.

The playing pattern never varied. The bass beat went one, pause, two, three, while the fundue kept the steady heartbeat one-two stroke. The first beat of the bass and the fundue was synchronised. The fundue's second beat filled in the space before the bass's second beat. The repeater – the smallest and highest-pitched drum – played over the top in a free-form melody. If a third or fourth drum is added, these stay in the pattern of the fundue or the repeater.

Nyabinghi originated in Uganda. The British, who were the colonial power in Uganda from the late 1880s until the country's independence in 1962, attempted to extend forced labour – the compulsory cultivations of certain crops for exportation for British profit – and unjust taxation on the people. The Kigezi people of south-west Uganda would have none of it, however, and their queen, Muhumusa, went *mano a mano* against the English Queen Victoria. Queen Muhumusa ordered her warriors to fight the oppressors. The British, not wishing to soil their hands, tried to impose indirect rule through the use of Buganda agents. The local kingdom of Buganda, neighbouring the Kigezi kingdom, had been in the pocket of the British East African Company, one of the first multinational corporations, since the kingdom was declared a British protectorate in 1894. Using Buganda as a base, the British extended their power over other native kingdoms. The Kigezi branded the black Bugandans and the white British as equal oppressors. Nyabinghi means "death to black and white oppressors".

Queen Muhumusa was captured, but that didn't stop the revolt, which continued for 20 years. Unable to defeat the Nyabinghi fighters by military means, the British banned the movement under the Witchcraft Ordinance of 1919. According to Elizabeth Hopkins in her essay "The Nyabinghi Cult Of South-western Uganda", which appeared in *Protest And Power In Black Africa*, the British tried to undermine the Nyabinghi politically by promoting a cult of rainmaking and fortune-telling. In the essay, she quotes a British report: "Since purely military efforts have proven useless against the Nyabinghi, it would appear that a considerable influence might be enlisted for European administration by a more sympathetic handling of a conservative cult and the powerful but innocuous local fortune-telling relating to an institution which enters so deeply into the lives of these people."

Rastas, who also refer to themselves as "Nya men", identified with the anticolonial movement of the Kigezi. They saw themselves as fighting a battle on the spiritual and mystical plane against anyone who attempted to rob them of their dignity and identity.

In the mid '50s, in Kingston, the Youth Black Faith – the Black Muslims of their time – introduced a ritual Nyabinghi dance. The dance was a strenuous shaking and tossing of the dreadlocks, and was meant to unleash the "earthforce" of cosmic energy that pervades the universe. This earthforce was directed against those who historically oppressed the African people. Bob Marley's prancing on stage, whipping his dreads around his head, is said to be associated with the Nyabinghi dance.

Bongo Cutty and the drummers played five songs and stopped. Bongo wanted to strike a deal for information exchanged. He tried to determine how much material from him I would use, like measuring out flour and charging by the pound. If it was to be a chapter or two with photos, this was equivalent to five pounds of flour. He kept defining how much material – "two chapters on our drumming" – that I would use. I kept reducing his top line. "The material will be included in a chapter on drumming." I would make money from his information, he said. To take it and leave without compensation would be like a mining company taking raw resources for their profit and leaving nothing behind for the local people, he explained. Using Queen's English, so that I'd better understand, he kept making the point that I would pay a "gratuity", to which I readily agreed. I suspected that he was angling for some of the book's royalties, which was why he kept trying to inflate the amount of his material I would use.

Finally, it came down to plain talk. "How will you pay?" he asked.

"I'll pay you Jamaican dollars."

He took offence. He said that he felt insulted. He was embarrassed for his drummers. He was stern in his admonishment, trying to portray me as being less than forthcoming and somehow devious, whereas he was looking straight ahead into truth, not around corners. I later came to understand that Bongo Cutty and Zaccheus were intrigued by the concept of reverse psychology. I took no umbrage. I looked him firm and steady in the left eye, matching his firm and steady gaze. We went around and around for another half hour, with him not asking outright for a fixed sum or percentage of royalties and me agreeing to pay but waiting for him to set the price.

While all of this was going on, Cutty would launch into teachings about the drums, about the danger of the bass if its player didn't have higher understanding and clear heart. The drums were spiritual. They were part of the meditation. They were the transporter and cleanser. They were praise drums, by which to honour the divinity in Haile Selassie.

I asked again, "What is a fair exchange for the information you will give me?"

"Whatever you want to give," he replied.

"Fine."

We left it at that.

Several more songs were played, including a cover of 'We Shall Overcome' with Rasta words and the Wesleyan hymns 'I Write My Name/Good Morning' and 'On Mount Zion', which had been brought to Jamaica by Pentecostal missionaries. These songs also appear on the Keith Richards, Justin Hinds and Nyabinghi drummers' 1997 album *Wingless Angels*. Hinds and the drummers live in the hillside Steer Town above Ocho Rios, about 25 miles from Bongo Cutty's hillside. Hinds, who still tours internationally, was a ska pioneer with his band, The Dominoes. He was St Ann's first pop star with 'Carry Go, Bring Home' before Marley and Burning Spear made their names. Winston "Blackskull" Thomas, who has played with Talking Heads and Bad Brains, and who is Hinds' neighbour in Steer Town, also played on the album.

Nyabinghi drumming has a slow, steady pulse, with spaces to allow for the preacher to call out the next line of the song or to insert a line from the Bible. It provides a rock-bottom bass line to any song. To tell the truth, though, I found it soporific as entertainment. After a few songs, the sound became a sleepy morning in a too-warm church.

After Cutty and the others put away the drums, we fell into a five-hour discussion. In Rastafari, according to Cutty, there is no heaven and hell. Life is a continuum. "We don't fear death," Cutty said. "We just drop this form" – he indicated his body – "and pick up another. Death is life. We come back to resume the lessons we are to learn to be clear with the Divine."

There is one supreme God: the Creator. That Creator is Haile Selassie. "We believe without reservation and without apology that Haile Selassie was God," Bongo Cutty declared, "but each person is responsible for his or her own coming to that understanding. Jah is not there to be prayed up to, asking for mercy and to be saved. The person must look into the self for the true being."

Fine. If a carpenter's son can be God, why not an African emperor?

"The li-on and lamb must live peacefully together," Bongo Cutty said. "This," he said, pinching the flesh of his arm, "is the lamb, this outward form we have. The li-on of Rastafari lives within. The li-on gives man the courage to seek the truth."

Rastafari uses meditation as a method of seeking the inner self, much as Buddhism does. Rastas have a meditation space, a quiet place without disturbance, such as Marley's rock on his Mount Zion. "A place where you don't hear a radio," Cutty said. "You might hear a bird song, and that's all right, because it's natural, but it's best not even to hear a bird song."

The intent of the meditation is to achieve a quiet mind, a mind without ego chatter, as in the Buddhist precept that the mind is the cause of confusion. By transcending confusion, one attains the enlightened state. Bongo Cutty was very aware of the power of the mind to seize control of a person, to keep the distractions going, and of the mind's power to inflate its self-importance. Meditation can be performed while sitting, although the Rastas don't subscribe to the posture of the Buddhists, who sit rigidly. To the Rastas, meditation can also be done when walking, and part of this meditation is to always be aware of the vibes you are giving out, even when walking a crowded street. The intent is to be in harmony, not to be aggressive, not to be negative. "In the Rasta way, aggression is met with gentleness," Bongo Cutty said.

I said, "The Buddhist teacher Chogyam Trungpa said that spirituality means relating with the working basis of one's existence, which is one's state of mind. We continually try to grasp onto some solid image of ourselves, and then we have to defend those particular fixed conceptions. Spirituality is cutting through our basic fixation, that clinging, that stronghold of something-or-other, which is known as ego."

Cutty nodded in agreement. "You no longer want to be excited or depressed by the mind," he said. "That's the spiritual state. We believe in the discipline of that ital life. You must be careful what you eat. How you think about your fellow man. That's why it's important Nyabinghi comes back stronger in the music. And not just anybody plays the Nyabinghi drums but those who practise and understand the true Rasta way. Then the message becomes clear, and the music will have more power. That power is in each of us. We must find our way to it."

The power of colours is important in Rastafari, Bongo Cutty said. There must be balance and harmony in the colours of all things. It is especially important to balance the colours of the seven *chakras* within the person and bring the harmony to those colours.

"You can see the colours through here," Cutty said, placing a finger in the middle of his forehead, the site of the intuitive knowing of the Third Eye. For Rastas, there is a distinct difference between rational knowing (the school education) and intuitive knowing. This is a characteristic of all mysticism- and nature-based beliefs. Bongo Cutty finds nothing mystical about knowing the world in a fuller way by communicating with the spirits of plants, rocks, people and animals.

Paraphrasing Chogyam Trungpa again, I tried this out on Cutty: "The intellect is completely intuitive as well as intellectually precise. The working of intellect is such that, when we pay proper attention to persons or situations, they automatically give us answers or understanding."

"Yes, that is it. Simply look at the world for what it is. Then you'll know how to change the world. Rastafari! Haile Selassie!" he exclaimed.

"We need to know where we are through knowledge, compassion and wisdom," I said, drawing again on Chogyam Trungpa. "We have to explore our environment, our particular location in time and space. Once we have knowledge as to where we are, then we become wise, because we don't have to struggle with our bearings. We don't have to fight for our position. So, in a sense, wisdom is an expression of non-violence."

"The Rastaman doesn't use violence," said Bongo Cutty. "You push me and I won't push back. I know other ways to struggle against evil and injustice. Yes, we have to know the past. If I don't know the past, I don't know how to drum Nyabinghi. I can't forget the past, but I can forgive it."

"All the world we see is an illusion," I replied. "It's an illusion each person creates through his or her own filters, judgements, fears, desires, and expectations. You must not be deceived by those judgements into believing that they are reality."

"This is what you know," Bongo Cutty said. "All persons know this. This is not something you learn in books. One of the dangers of so-called education is that you are brainwashed. You are taught false things. You are taught only those things that are useful to Babylon, like how to make money at the expense of others, how to serve the master of materialism. You are not taught in schools how to see the true self.

"It's the duty of each person to go inside and confront and tear down those self-created forms of illusion. That's each person's Babylon. That's the personal fire and brimstone, the earthquake and thunder and lightning, the fire of burning away the illusion to see the reality behind the illusion, that's the Divine love that sustains all. There's nothing more. That's the source. Be within the embrace of that love and you are that love. You are the embrace to others.

"Don't corrupt the body with false food or chemicals or with the flesh of dead animals. You cannot be pure and clear if you pollute the body, as you pollute the mind. A polluted mind is unclear in its motivation and intent, or is motivated by self-interest. Don't pollute yourself with pride. Pride is a form of shame. Pride is used as a shield because the person is shamed that he or she looks down on another for whatever reason. Pride is holding yourself aloof from another's need and misery, so you don't offer help. Then you are ashamed of not having an open heart."

★

All this sounded wonderfully enlightened and high-minded. I was quite impressed. However, I had reason to temper that first impression during the following week I spent with Bongo Cutty and Zaccheus as they travelled on Rastafari business.

One stop was at the country home of Delron Scott, a strikingly handsome man with strong features and Medusa dreads tinted red by the sun. In a small, cluttered room, spliffs were toked and praise given to Rastafari. Delron had stacks of books on herbs and their use. He showed me a notebook, in which he had written detailed notes of his own studies and work in preparing herb medicines. He was a serious student.

The card table in the middle of the room was littered with a hodge-podge of stuff. The flame of the Bunsen burner represented infinity, the ability to see clearly, Delron explained. The unopened bottle of clear soda symbolised keeping the elements in their form, contained within their vessel, as it were. The bits of quartz represented magical and healing properties. The green lime was to break down the elements of Satan, to bring infinite clairvoyance, luck and meaning to come through inspiration. The small cob of maize evoked the higher spirits of rain and breeze. Various bits of herbs held integrity and intelligence, he said. Meaningful symbolism is standard among all mystic traditions. In this, Rastafari is in good company.

He declined to explain the nature of other objects on the table. Perhaps if I came back and paid for an understanding into the higher levels, he would explain.

As we drove through the towns in the following days, Bongo Cutty flew a small Rasta flag out the window. He called out to everyone "Rastafari! Fire! More Fire! Haile Selassie!" Most people greeted him good-naturedly. Rastas reacted with the enthusiasm of lonely people finding a long-lost brother. What an odd sight we had to be, I thought: a bearded fellow wearing a huge, funny hat right out of *Alice In Wonderland*, waving a flag from a car and shouting the equivalent of "Praise the Lord! Jesus Saves! Believe in God!" I felt that I was in the lead car of a crusade caravan. In fact, within the context of fundamental evangelism, such behaviour was not off the scale.

Bongo Cutty and Zaccheus gave freer range in expressing their vision for Rastafari as they relaxed with me. The millennium of the Rasta is here, they proclaimed. The Rastas are here to save the people. Rastas are here to lead the way to a rightful life, they explained, with the zealotry of true believers.

Ping! Ping! A small alarm bell went off in my mind.

"We keep the ital ways so the others know how to follow," Zaccheus said.

The country Rastas are the true keepers of the flame; city Rastas are distracted by the material world. The country Rastas keep themselves apart from that world so that they can develop their spiritual being.

"Now, many others were seeing and acknowledging that Rastafari was the only way to be saved," Zaccheus said. "All other belief systems were corrupted by centuries of deliberate misinterpretation that served white colonial masters."

Ping! Ping!

When I asked if their condemnation also included Buddhism, Zen, Hinduism, Islam or Judaism, they admitted that they didn't know about those beliefs. For them, all religions were the religion of their colonial oppressors.

Ping! Ping!

On the grand scale, they envisioned opening Rasta schools, much like fundamentalist Islam schools in Iran, in which boys and girls would be educated separately. They spoke of bringing discipline to the people in order to save them and the society.

Ping! Ping! Ping!

"Jamaica is the new Jerusalem," Bongo Cutty said with the certainty that his sun was the centre of the universe.

I had been told that, if you ask ten Rastas about Rastafari, you'd get ten different answers. One Rasta told me that the Queen of England should send a ship and transport all Rastas to Africa free of charge. And give them new clothes. And money. It didn't occur to him to question whether the Africans – whose economies are already under strain – would welcome several thousand Jamaicans competing for scarce jobs and land.

At another time, a Rasta pointed to two women in short skirts and indignantly declared, "We would put a stop to that. We want women to wear long skirts and be modestly covered."

Blaming the woman for arousing man's temptation and lust is an old dodge to make the woman responsible for the man's behaviour. "How can a man who doesn't take responsibility for his own thoughts and actions be trusted?" I asked. "Why make women guilty for your inappropriate thoughts?"

The answer was, in various versions, we are men and we sit in the catbird's seat. We love our women, call them "Queen", respect their duty as mother and housewife, but we find that the patriarchal social and family structure suits us as men.

There are three main factions of Rastafari in Jamaica, of which the Bobos (also called Coneheads, because of the shape of the turban that wraps their dreadlocks) are considered the most Puritanically extreme. Their main base is between Kingston and Yallahs. The 12 Tribes Of Israel, meanwhile, are a moderate, largely urban-based group that appeals to the professional class, and the island-wide House Of Nyabinghi gives show-and-tell performances at schools, and otherwise spreads their message through drumming exhibitions. The three groups jockey for the national leadership position at the expense of a unified front. Zaccheus confirmed that it is politics, rather than a theological disagreement, that keeps them separate.

On their album *One Calling*, Morgan Heritage has a song, 'Number One Bingi Man' (with a melody reminiscent of 'Ten Little Indians'), that addresses the disunity within Rastafarian ranks. The song calls for the Bobos, the House Of Nyabinghi and the 12 Tribes Of Israel to work together in unity. The line "segregation amongst ourselves makes no sense" has a double edge: the universal everyone should unite in Jah, and the Jamaican Rastas should unite in harmony. "When a Bingi, a Israel, a Bobo, we are all the same,/but the truth, I 'n' I we got to live it for,/battle getting hot in the end," the group sings. "Every Rastaman should know/only united of I 'n' I got chase them [wicked people] away./Our liberty will show them we're the same" reprimands the song, calling attention to factions within the Rasta community.

Zaccheus showed me a five-page questionnaire which the House Of Nyabinghi – "the Rasta government", in his words – plans to send to every household in Jamaica, although the practical aspects of how they would do this were vague. The questionnaire is an opinion poll, Zaccheus explained, designed to discover how people feel about certain issues.

It read more like a revolutionary call to sweep out the present government and all other Jamaican institutions tainted with the smudge of holdover colonialism. One question asked if people agreed that the entire police force should be replaced, because they were tainted by British colonial mentality. Another question asked if the entire government should resign because the government was based on the institution of colonialism. The "questionnaire" was more of a rant, promoting the Rasta viewpoint, than an objective poll. In short, it called for the overthrow of the government.

The Rastafari movement has made great strides in Jamaica over the past 60 years. In as late as 1963, Rastas were hunted as wild animals and killed. Military snipers in helicopters flew over the countryside, searching for Rasta targets. They were the lowest of the low in Jamaica, bogeymen and evil incarnate. Today, the Rastas are highly visible and in general are seen in a positive light, or at least tolerated. After a period of growth, fuelled to a large extent by the success of reggae music, the movement appears to have reached a plateau.

To the ordinary Jamaican, the Rastaman is a bit too far on the edge. On the whole, Jamaicans are deeply religious and conservative. The Christian faiths – Seventh Day Adventist, Methodist, Baptist, Catholic, Anglican and Pentecostal – dominate the island. The majority of Jamaicans are fundamentally distrustful of anyone who transforms Christ into a dead African head of state.

15 Rasta Culture

Ken Booth, Mr Rock Steady, recipient of the 1999 Jamaican Living Legend award, lives in a modest corner house with a mango tree in the front yard. The neighbourhood in Kingston is unpretentious, middle class, and not somewhere that I expected to find a star of his stature. A low, white cement-block fence encloses the yard. An iron security gate – *de rigueur* in Kingston – blocks the driveway. The driveway is painted in broad green, red and yellow stripes, the colours of the Ethiopian flag.

Ken greeted me on the small open porch off the carport, wearing a white V-neck T-shirt and shorts. He has a round, handsome face and no grey in his short hair, although he is a grandfather and of the age when white hair betrays you. People call him Mr Evergreen for his forever-young looks, and Mr Smooth for his stage persona. *Smooth* is the title of his album released in June 2000.

Photos of Haile Selassie as a boy, as a teenager and as a man cover the walls of the small porch area. A framed copy of a speech His Majesty gave on education hangs next to the door leading inside. (Haile Selassie once held the portfolio of Ethiopia's Minister of Education.) The excerpt is on the theme of self-reliance through education, and how the truth will be known through education. Ken reads the words with the reverence of a man reciting holy script. "Haile Selassie is a teacher. His Imperial Majesty is the living Christ, Christ made flesh. You can't worship what you can't see. Those duppies and ghosts – how can you worship those?" he asked dismissively.

He led the way into the main room, which he has converted into a museum to his career and family. The walls are painted swirls of green, red and yellow, as are all of the interior walls of the house, so Ken is continually surrounded by his awareness of His Imperial Majesty. Ethiopian flags hang over two doorways on each side of the room. A flag with the portrait of Haile Selassie hangs over the door at the far end, next to an altar-like affair with vases of small stones and an American flag. Covering the walls are framed photos of Ken performing, of him getting married, of his two boys when they were young onstage with him, of friends in the music business, and several awards, including his crystal sculpture Living Legend award. The room is bare of any furniture except for the pot of cloth flowers in the centre of the floor.

After the tour of the shrine room, we settled around a table in a small back room. Ken prepared a chalice and fired up, generating billows of ganja smoke.

"When I smoke herb, I eat and drink better," he said. "If you don't eat and drink well, you won't be healthy." He held up a clove of garlic. "The bush doctor told me to take this." He put it in his mouth and washed it down whole with a glass of water.

"I am a Rasta man. My mother was one of the first Rasta women, so I grew up Rastafari from a little boy. The Rasta man smokes for wisdom. The herb is a sacrament that helps uplift the mind. Herb can make you more observant; you know what I'm talking about? The herb is so humble. It is a stimulant that has humbleness in it. The herb has saved a lot of people, even wrongdoers, criminals, you know. When they want to do something bad, they smoke a spliff and the spliff calms and relaxes and they forget that they want to kill the poor man on the corner, you know what I'm saying? The herb automatically saves his soul because it makes you procrastinate. In that, formula is good, you know?

"But the herb is not for everyone. Some people should not smoke it. It don't agree with them. The herb can be used for fun or it makes procrastination. Then you must have the will to do what you will. You must have that discipline. I can take the herb and then go about what I need to do, go where I need to be.

"Not everybody must smoke herb. Little children shouldn't try to smoke herb when they are 10 or 15. First, they have to understand themselves. Before you approach anything at all, you must know what you are doing. That's your responsibility. That comes first. Then you can take up trying other tings.

"But not everything you must venture. For example, cocaine. I ventured cocaine already and realised that it's not for me. It's not right. It does something very different than herb. It's negative. Its didn't get me that way. But I saw what it does. I'm an advocate now when it comes to cocaine. I'm a man who tells people why they mustn't do it. I feel I have the right to do this. I know of this. When you don't know about something you don't have the right to tell people, but since I've had the experience I'm ready to go on the radio and talk about it. I want to tell the world so the children can understand to say no to these things. Even to herb, the children should say no to.

"I advocate legalisation of herb. I agree to legalise, but that's not to mean a man can go into a place and smoke where everybody don't smoke. Go smoke someplace where you don't interfere with other people, who don't smoke. I don't believe that if it's legalised you just go into a theatre, smoke herb before a lot of people who don't smoke it. I don't think it's right to walk around on the street with a spliff. It's like with the cigarette. They've banned smoking the cigarette in most places because, if everyone in that place did smoke, they don't need to ban it, but you go into a place where some people don't smoke, so you don't have a right to smoke there. You can carry a spliff with you everywhere, even in the White House, but you must not go into the White House and smoke it because not everybody smokes it there."

The values and symbols of Rastafari and reggae have become so intertwined that they are widely regarded as parts of the same whole. The Rastafari expropriation of the Ethiopian flag's colours (red, gold and green), the lion, the drum, smoking marijuana, wearing dreadlocks and the distinctive language were symbols of resistance – these symbols are now identified with reggae.

A cover of one Marley album has him wreathed in ganja smoke. Peter Tosh named an album *Legalise It*. One of the most promising current reggae groups, Morgan Heritage, on their album *One Calling*, sing, "We have licence to drive our cars/but still so many people die by cars./We have licence to use guns/ but when we use our guns life is done." Better to give a licence to smoke the spliff, for "herbal wisdom don't kill no one./Herbal wisdom help you understand./Herbal wisdom is a natural healer./Herbal wisdom life preserver." Herbal wisdom didn't kill President Kennedy or Martin Luther King Jr, the song goes. A man with his gun did.

There is a strong movement to decriminalise the smoking of marijuana in Jamaica, according to the newly appointed public defender, Howard Hamilton, QC, a tall Lincolnesque-looking man with eyeglasses. The legalisation of marijuana is moving, if indirectly, onto the Jamaican political stage. Hamilton has proposed that the Jamaican Constitutional Court recognise Rastafari as a legal religion. Once the right of religion is guaranteed under the constitution, the issue of ganja as a sacrament of the church can be addressed.

As the public defender, Hamilton's job is to investigate complaints of injustice or hardships suffered by any citizen at the hands of any government office, agency or ministry. However, he doesn't try cases in court. That is left up to other attorneys.

Forcing the marijuana issue through a legal case is not a new tactic. Dennis Forsythe, a Kingston attorney, Rasta and Rastafari scholar, brought a court action to have his right to use ganja accepted as part of his religious freedom. The court ruled that Rastafari is not a legally recognised religion in Jamaica, and that therefore he could not claim religious rights.

"First, get your religion accepted as a religion," Hamilton told me during a visit to his office. "Once you have that, you can go to Parliament, or back to the courts, and seek an exemption. There are exemptions right on the books for the medical profession to use ganja. An example I use is the Roman Catholic Church in America during Prohibition, when it was illegal to manufacture or sell liquor. The church got an exemption to use wine in its ceremony.

"Rastafari needs special constitutional recognition, because it has not been accepted as a religion in Jamaica. It has been regarded as a cult, or a faith. Once it is a religion, lots of benefits and privileges flow:

the right to hold land, the right to tax exemption as a church, and the right of the ministers to minister to the members of faith. Until that is done then you're on the fringe. You can't demand rights."

Rastafari is recognised as a legitimate religion (for legal purposes) in Great Britain, the United States and other countries. In the United States, this legal status was granted in a court ruling in a drug case. Three federal judges of the US Court Of Appeals For The Ninth Circuit in San Francisco reversed the marijuana possession conviction of Rastafarian Cameron Best of Billings, Montana, "citing violations of the 1993 Religious Freedom Restoration Act". The judges argued that, "Best's use of marijuana as a Rastafarian sacrament was largely and wrongly proscribed by the lower court as an element of his defence." The Native American Church, which uses peyote as a sacrament, won religious legitimacy on similar legal grounds.

"I don't think anybody objects or argues against the Rastas' right to their religion," Hamilton said. "Freedom of religion is guaranteed under the Jamaican constitution. All the arguments I've heard are in relation to 'This is going to open the floodgates to the use of marijuana,' which I don't believe. This doesn't mean that, if Rastafari is granted the status of a religion, that a Rasta can be seen walking down the street smoking a spliff and claim to be meditating – that would be a misuse of the sacrament. When you're together at your church, celebrating, you can smoke marijuana. If you leave the church and are still smoking a spliff then the police can prosecute you. You have the right to do it in a prescribed and regulated manner.

"The Rastafari have clung to their beliefs for years. The movement has grown in members. They are all over the world. I've been in the practice of law since 1959. I have seen the tribulations that have beset the Rastafari. There was a time in 1963, the Coral Garden incident in Montego Bay, when people who resembled Rasta in their hairstyle committed some robbery. As a result, the entire strength of the police force was turned out on the Rastas. They were hounded. They had to hide, had to run. Still, they never gave up their faith, never gave up their wearing of locks. There were times when the police would raid them and kick over their food while it was being cooked, claiming they were looking for ganja. They were deprived of employment. They were told, 'If you cut your hair, you'll get the job. If you don't, you don't get the job.' There were situations of wholesale discriminations.

"I always like to tell this story. I once defended a Rastafari in the '60s because he was barefooted, riding a bicycle, and when the police stopped him and searched him he had $20,000 on him. They charged him with unlawful possession of money because he refused to explain where he got it. He said, 'It's mine,' and refused to give any explanation. The court convicted him. It was just that that was too much money for a Rastafarian to have. He took the matter to the appeals court. They laid down the law that there can be no presumption that any amount of money is too much money for one person to possess. It's like if a banker had been robbed across the street, and you're just walking away with a bag with $100,000, you might be charged with suspicion of robbery but not possession of too much money for one black man to have. He was acquitted.

"I'll tell you another reason I'm going to bat for the Rastafari, quite apart from as a lawyer. The genuine Rasta is non-violent, disciplined, respects his women folk and takes care of his children. These are the people who I am looking to to set the tone of the return of discipline in this country now. That's why I'm going to bat for them. If the rest of society could exhibit that kind of discipline in their home life, and in their work ethic, we can turn this country around." Hamilton predicted that the case to get Rastafari declared a religion would be before the court within a year.

The Rasta community seems to be of two minds about the attempt to legitimise Rastafari as a church. They stridently insist that their spiritual beliefs are above the constitution and any man-made institutions. They don't need approval to smoke ganja, they say. Jah has given them herb and His approval. They are suspicious of a conspiracy to regulate herb and control them by making Rastafari a legal religion. They recognise the benefits, though, and so don't reject Hamilton's effort out of hand, but at the same time they dismiss the whole notion.

The Spanish introduced ganja to the New World in around 1545, but it was the British who championed its use. The British offered

Jamaican planters generous subsidies to grow the hemp, the fibres of which were used to make strong ropes, prized by the British Navy.

The term *ganja*, a Hindi word, became widely known in the early part of the 20th century, when the British colonial administration chose the already-familiar word while drafting anti-cannabis legislation. The herb has many names, including Asian hemp, marijuana, lamb's bread, *kan* in the Amharic Bible, brain food, wisdom weed and *kali*, a particularly potent grade of dark-coloured ganja named after the Hindu goddess, who is often portrayed as black and who slays illusions – including death – so that one can see with brilliant clarity.

The Rastas quote numerous biblical passages to attest to its sacramental properties: "He causeth the grass to grow for the cattle, and herb for the service of man, that he may bring forth food out of the earth." (Psalms, 104:14.) In Psalm 18:8, "Smoke went up from his nostrils, and devouring fire from his mouth" gives evidence for the Rastas that God smoked the herb, even though this passage refers more to dragon fire than to smoking ganja. In Revelations, they say, it appears as "the leaves of the tree for the healing of the nations", and in Genesis, Deuteronomy, Isaiah, Proverbs... The Rastas will quote a mouthful for their herb. They call it wisdom weed because marijuana was allegedly found growing on the grave of King Solomon.

Ganja represents a strong cultural link between Jamaican and African rituals and practices. Among the central African tribes the Batetala, Basakata and Bakongo, cannabis has played an important religious role, similar to the one that it plays among the Rastafarians. The Kung of the Kalahari smoke cannabis throughout their nightly healing dances so as to facilitate the onset of *kia*, an enhanced state of consciousness that a healer must reach before he can access the power to heal. In the Kumina rituals in Jamaica, ganja – referred to as *diamba* – is used in the seeking of spiritual guidance and inspiration.

The Youth Black Faith institutionalised ganja as an integral part of the Rastafari reform movement. At that time, in the mid '40s, the British authorities were cracking down on the trafficking in and possession of ganja. This provided a convenient smokescreen to also crack down on the anti-colonial Rastas, who were becoming more and more vocal and militant in their opposition. The Youth Black Faith reasoned that the government's insistence on making ganja a political cause was an attack on the people, especially the Rastas. The crackdown was the government's excuse to suppress the people, which gave them all the more reason to smoke it, claimed the Youth Black Faith, but only in religious practices. Members of the Youth Black Faith were instructed not to carry the herb on their person but to leave it at their places of worship.

In my considerable experiences with Jah Earl, Zaccheus, Bongo Cutty and the other Rastas, I found it difficult to discern the difference between social and sacramental uses of ganja. For the most part, they rolled a spliff whenever they felt like it, whether driving the taxi, riding in a car or visiting friends. There was no ritual involved in its preparation, no prayers mumbled, no ganja dropped to the ground as an offering. Of course, they may have considered any use of ganja in any situation as partaking in a sacrament, but such a broad stroke dilutes the significance, and is much like one claiming that onanism is profound, soul-sharing lovemaking.

So how did the dreadlocks start to be part of Rasta culture? There are two schools of thought. One says that, in the '40s, the Rastas at Howell's Pinnacle commune began wearing locks after seeing magazine photos of Jomo Kenyatta's Masai freedom fighters, who wore matted hair, battling in the wilds of Kenya. The hair made them look more ferocious, fearsome – a look that Howell's Ethiopian Warriors, who guarded the commune, wanted to cultivate. The African connection is also linked to Somalis and to the Gallas of southern Ethiopia, who wear their long locks plastered with ochre.

Wearing matted or twisted locks of hair is fairly widespread in Africa. Ethiopian monks have traditionally worn dreadlocks. The royal soldiers of the pre-Islamic Wolof society in Senegal and Gambia, the *tyeddo*, also wore dreads. The Islamic-based Baye Faal sect of today wears dreadlocks. In Ghana, many of the traditional Akan fetish priests and priestesses, the *okomfo*, wear dreads. Matted hair is associated throughout West Africa with those who are traditional healers and priests.

The other school of thought credits the style of Rasta head hair to the House Of Youth Black Faith, the group of young radical Rastas who, in their most influential period from the late '40s to the '60s, enforced reforms on the movement. The Youth Black Faith insisted that its members should return to the practice of growing beards. In the mid '30s, it was believed that those with beards would be repatriated to Africa on 1 August 1934, although that date came and went without deliverance. In the '40s, due largely to the Youth Black Faith, beards came to be identified with the Rastafari, much like turbans are associated with Sikhs.

A main thrust of the Youth Black Faith reform was the denunciation of traditional practices of superstitions, especially those of Kumina and earlier Revivalist beliefs. The purging of Revivalist rituals and attitudes also challenged many of the social and religious norms that were taken for granted, such as the superiority of the white Christian God. One result was to stir the poor and rural people from the mental apathy of the colonial status quo. Having dark skin no longer meant being a slave in any sense, or being inferior to the more light of skin and economically powerful, whether Jamaican or foreigner. This undermining of racial values remains a hallmark of the Rastafari movement and a constant theme in reggae music.

A faction within the Youth Black Faith who called themselves the Dreadlocks espoused strong separatist leanings: "Black, white/and here's the line:/you on your side/me on mine." The Youth Black Faith purged short-haired people – referred to as baldheads – from the Rastafari movement, and began the process of clarifying and consolidating male and female roles. One criticism of Rastafarian is the largely domestic (ie subservient) role given to women, despite them being called "my queen".

According to author and Rastafarian scholar Barry Chevannes, members of the Youth Black Faith grew their locks as a direct assault on the Jamaican social norms. If society was going to treat them as outcasts, as antisocial madmen, well, then, they were going to take the image and run with it. The long-haired hippies of the '60s – often referred to as freaks by disapproving society – took a similar stance by becoming even more freaky looking, thus showing that they weren't intimidated. By adopting with pride the very negativities attributed to them, they took some steam out of their opponents' attacks.

The purge and control was important in solidifying male ownership and control of the Rasta movement, on which the Youth Black Faith also adopted a militant stance. The members conceived themselves as people who were "struggling to leave a society to which they felt they did not belong", writes Chevannes. "They took a more aggressive, non-compromising stance, symbolised by dreadlocks. The Dreadfuls, or Warriors, were the first to start the trend, and as their hair grew they became more dreadful." The Dreads went out of their way to invite confrontation with governmental authority, most often the police. They claimed that colonial-imposed laws did not apply to them, or to any free Jamaican. It was their duty to show contempt for such laws, and the society that bowed down to those laws, and they did so with religious zeal.

Rastas who distinguished themselves with exemplary ascetic discipline, keeping the ital way of life, were honoured with the title "warrior" or "dreadful". "Dread" or "dreadful" was synonymous with "upright", and was applied to an honourable and honest person who was motivated by a deep sense of religious conviction. A "warrior" or "dread" was someone who inspired dread in others because of his forthright and frank critical remarks and defence of the faith. The warriors were also called Bonogee (Boanerges), or "Sons Of Thunder", the name that Jesus gave to the brothers John and James, who became his apostles. (See Mark 3:17.) A Rasta may refer to his or her locks as their crown, an association to the real crown of Haile Selassie. The locks are also symbolically compared to the mane of a lion, a symbol of male strength.

The Youth Black Faith institutionalised dreadlocks at a time when wearing such outlandish hair was not in vogue. By the end of the '50s, dreadlocks and their dreadness lifestyle became entrenched in the Rastafari community. Locks marked the members as outcasts, cultists, isolationists and difficult people. No one outside the movement wore dreadlocks. Fashion dreads and wannabe Rastas didn't come along for another 20 years.

In the '50s and '60s, dreadlocks were a Rasta-owned symbol of uncompromising opposition to the materialism and superficiality of Babylon. The very sight of the locks was supposed to strike fear in the hearts of Babylonians, and this is part of the reason why they are called dreadlocks. Shaking the locks, or tossing them back and forth over the head as Marley did on stage and Burning Spear still does, is thought to release spiritual energy to bring about the destruction of Babylon. The locks are a psychic antenna, a mystical link to what the Rastas call *earthforce*, which connects Rastas with their God and his power.

Rastas quote biblical sources to support their unshorn hair. "All the days of his separation there shall no razor come upon his head" (Numbers 6:5) is one such directive, as is Leviticus 21:5: "They shall not make baldness upon their head, neither shall they shave off the corner of their beard, nor make any cuttings in their flesh," and "He shall be holy and shall let the locks of the hair of his head grow." The locks were a witnessing to faith with the fanaticism of the old biblical prophets, men gone mad with the spirit.

However, in the '50s, the hair issue split the Rastafari movement into two factions: the House Of Dreadlocks and the House Of Combsomes. The Dreadlocks prevailed, though, and within a decade the Combsomes had all but vanished. One reason was the visibility of dreadlocks as an antisocial and anticolonial statement. Although many of the leading figures of Rastafari were schooled in Youth Black Faith values, the movement broke up in the '60s. Some of the leaders were arrested for various reasons, and many of the followers dispersed throughout the Kingston area.

David Hinds, lead singer for Steel Pulse, wears impressive dreadlocks. From a distance, they look sinewy, heavy, like thick arms of an octopus, but his hair is soft, fine and light. On one morning, between running errands at his home in Birmingham in the UK, David explained to me the personal significance of his dreadlocks. "For me, they take on both spiritual and mental connotations. When I started out being a Rasta, to me, physically, the locks were a symbolic way of identifying who I am. There is always a tendency to meet an antagonist when one wears dreadlocks. My locks are an identification of self and letting others be aware that there is a certain mind-set going on. When it came to my enemies, or people I have problems with before it comes into any conversation, they know where my mind-set is, by physically seeing. Wow, this guy's got dreadlocks!

"Spiritually, when you go back to the biblical context, where we read about various people in the Bible – whether it's Samson or Jesus Christ or Moses or all these prophets and seers – they all had long hair. Jesus Christ is painted white in the eyes of the Western world, but at no time at all did they dismiss the fact that he had long hair, although the right-wing-orientated Western world – ie Reaganists and Margaret Thatchers, all those people – tend to be against long hair, the whole hippie scenario, Flower Power and everything else. The status quo still acknowledges that Jesus Christ had long hair. You read in the Bible about having long hair and not cutting it. Some kind of strength within.

"I am a rebel, and I've noticed that every institution, where the system tends to have the upper hand over individuals or people collectively, those institutions have those people's hair cut. The army, the marines, in prisons, mental institutions, all the institutions where they want to control people in masses, the hair has to be cut. The institutions which want to hold the status quo – that is, they're in control – their policy is to have the hair cut. This is another reason why we're against cuttin' the hair, because the institutions always preferred to have the country be shorn.

"It's really hard to give a direct reason for dreadlocks. I see Rastafari and dreadlocks as being a fingerprint. Every man has a different fingerprint. I also see that every man wears his dreadlocks differently. If you look carefully on how dreadlocks are formed, there are no two dreadlocks that are identical because, even if it's shaped the same, there are different grades of hair.

"As far as I'm concerned, when every man decides to take on Rastafari, he does so because of what he himself has experienced. The only thing we've got in common collectively, as Rastafarians, is that we tend uplift our minds to a higher level of consciousness than where we started out individually to where we can work collectively, so every man, to me, has a reason why they wear their dreads. At the end of the day, the heart knows. That's the most important thing.

"Rastafari has been through many transitions now, through many types of development. I've always believed that any culture or consciousness or religion – whatever terminology one wants to put Rastafari under – always moulds itself according to the social/political climate at that time. I think now it's a little bit easier, as far as the physical tension that Rastafari has suffered over the past 20 years – ie the incarnations over having a spliff, or this whole idea of having dreadlocks, where one was just thrown into jail and beaten. On certain Caribbean islands, Dreads got killed for having locks. That kind of tension isn't quite there as it used to be. So you find certain things have adapted [because] of what social/political pressures there are.

"I think Rastafari has reached a stage now where it's more – as far as I'm concerned – being politically aware of what's going on. Rastas have become a catalyst for political consciousness, strengthened by a superior being. It's reached a point now where, to me, you don't have to be a Rastafari direct to share those sentiments."

Perhaps the most dangerously revolutionary action of Rastafari and its sword carrier, reggae, is the deconstruction, and reconstitution, of language. One simple example: the Rasta word "polytricks" or "politricks", for politics, is devastatingly descriptive.

"Their use of language is totally turning things on its head," Kwame Dawes said during one of our early-morning talks. "Rasta is actually challenging the fundamental basis of language. It's remarkable, beautifully done, articulated and powerful. To be effective, the Dread talk does not have to come into general use. If it comes into general use, it's defeated. The point is to stay one step ahead. That's why the language is always changing. The terms and idioms of the street change rapidly, because it's propelled by the music. This is where the language is created and heard: in the streets.

"Language is the most powerful long-term weapon of the Rastas.

Not in that the actual words of the language may change, but that the perspective is shifted by images of the words. This happened when the feminists tried to change and influence the language, with some success, in reminding us how we use language, and that language has power. The Rastas keep prodding language because what is being said has implications every time you use those words. Rastas are not interested in literally changing the language, but they are certainly interested in the way we look at language."

Along with Mutabaruka, Jesus Afari is Jamaica's best-known dub poet, followed by Natural Cherry. I met Jesus at the Black Scorpio Studio, where he was editing the playlist for his newest album as if he was structuring the rhythm of a poem.

"Tell me which one you like best," he said to me, handing me two contact sheets of possible cover photos. There was Jesus professionally lighted and studiously posed. His massive dreads were bound in white, looking like a heavy coxcomb arching off the back of his head. They are his trademark symbol. He is not a tall man but broad in the shoulders and chest, which makes him appear powerful. He has a strong face with striking honey-brown eyes. He wore white in some of the photos, and black in others. He had his chin thoughtfully resting on a fist, much like a book-jacket photo of an overly self-conscious writer trying to convince the world that he is a serious artist. At the top left-hand corner of the contact sheet there was a photo of Jesus looking directly at me with a light, playful smile – an invitation.

"This one." I pointed.

"I had selected this one." He pointed to one of the pretentious scholarly photos.

We got into a half-hour analysis on the merits of his publicity photos, as if we were dissecting a PhD thesis.

Jesus Afari is a serious artist. His records are not just recitals of poetry but compositions of sounds, both instrumental and spoken. His love for jazz is obvious in his poetic phrasings. He has worked with full orchestras, with big bands, with melodic songs and with stark soundscapes. His albums include *Mental Assassin*, *Dancehall*

Practice, Man's Gonna Crawl Away, and the recently completed *Rastafarian Friends*.

"Language is the most revolutionary tool that can be used to cast out and recast an identity," he said, setting aside the photos. "That is my major pre-occupation. Let us examine language. The best and most. effective language is that which is most picturesque. Language is meant to create mental images and impressions so that you can see what I am saying. You can, by virtue of seeing what is spoken, visualise the images that the thought process paints on the canvas of your mind.

"How you think, how you speak, the language you speak, is a reflection of how you perceive yourself and others, and the value and self-esteem that governs your life and your relationships, so if we are to liberate and free ourselves we must evolve a language that is particular and unique to our own circumstances. Language will help to bring a certain level of identity. Since we Jamaicans have been through an experience that is unparalleled in history, then we must evolve a language that is unparalleled in history.

"The colonial masters deliberately forced out a language and forced in their language, so de-colonialism is what we're about now. We are de-colonialising colonialism. We are reclaiming. We refuse and expel that alien concept and reality and reinstate what best fits us and allows us to be the best that we can be.

"We use language to cultivate and recultivate, to align and re-align the mind. You think in the language that you speak, so the language in which you think and speak shapes and directly conditions your thinking, and by extension your life and your culture. So I really attempt to use my poetry, my music, to create that mind-set which will lend itself to healthier thinking and a healthier life, ultimately.

"I think that poets are scientists, or doctors. We use poetry and music similarly, as a surgeon uses his surgical instruments. We are linguistic practitioners. We practise psycho-cybernetics, where we reshape and refashion the mind and the mentality. We do that through language and other concepts. We associate ourselves similar to a mental assassin, that will eradicate and expel and reject negative concepts out of the mentality, out of the mind, out of the people and the culture. By extension, we see ourselves as mental farmers who replace that which is expelled with healthy seedlings to cultivate and recultivate the mind and mentality.

"The whole idea of dub poetry is to take out and put in, so we consciously make a decision to extract negative elements and concepts – demons and witches and wizards – out of the mind and to replace that with factual information – love, knowledge and inspiration – so that at least we can recultivate people's thinking. Recultivate humanity. Recultivate our social culture and social life.

"The diseases we experience in the human family now are real lifestyle diseases, so the benefits must be the lifestyle you live. So we think that this is a scientific approach. We think we need to subject our thinking to scientific scrutiny so that only the best will be used and dispensed in our job.

"We have a proverb that says, 'Dance a yard before you dance aboard.' Charity begins at home, so I'm concerned with the betterment of my individual life, and my family, and my nation, and country. I recognise that we are part of an integral whole. We are part of a region and an international community and a human family. Jamaica occupies a certain focus, as it relates to music in the international community; so my extension of my work concerning Jamaica concerns the whole. While we fulfil our responsibility to Jamaica, we fulfil our responsibility to the region and the international community.

"As an artist, I 'n' I is about creating and recreating sounds that will catch people's attention back to the message, to make it fashionable to be righteous and good, to be fashionable to talk of love. Check Jamaica now. The sociological inversion that takes place is due to the contradiction of this state of symbols that they hold up for society. In the ghetto, when something's good, the man him say it's bad. That's an inversion. The people who are supposed to be the models, they caught them red-handed in the cookie jar.

"In the context of a Shambhala warrior, and in the context of the liberation of the I 'n' I people, I consider myself a warrior. Then I 'n' I is a mental assassin. We want love and goodness and unity and tolerance and overstanding and wisdom and truth and togetherness.

That is what we want to implant in the institutions. In that context, I'm a warrior warring against evil and corruption and injustice. Still, we are a love-maker because we strive to instil and spread love and harmony and goodness. At the same breath, I'm a warrior; I'm a love-maker."

The phrase "I 'n' I" didn't come into general Rasta use until the '50s. It is a means by which Rastas communicate their basic philosophy or concept of themselves, their community and the world. Out of it comes a new sense of self that leads to a new vision of values.

"I", the most central word in Rastafari speech, transforms many words. The first-person I replaces the *u* or *you* sound in words such as *unity* and *human* to create the words I-nity and I-man, similar to the word sounds *Itrol* and *Iscious*. *Brethren* – pronounced *bredrin* in dialect – becomes *Idrin*; *eternal* becomes *Iternal*; *hour* transforms into *Iowa*; *times* becomes *Iimes*; and *creator* is *Ireator*. The psychological power of *I* is important in Rasta talk; *Iman* equals Rastaman; *Ifric* equals Africa; while *Itals* are foods produced from the ground and unspoiled by preservatives, such as *Inana* (banana) and *Ilaloo* (callaloo). One of the ills of Babylon, according to the Rastas, is its departure from naturalness and its commitment to artificiality.

To the Rastas, the personal pronoun is associated with the Roman numeral I, as in the title Emperor Haile Selassie I. *I* is a substitute for *me* and *mine*. The religious meaning behind this substitution is that the Rastaman is also part of God, and that, if God is a visible, living man – as is expressed by Marley in 'Get Up, Stand Up', and by others in reggae songs – it must mean that the Rastaman is another Selassie, another I, another divinity. The incarnation of I in Jah Selassie I invokes the biblical expression of "the Word made flesh" (John 1:14), referring to the ministry of Jesus. This word of flesh, power and life provides the context for all significant and definitive Rasta discourse.

I in Rastafarian thought signifies the divine principle that is in all humanity. "I 'n' I" is an expression of the oneness between two or more persons and between the speaker and God. "I 'n' I" indicates a rejection of subservience in Babylon culture and an affirmation of self as an active agent in the creation of one's own reality and identity.

For Rastafarians, language is an arena of political struggle and personal transformation. Since English was associated with the enslavement of African people, its grammar, phonology and semantics weren't considered to be *heartrical* – that is, capable of expressing African culture and consciousness.

Rastas "penetrate" the phonological structure of English words by sounding out, then re-assembling the sounds into new words called "up-full" sounds. For example, the *de* sound prefix in the word *dedicate* (pronounced *dead-di-cate*) was deleted because of its sound-sense, which is similar to the *de* sound used in the English words death and destruction. The *de* prefix was replaced by a sound that signified its opposite, as in life, creating the up-full sound *liv-i-cate*. The *un* sound in words such as *understand* was replaced by the *o* sound of over, as in *overstand*, implying that all the speakers are competent – ie no speaker of Dread talk is under or down, as in *down-press-I*.

Meanwhile, the *con* sound in words such as *conscious* and *control* was associated with the k sound in the Creole word *kunni*, meaning clever. It was replaced by the first-person pronoun, I, as in *Itrol* and *Iscious*. Similarly, the suffix *dom* was deleted from the word *wisdom* because of its similarity to the word dumb. How can a man be both wise and dumb at the same time? The Creole mon (ie man) replaced the dumb suffix, creating the word-sound *wiz-mon*.

In Jamaica, music is often referred to as "sound". That sound, more than the word, has the power. You don't necessarily have to understand the words to feel the power of the sound, which is often true from the old-time reggae of Lee "Scratch" Perry's to much of the current DJ music. That sound translates the ineffable spirit. The limitation of words can never fully articulate the sound of the spirit.

In Jamaica, this spirit speaks through the music and rituals of Kumina, Pocomania, Revivalism and, most importantly, the drum. The spiritual and secular forms of Jamaican music were fused together in the evolution of reggae. This fusion of sound and spirit continues to be an undertow causing new currents in the music.

16 The Walking Corpse

Dancehall is a walking corpse. A very animated corpse, I admit, bouncing up and down like a hyperactive teenager on a turbo pogo stick, waving gun-barrel fingers over its head and shouting *bam! bam!*, flicking Bic-blasting three-foot-long jets of flame from big bamboo aerosol cans and with women blinking like neon signs advertising *sex!* how can you call this *dead, mon, be dead alive*, to the stompin', snortin', argo sound, every man for himself and dis the ladies along the way, because this's hard-metal-jacket bullet shattering the nervous system, so no talk DJ Ripem telling' you *don't listen, just do* the wave, jump to the right, the crushin' hop to the left, *get air! get air!*, so the sound carry you right away and don't look where you're gone, it don't make no difference, you'll be back from the beginning.

I went to a lawn dance, and it's still ringing in my head. The dance was at Bounty Hall, a strip village back in the hills with an enclosed sports complex and a capacity of 1,500. A "lawn" is the country version of an urban street dance, with sound system and dancehall music. The raucous all-night dances are now forbidden in Kingston, victim of their own violence and a 2am noise curfew. The famous Rae Town street dance was closed down years ago for such reasons. Rae Town, a cousin to Trench Town, was a place to avoid most the week, but on Sunday nights people from all over Kingston, from all walks of life, in rich clothes and poor clothes, came without fear to party on Rae Street.

The gunfire associated with dancehall began when security guards at the outdoor street dances fired their pistols into the air signifying support for an artist. Soon others came to the concerts dressed with their own applause meters. Bullets falling out of the night sky wounded innocent bystanders. Men purposefully shot and killed other men at the concerts. People stayed away. The performers, feeling the economic repercussions, asked their fans to leave their guns at home. The hand-as-gun salute and the verbal *bam! bam!* replaced the real thing.

Showtime at Bounty Hall was advertised as being 9pm. At 10:30, I took a series of collectivo taxis into the dark countryside. Several hundred people milled around the front of the sports field sealed behind a tall fence. Quick-buck artists had set up dice tables and lit kerosene pressure lamps to see their money better. Chicken was grilling on jerk barrels along the two-lane road, which was quickly squeezed to one lane for two-way traffic. A peanut vendor, the steam whistle of his roasting cart shrieking like a pig being castrated, shoved his annoying contraption over rough ground, herking and jerking through a crowd that was now, at midnight, numbering close to 800 bored people, by my rough count. The sound system blasted behind the zinc fence, with the unseen DJ causing coitus interruptus to songs while shouting out his own ejaculations.

People, many with a beer bottle in one slack hand, stood without a twitch to the music. Little kids, normally long to bed, played their games off to the side while their mothers and brothers and sisters stood – beer bottle slack in one hand – and waited. Men outnumbered women ten to one. The women who wanted to be seen wore their guarantee: tight, tight, tight cellophane wrapped in faux leather and sequins. I, not culturally adapted, mistakenly thought that I was at the Bad Taste Costume Ball. One woman, naked except for a butt-floss G-string, had draped herself with fine-mesh netting. Men laughed at her.

There were fine-looking women in skimpy flash-and-dash, but I knew better than to let my eyes linger. They may be a single, or with an equally adventurous girlfriend, but to make that dangerous assumption would be like assuming the chamber is empty before pulling the trigger of the gun at your temple. Umbrageous males populated the shadows, claiming ownership by telepathy.

By three o'clock, a herd of over 1,000 people shifted from foot to foot. At 3:30, a single door opened in the fence. The crowd swirled towards it like bugs being sucked down a drain. I hung back on the edge. It felt like a loaded gun to me.

Dancehall is the flagship of Jamaican music, supplanting reggae. It has legions of ardent fans and legions of equally ardent critics. Jamaica dancehall performers have been banned from other Caribbean islands. The Cayman Islands government forbade Capleton, The Fireman, Jamaica's hottest DJ, from performing in the Cayman Islands. He wouldn't agree to tone down his 'Fire Can't Cool' show that was scheduled to take place in Georgetown. According to newspaper reports, Capleton refused to assure that he would not "spew inflammatory lyrics about the Pope and the Queen of England during his show". The Caymans are a British colony, and the Cayman authorities, fearing that he would make "utterances to corrupt the morals" of the Caymanians, refused him a visa. The authorities finally agreed to let him perform if he would not refer to persons in positions of authority. He cancelled the show.

In the spring of 2000, the Barbadian authorities banned all reggae shows from Barbados national venues for 18 months. Dub shows – ie eastern Caribbean reggae – were also banned from all of the island's schools. Government authorities said that the ban was enforced because of the use of drugs, unruly behaviour at the shows and lyrics that taunt the police. Jamaican DJs Cocoa Tea and Cobra have been arrested in Barbados for "unsocial conduct" onstage.

Allison Hunte, of Las Islas Productions, based in the Barbados capital, Bridgetown, was quoted as saying, "As we all know, Jamaica and its music have been associated with a lot of negatives. Reggae has unfortunately been caught in that trap. When they [the authorities] hear reggae, they tend to associate it with drugs and violence. The people who have called for the ban have come from an older generation and are not in tune with what is happening today. There is a lack of knowledge, and they don't understand what the artists are saying. They think it's a conspiracy to infiltrate the minds of the young people with drugs and violence."

Freddie McGregor, the Jamaican international reggae star and a supporter of dancehall since its formative stage, is sympathetic with the Cayman and Barbados positions. "The DJs have made it bad for themselves, and now things just get out of hand," he told Kingston's leading newspaper, *The Daily Gleaner*. "When you go into another man's country, you should yield to the rules; we in Jamaica should do the same thing."

Myriad sins are laid on dancehall's doorstep. The climbing crime rate and shocking immorality among youths (schoolgirls cutting out the bottom of the pocket in their jumpers so that the bus conductor can feel them up) were evils spawned by dancehall, claim the critics. It's true that, in as early as the '60s and '70s, dancehall was lustful and explicit in its sexuality. The attitude of antagonistic youths, people shunning work – all of this and more is blamed on slack dancehall music.

But dancehall is just a Darwinian creature. Economic, social and cultural conditions evolve, and the music shifts with the situation that requires new gods and symbols. Music adapted to the changes in Jamaican society, as animals adapt to changing environmental conditions, and raggamuffin/dancehall emerged. The word *raggamuffin* indicates hardcore dancehall with the mechanical repetition of the dub instrumental, characterised by a heavy bass. Dancehall and raggamuffin are used interchangeably to describe the computer-driven music that followed (and, to a large extent, pushed aside) traditional reggae. The difference between ragga and dancehall is much like the distinction between hip-hop and rap. Ragga belongs to a culture more disdainful of popular acceptance. Dancehall is more commercial in its grab for mass attention, and has linked its definition of success to popular tastes. Ragga artists are not primarily concerned with sales; dancehall musicians want to win a Grammy.

The rude boys – or rudies – of the early '60s, before the Rasta-conscious reggae dominated, were the voice of ragga. Marley himself did a turn as a *faux* rudie. The rudies modelled themselves after the attitude of American cowboys and gangsters. Raggamuffin DJs named themselves Clint Eastwood, Al Capone, Josey Wales, Dillinger and John Wayne. They dressed sharp, swaggered with chips on their shoulders, talked tough, treated women as cream-filled buns to be licked up and discarded, carried weapons and, like today's American street gangs, weren't shy in blazing away. Unlike the Rasta reggae performers, who preferred to be elsewhere – Africa – the rude boys stuck to the "strict reality" of Kingston urban ghetto life. Life was raw, fast, loud, unforgiving and brutal. That was the place to be. That's where the action was. And that was their music.

In 'Shine And Criss', a gun-talk dancehall chant named after a famous Jamaican gunman, Shabba Ranks sang, "Oil up all a the gun dem, keep them shine and criss./A coppe shot, you fe carry inna you gun./Mek a bwoy turn purple any him get it, Lawd…"

When Shabba Ranks became very popular in America, some of his songs were banned in Jamaica. Nobody in America knew that pom-pom was a derogatory term for a woman's privates, a well-understood slang term in his home country. Shabba Ranks, Yellowman and Ninja Man are fingered for popularising the lewd and violent dancehall songs of the '80s.

Ragga spurns the Rastafarian mythos that celebrates – indeed, encourages and nurtures – the idealised notion of a universal black racial and cultural identity. Such a notion is more an abstract concept than a practical reality, as many North American and Caribbean blacks discover when visiting Africa. Jomo Kenyatta and other African leaders who fought colonialism and won independence for their nations had a sentimental vision of pan-tribalism, a people unified under the colour of their skin. The vision of Kenyatta, Nyerere (former president of Tanganyika) and Nkomo (African nationalist and Zimbabwean politician) took on this rosy hue while they were in exile, removed from their homelands, the tribal factions and the racism that exists amongst the various shades of black even today, and certainly in Jamaica. Pan-Africa Rastas such as Marley, Burning Spear and others indulged in the deception that all black people are brothers and sisters, that their shared oppression is the basis of friendship and shared ideals. Reggae constructed rhetoric around the dignity of the black race and of Africa as a utopian heaven, a mythical place of ultimate beauty and peace. The ragga musicians blew holes in that pretty soap-bubble view of reality.

For the dancehall generation, sharing colour doesn't mean sharing culture. They pulled those two tired old shibboleths apart and inserted their notions of belonging into the newly created space. Africa, black skin and the pre-colonial utopia of Ethiopia were not a cultural commodity to the Jamaican dancehall generation. They were more concerned with First World materialism and music created by First World technology. They didn't even share hatred of the tried-and-true bogeyman Babylon. The dancehall crowd relished the spoils of materialism, just as United States rap stars flaunted diamonds and Mercedes limos.

The "new Africa" of the dancehall generation stretched from the shoot-'em-up poverty of Kingston to the depressing housing estates of south London, the sandcastle exile world of Brooklyn and the bleak winters of Toronto. Those regions of the non-geographic culture were linked by the "sound", which created a sense of belonging beyond boundaries constructed by politics and geography. Outside the old definitions, but within the space they called "borderline", the rudie gangbusters created a nervous, jittery music that had nothing to do with playing the guitar or drums. Machines did that mundane work. The artists just had to run their mouth.

Why are people drawn to this music when they don't necessarily understand the words? Because there is a power to the sound and rhythm of dancehall music. When Shabba Ranks does a DJ *a cappella*, he creates the rhythm that becomes reggae. On his *Trailer Load* album, he performs different versions of the title track, from *a cappella* to hip hop. You're dancing funk at one moment, but as soon as Shabba comes on you're dancing reggae. He walks into the spaces and creates different accents, and suddenly you're in reggae. That is the phenomenon of dancehall. The control of rhythm in dancehall is a remarkable thing. That rhythm moves you. It takes you up, throws you back, and makes you shift and shake even if you don't understand a word of the song.

It's a mistake to dismiss dancehall as a simpleton's music performed by somebody who hasn't bothered to learn the guitar. Good dancehall – that of Beenie Man, Tony Rebel, Buju Banton, Sizzla, Bounty Killer, Steely And Clivie, Lady Saw, Capleton and a dozen others – is meticulously constructed and orchestrated. As in reggae, the space and the breaks within the music are important in dancehall. Steel Pulse and Awad, to name only two examples, pull out the drum and bass and leave the light beat that keeps you on edge, before the bass comes back. The breaks and interruptions in dancehall are part of a conversation between the band, the soundman, the DJ and the audience.

The pause, the created space, allows the listener to become one with the performer, to add a free-form image, a shout, a dance step, a *bam! bam!*, and in that they claim part of the song for themselves. The listener claims part ownership, and with that ownership reserve the right to give the music another individual colour and interpretation. This reworking and adding to the sound in the pauses binds the new "culture" of the music more than race, social and economic background or political posturing.

The current crop of DJs learned all this from the *ur*-DJ, U Roy, "the Teacher". U Roy was the first original DJ, back in the '60s, starting with the first sound systems. I had previously visited U Roy at his home in the Coalburn Pen, also known as Cockburn, section of Kingston. The driveway was painted bright blue. Mango trees and foliage gave coolness and privacy. During our talk on his front veranda, with a pretty black-and-white marble tile floor, he was antsy, waiting for the man to fix his hot-water heater. The man had gone for supplies an hour ago and hadn't returned.

U Roy wore a dark-blue knitted cap over his grey locks, which hung down his back in thin braids, and wore shorts and a net tank top. A gold-plated chain with a rectangular plaque hung from his neck. The plaque was filled with Amharic script, which resembles Arabic characters.

His bottom front teeth were long, uneven and protruded slightly. His upper front teeth looked as if they'd been straightened, although he didn't seem to be a man who cares about a pretty smile. I imaged some publicist telling him, "Get a smile, Snaggletooth!", and he was professionally savvy enough to take the advice. He's a slim man with a slight concave chest and worn-looking face. It wasn't hard to see him as a street vendor behind a pushcart.

"When I started as a DJ, as a young man, I used to play sound systems for dance and I get no money," he said. "I couldn't buy clothes off the music. I do that because I love it. If somebody tell me at that time, if they tell me that, you know, there will be come a time when you can buy two shirts off of DJ, I'd tell him nothing like that can be possible. I live to see, at this time, nine out of ten things that I buy, I buy out of my music, including this house.

"The music come a long way. My biggest dream is that the music reach the highest heights, like how hip-hop come the other day and reach high heights. DJ is reggae, so I think reggae come to the same thing. Sell some millions. That is one of my biggest dreams. It needs more marketing. Reggae need good proper promotion worldwide. Promotion is the key to any marketing stuff. You cannot over-promote.

"But there are producers who say, 'You do this music because that's what sells. If you do other music, I won't promote it.' That's a little problem here. I think promoters are supposed to accept what the singer have to offer, and try with that. If a man sing jazz, you can't expect him to come sing hip-hop. That is not his profession. The producer must respect me as a DJ and not as a soca singer. Why not promote what you hear? If you can work and mix in a little thing, touch a little soca into the reggae for the sales purpose, that way we deal with it.

"The producers don't give – especially the reggae singers – no choice. No, they don't give them a choice. They say, 'Try this rhythm. Sing reggae and work with this rhythm.' They say, 'Violence sells, so sing me violence.' So right away you're promoting violence. You're not promoting music. They want violence because that's what's selling. To me, I don't believe in that, so I know there are a few producers who do the right thing. Their money is not that big. Their promotion is not that big. I prefer to work with those producers to those who say some things to make the youth fire the guns. That would sound so stupid to the people who know me. I would be an as-s-shole to those people. I don't want to be that because some people offer me two million or five million dollar.

"The producer decides if he wants to sell conscious music or gun music. Right now, violence is selling, so they want violence, but that will change. After a storm, there's got to be a calm. People have a time when they get really tired of some shit, really tired. Fed up. They don't want to hear that any more. So, in my book, if it's not conscious, it's not going far. With the hip-hop, you have some new ones this week, and next month come something else, because they don't have lyrics to carry it far. It's all about 'motherfuckers' and 'niggers'. Some people don't want to hear that. Period.

"We have so much reggae in our country we don't know what we have, so just throw it away. It's like you have five mango trees in your yard so you don't even look for mango, and some other people, who it makes some sense to, who just love it, come pick it up. When those people start to make progress from it, we start to cry. Cry our eyes out. You're not going to know what you have until you lose it. My grandmother always tell that a cow never know the use of his tail until it got cut off. And when the flies start messing around his tail, he don't have nothing to fan the fly. No shit. Lose the tail. That's what will happen to this music with some of us. You not going to know what you lose until you lose it. If you don't know what you have, don't respect what you have, you're going to lose it. And don't cry when you lose it.

"Reggae is a link back to Africa. My music helps link the memory between Africa and Jamaica. I have my biggest hits in Nigeria and Cameroon, places like that. I try to keep that conscious connection. It's important. Very important. If you lose the music, you lose the link. The Africans know the music comes from here. They're not going to have much respect to you again if you lose it. You sit your ass to one side and shut up and watch what's going on. That's how it's going to be if we lose it.

"I want to see the culture to continue. That's how I learned it and that's how I want it to be. I know right now the new generation of people we have right now. I don't expect things to be perfect 100 per cent. We have to respect what the youth do. They're people, too. I give big props to youths who preach consciousness, all singers and DJs. Buju, Tony Rebel, Luciano – they do that. We have quite a few young people who sing with conscious belief. Dancehall music is forever.

From the '60s, put on the turntable and no other man has that, it is so exclusive. That is dancehall music, brethren."

The sound pioneered by U Roy was taken to the United States by Clive Campbell. As a 12-year-old boy, in 1967 Campbell moved with his family from Kingston to the Bronx. He so missed the Jamaican sound- system music that he sought to replicate it by building powerful banks of speakers hooked to turntables. On one evening, he set up on a street corner and began to imitate the Kingston DJ sound-system style of U Roy. Campbell named his sound system Herculords, and tagged himself Kool DJ Herc. The rest is musical history. The synthesis of the Jamaican DJ talking over the music and the American funk sound evolved into hip-hop and rap. A new musical genre was born.

So why, in my opinion, is dancehall a walking corpse? Because so much of it is inauthentic. The DJs who shout out about being an armed cowboy, driving women down under the male thumb, committing violence against gays, calling for *more fire* to burn down the Babylon system – these DJs don't live any of that, except perhaps in how they treat their women, and I can't personally comment on that. They depend on the Babylon record industry for their livelihood and commit the polite violence of perpetually aiming for the lowest common denominator in order to line their pockets. It can be argued that these DJs are voicing a reality, much like gangsta rap speaks to a reality; but to glamorise violence, to champion brutality – both physical and emotional – against others is not living in the fundamental truth of human nature.

Beenie Man, the headliner at the Bounty Hall lawn dance, made me modify my opinion about dancehall a bit. He started being a DJ as a young boy, a tiny fellow, no larger than a bean, hence the name. As a grown man he is diminutive, making "Beenie Man" even more apropos. He now wants to be called Ras Moses (Moses being his given name), and has titled a CD *Many Moods Of Moses* to underscore the point. Hardly anyone calls him Ras Moses, and certainly not the outlandishly dressed women who gathered in front of the stage. "Beenie Man! Beenie Man!" they chanted, hoping to catch his eye, or catch whatever he might throw to them. A sweaty T-shirt or a handkerchief would have been a coveted prize for their bragging rights.

He was dressed in a zoot suit, which was oddly formal attire for the normal reggae/dancehall performance. Without so much as a how d'you do, he launched into the show. He is a wonderfully talented performer who can do the country and western tune 'Handful Of Ashes' straight out of Nashville, without a trace of Jamaican accent, and then rattle off rapid fire a song in patois in perfect rhyming couplets. He's the most successful DJ on the island, riding a string of hits. At the May 2000 19th Annual International Reggae And World Music Awards, he was given the Bob Marley Award for Entertainer Of The Year.

By the third song, he had flung off his hat, but not to the ladies. By the fifth song, off came the suit jacket, but not to the ladies. The crowd was jumping and shouting and laughing, having a good time. Even Beenie Man's occasional political rant and moral lecturing didn't turn into a political rally or a tent show. When he sang his pop-Christian hit, urging the crowd to "shake your booty for the Lord" (based on the ridim of the hokey cokey), booties bounced and jiggled. The tall, drop-dead-gorgeous young woman in front of me was trying her best to get me in trouble as she shook her bootie for the Lord. Lawdy, lawdy, what would her preacher say? More to the point, was there a boyfriend lurking around who might have more than something to say? She gyrated around to face me and gave a quick smile, her slim bare shoulders beckoning like the Devil's call. Man, I tried hard to keep my eyes on Beenie Man, but she was so tall I couldn't see over her to the stage.

She looked the classic Nubian princess, so regal was her profile. She wore simple, form-fitting black jeans and a white off-the-shoulder tube top – nothing provocative, really, except on her. The casual modesty, and the shyness of her quick smile, was part of the allure. I was desperately trying to be cool, boppin' along with the music, checking out of the corner of my eyes for a boyfriend somewhere unseen. She knew I was looking at her. I could no more ignore her than I could ignore a stunning sunset. She swivelled from side to side with the music, and every third or fourth beat threw a smile over her shoulder to where I could catch it, but not a deliberate fastball, so no one could accuse her of sending an invitation.

She had the gift shared by so many Jamaicans: the ability to make a friendly smile shatteringly seductive. Men, women, kids, old people – no matter. They can all put you on your knees with their natural voltage that sends the good-feeling meter right off the scale. Beenie Man pumped out good vibes, and the crowd caught them and tossed them back and forth so that everyone, including myself, had that seducing-life smile. The night lightened up, and everybody cheered the sun. The Nubian princess turned right to my face and laughed, and I laughed, and nothing more – not a name or a touch – could make the moment any better. It was one of the best concerts I've ever attended.

17 Coffee Reggae Blues

The all-night lawn dance did me in. I needed a coffee break, a day off from chasing music all over the island. That meant a trip into the Blue Mountains. Chocolate lovers pay homage in Brussels. Truffle gourmets rejoice in France. I sought satisfaction in the Blue Mountains, home of some of the most expensive coffee in the world. A pound of Blue Mountain costs $28-$40 at home, when I can find the real article. I wanted to buy a couple of pounds of the premier beans cheap, fresh out of the oven, directly from the source. Jimmy, a friend and a born-and-bred Jamaican, agreed to drive me to Marvis Bank, one of the island's coffee-sorting and curing centres.

We drove up the colloquially named All-Year Road (so called for its 365 curves) in the direction of Blue Mountain Peak, which, at 7,402 feet, is the highest point in Jamaica. True Blue Mountain coffee is grown at altitudes above 2,000 feet.

"You know why you pay through the nose for Blue Mountain?" Jimmy asked. "The Japanese. The Japanese have cornered the Jamaican coffee market." Japan imports 85 per cent of the Jamaican coffee crop, including nearly all of the best Blue Mountain beans, he explained. Only ten per cent of the crop is sold to US buyers. "The Japanese offered growers cheap development money at four to five per cent interest. Cut down the pine trees and expand your crops, they told the growers. We'll give you the money. In exchange, the Japanese got long-term leases on 10,000 acres of prime coffee bushes. The Japanese don't quibble over the price, like the US buyers. US buyers are always trying to get the cheapest deal. Americans get the coffee they deserve."

"That's what I'm thinking about the Jamaicans," I countered. "They get the music they deserve." I had been flipping through the radio stations. All I'd heard was covers of US R&B, covers of schmaltz, golden oldies rock 'n' roll, derivative dancehall, and muzak reggae.

"Yeah, well," admitted Jimmy. "But there's a new crop coming."

The higher we went, the more the mountains took on a distinct blue hue. It's the pine trees, Jimmy explained. They have more of a blue cast than the banana tree or other tropical trees. The pines also give the coffee its distinct taste. As the coffee berry ripens, it absorbs from its surrounding environment, which is why the quality of soil and air is important.

In the Blue Mountains, the cool air encourages a vibrant bean with a smooth flavour. The mountain peaks catch morning and late-afternoon clouds that shield the coffee bushes from the hot sun, which can burn the maturing beans and impart a harsh taste. The volcanic soil produces a full-bodied coffee with less acid, and thus a more mellow taste, than most Central and South American or African coffees.

We rounded the final curve, splashed across a stream and stopped at the Central Coffee factory, a modest building set against the side of the mountain. "Come on, I'll give you a tour," Jimmy said, as if he owned the place.

We started at the cement tanks, where fresh-picked beans soaked for 20 hours in water diverted from a mountain stream. This "wet process" makes the coffee taste softer than the dry-roasted Brazilian or Haitian coffees, Jimmy explained. "Clean water is the key," he said. "Contaminated water will spoil the fermenting beans' flavour. There is concern that the use of chemical fertilisers will eventually damage the quality of the coffee."

"How do you know so much of this?" I asked.

"John Martinez is an old friend."

My look told him that the name didn't ring a bell.

"The Martinez family is an old-time Jamaican family, like mine. They've been into coffee forever. John moved to Atlanta, where he has a coffee-exporting firm specialising in the finest gourmet coffees. He's a real crusader for better consumer protection from coffee frauds."

"Coffee frauds?"

"A roaster can put one Jamaican arabica bean in the mix and label it Jamaican blend. There are no industry-wide labelling standards. That's one of John's pet peeves. A can of '100 per cent Colombian' tells very little about the actual coffee. All the consumer knows is that the coffee comes from Colombia. It could be a mix of beans grown at low and high elevations, or contain a high percentage of low-grade beans with a handful of higher-quality beans thrown in."

Arabica and robusta are the two main types of coffee beans. "Arabica is a Rolls-Royce. Robusta is a bicycle," Jimmy said. "In Jamaica we have predominantly tipica beans, a subvariety of arabica. Tipica is the Silver Cloud model of the Rolls-Royce. We also have katurah – another subvariety of arabica – and some robusta. The Japanese want all the robusta plants torn out and replaced with arabica plants."

Jimmy led me to beans drying in the sun on a cement pad. "After soaking, the beans are spread out here for two or three days. If it rains, the beans are mechanically dried for 20 hours at sun temperature – that is, 190°F. The timing and temperature is calculated to leave 12-13 per cent moisture in the beans."

Jimmy picked up a handful of beans. "This tipica is a big bean, fairly uniform in shape, which is important in roasting. The katurah bean is smaller. It's used as a blend in the less expensive brands. The bean is a little more acid tasting than the tipica. The robusta bean is used mostly as filler, with no taste and little aromatic qualities. But they have more caffeine than the arabica beans. That's why weak-tasting swill made from robusta has more kick and a stronger taste than arabica coffee."

We went into a small room where a mechanical drum shook beans – two per pod – from their casings. A few feet away sat two women wearing facemasks, winnowing chaff from the beans with hand-held sieves. In an adjoining room, men and women sat at banks of high tables hand grading beans for size and uniformity. Beans of similar shape and size roast more evenly, giving a consistent taste.

"Most of the beans are shipped green," Jimmy said. "The length of time and the temperature beans are roasted at are crucial to the taste. Most processors roast beans for 15 minutes at 500°F. I prefer beans roasted at a slightly lower temperature, say 430°, and for a longer time, maybe 20 or 30 minutes. That preserves the flavour and makes for more robust coffee. The shorter, faster roast cooks the beans and destroys the oils, which makes the beans bitter. When the oil comes to the surface, the bean is burnt. Some people like that taste. French roast is burnt bean. That's another one of John's crusades, to have the roast degree – which is determined by time and temperature – stated on labels. Most roast masters claim that revealing their roast degree, which gives coffees an individual taste, would be revealing their trade secret."

Jimmy led me to an upstairs office, where a man from the Jamaican Coffee Industry Board – which certifies the quality of all coffee beans for export – was preparing for a tasting, dressed in a white shirt and tie. The smell of fresh coffee made me salivate. I was at the fountainhead of Blue Mountain coffee. At any moment, a freshly brewed pot would be set before me.

The official taster scooped handfuls of green beans from sacks and examined their size, colour and uniformity. Then the gentleman sat at a small table. Three cups of fresh coffee were set before him. He sniffed a deep draught of aroma from each and carefully looked at the colour. He then sucked noisily from the first cup, swirled the coffee around in his mouth and spat it out. He repeated the process with the remaining two steaming cups.

"You lose your palate if you swallow," Jimmy explained. "Just like in tasting wine."

The taster waited for the coffee to cool, then again went through the tasting process. As coffee cools, the acidity comes through, giving a more pungent taste. If the flavour is too sweet and mild, the beans are too green.

The taster gave a brief nod and left the room without a word. Now was my turn, I was sure. A man cleared the table. As soon as the fresh pot of coffee appeared, I'd sit down and reward myself. I waited. No one was in the room except Jimmy and myself. I was confident that our coffee was being brewed in the back room. We waited. Finally, Jimmy called out and the serving man reappeared.

"We'd like a cup of coffee," Jimmy said.

"We don't serve coffee," the man replied.

"But," I protested, "this is a coffee-processing plant. Surely you have coffee."

"Only for the Japanese," the man said.

He must have seen the obvious disappointment on my face. "Here," he said, and offered me a big, dark, evenly toasted tipica bean. "A souvenir."

Jimmy laughed. "Come on. We'll find organic coffee farmers up in the mountains."

I could have eaten nails. Or coffee, in this case. Africans eat coffee. They'd combine the beans with animal fat and chew them, like nuts with a sweet taste, or they'd make thick, flat cakes of pulverised coffee beans mixed with dried fruit and salted butter. Coffee is grown in Africa, of course, so I suppose that's another back-to-Africa link to Jamaica. Eighty per cent of the Jamaican population is of African descent, which explains the African influence in Jamaican folklore and the constant presence of African patterns in all Jamaican popular music – mento, bluebeat, ska, rudie, rock steady, and reggae, although the African influence is not as distinct in DJ reggae. In DJ, the Old-World, human-played drums have been replaced with New-World, computer-driven syncopation.

One of the enduring and endearing qualities of roots reggae is the direct link to the African background. African traditional music is usually based on a five-note scale that gives a certain minor tonality to African melodies. Many reggae artists compose and play in the minor-sounding keys. Roots reggae lyrics also express the emotionalism, spiritual vitality and pithily clever lyrics that have been borrowed from the African oral tradition, most often via the Anancy stories brought to Jamaica in the 1600s by slaves from the Akan people of the Gold

Coast (now Ghana). These stories were told primarily in three Twi dialects: Ashanti, Fanati and Akwapim, the most important African sources of Jamaican patois, the forerunner to Dread talk. Anancy, the trickster, is an impish spider that can alter his physical form at will. He is cunning enough to outsmart the slave master, and can even deceive God. Anancy evolved from a folklore character into a crucial symbol of courage embodying the concept that the supposedly lowly creature can outwit his formidable adversaries. Anancy must never show itself for what it is. What you see is not what you get. That's what I felt about the Central Coffee factory.

Marley, who was seen as an Anancy trickster, borrowed liberally from the African allegorical storytelling form. The song 'Small Axe', written with Lee "Scratch" Perry, is a good example of using music as a double-edged sword. In the song, a woodman tells a large tree that it is about to be chopped down, on orders of an overlord authority. This echoes back to the old plantation days, when slaves were ordered to cut down the gigantic silk-cotton trees, which were held sacred by the Africans. The slaves would sprinkle rum on the roots of the tree and sing a woeful song to assure the spirits lurking within the tree that the destruction was the master's idea, not the slave's. The song's central image is that of felling a big tree with a small axe. Jamaicans understood the allegorical warning to oppressors everywhere. People will cut them down to size. Marley aimed the message at the Jamaican record companies.

My coffee blues set me to thinking about music blues.

The novelist LeRoi Jones wrote, "To go back in any historical (or emotional) line of black music leads us inevitably to religion, ie the spirit worship. This phenomenon is always at the root of black art, the worship of the spirit – at least the summoning of, or by such a force."

In Jamaica, this spirit spoke through the music and rituals of Kumina, Pocomania, Burru, Etu, Goombay, Jonkonnu, Revival and Rasta music. In the United States, this spirit spoke through the blues. Both reggae and the blues were founded upon a spirit of survival. Much of reggae is blues orientated – a certain kind of lament, a certain kind of wit, a certain view of the world – and they share the chord progressions of G, C, D, A minor, E minor. Reggae and the blues take the language of oppression and translate it into a resolute call for persistence in the face of tragic abuse.

The blues, like reggae, puts the black experience at its centre, whether it's talking of walking shoes, lost love, roosters at the back door or the pains of hard labour and an unjust society, and both use the allegorical trope of making the individual experience a universal truth. However, there is a distinct difference in the social context of Jamaican reggae and American blues. The blues has a shadow of ambivalence with regard to its position within American society. It contains the competing desires to turn its back on the white world and also to demand admittance on equal terms. Reggae, as inspired by the Rasta worldview, calls for the ascendancy of the African identity and a complete retooling of white society. There is no ambivalence to its stance.

This parallel extends to the relationship between American soul music and reggae. Soul had a big impact on reggae music. Jamaican musicians covered a lot of soul songs and drew on soul love songs during the '60s, but the Rasta influence made a fundamental difference between soul and reggae. The Motown sound, which carried the soul song to mainstream America, is not distinctly pro-black, but rather sticks to the generalities of the human heart. It was music intended to cross over and appeal to both the black and white market, which it did with great commercial success. This is not to detract from the work of Marvin Gaye or Stevie Wonder, though, who wrote directly about the black experience; both artists have found a home in Rasta-influenced reggae, with its overtly black consciousness.

In soul music, the religious underpinning is understated. The work of Aretha Franklin, with its obvious gospel influence, or Sam And Dave, or Otis Redding, was religious in style but not necessarily in lyrical content. This never happened with reggae. There is not a distinctive religious reggae and secular reggae. Reggae doesn't divide itself. In reggae, the spiritual is secular, and the secular is spiritual.

The American influence on Jamaican music became pronounced in the late '40s and early '50s. In the late '40s, Jamaican musicians imitated Latin swing and American R&B. The 12-bar blues shuffle, with accents on the second and fourth beats and an afterbeat on piano or percussive rhythm guitar, resulted in an amalgam of mento and R&B. Miami's WINZ and New Orleans radio stations beamed out Fats Domino's 'Walking Blues', LaVern Baker, Louis Jordan, Nat "King" Cole, The Drifters, The Coasters, The Platters. Meanwhile, the sounds of New Orleans, as heard in Lloyd Prince's and other New Orleans musicians' strutting second-line approach to R&B, was heard in Jamaica. The tempo of New-Orleans-based dirges and jump-for-joy jazz at funerals, the Latin-tinged bass patterns of Jelly Roll Morton and the barrelhouse boogie-woogie of King Stormy Weather and Professor Longhair all found their way into Jamaican music. Jamaican bands took the nuts and bolts from the sounds, and in around 1956 the hybrid ska began to emerge.

While I was distracting myself from coffee disappointment with this musical musing, Jimmy drove up some "bad to 'ell" road to the top of a ridgeline. On the narrow ridge top, perhaps 20 feet wide, was a jerk chicken place. On the other side of the road was a rum shop, a "grocery", with packaged snacks, and dropping down the steep mountainside there was a coffee cottage industry. A man sat on an upturned plastic bucket holding a sheet of tin over an open fire roasting coffee beans. He shook the beans as if he were making popcorn, to keep them from burning. When he decided that the colour looked right, he dumped the beans into a plastic pot and poured more green beans onto his tin. A woman carried the roasted beans down ten steps into the lower level of a neighbouring building, where Richard (as Jimmy introduced him) weighed the beans into one-pound lots and packaged them in cotton bags.

"I refuse to sell to the coffee cooperatives, like Marvis Bank. I could get more money, but it goes out-country. Then, who my neighbours buy coffee from?" Richard asked.

He dumped beans into a hand grinder and ground them. A pot of water steamed on a two-burner propane stove. He put the ground beans into a cloth filter and let the coffee drip into a coffee pot, the kind seen sitting on a cowboy's campfire. Then he poured out three cups. "No milk. No sugar," Richard said. "Don't commit that sin to my coffee."

I was disappointed at the first sip. The coffee didn't grab me by the tongue and pull me to Heaven. But after the second sip I noticed a warm brightness at the back of my mouth. After the third sip, the coffee gave the same comforting feel as when I warm my cold hands over a fire. I held the fourth mouthful, letting the subtle flavours seep in. If the coffee had been chocolate cake, I would have chewed it, so rich was the flavour. When I swallowed, the taste didn't linger unduly, as if it were proud of itself. Instead, it lightly evaporated, making room for the next mouthful of taste.

"I'll take five bags," I told Richard.

"Sorry. Only two bags. My neighbours need coffee."

"Okay. How much?"

"Eight bills US each."

Trying not to gloat like a man who'd just bought a masterpiece at a garage-sale price, I handed over the money.

"Happy now?" Jimmy asked as we started down the Blue Mountains to the North Coast.

"A pig in cool mud on a hot day," I answered.

I also found good reggae on the radio. Reggae and Blue Mountain coffee. I was in Jamaican paradise.

"Ya, mon. Now you with a foot on each side of the ocean," Jimmy said.

"What do you mean?"

"You are here, in Jamaica, and you are there, in Africa, now. Jamaican coffee taste in your mouth and reggae music in the ear. That's how we Jamaicans live, both here and there. Same place."

That got me thinking about a conversation I'd had with Kwame Dawes, who made the point that reggae plays a role in creating the communal history to which Jimmy was referring. Reggae is in many ways the soundtrack for our community, Kwame had said, meaning that the music creates a shared sense of place and time and experience. Reggae is commenting on society. Reggae articulates what is happening in the community in which you live. Also, that reggae brings its own language to bear upon your relationship with that community. Because those things are happening, reggae creates that shared sense of community.

"When I talk with Jamaican friends," Kwame had said, "we don't just talk about the politics and so on, but we talk about the shared connection of reggae music. We therefore are creating an assumed community that was formed around the music. It gives you reference points and a shared history of a shared language. The rise of technology – radio, recording industry and television – in the Caribbean changed the sense of community so that there is a sense of a regional national community that is driven mainly by the reggae music that we all share. Reggae has created, for many, a communal history back to Africa.

"This positive connection within Africa was also true for the Jamaican aspiring middle class and upper class. That relationship was strained, largely on the basis of slavery and the colonial instinct to deprive people of their sense of their value by denigrating their sense of origin. That was very true in the educational system. What reggae did was compel the aspiring middle class and upper middle class to reassess their engagement with Africa and their understanding of Africa and to make it more positive. That is largely due to Rastafari, which transformed the notion of Africa. But it had to do a lot with what reggae had to articulate. That sense of communal connection to Africa didn't jump out of a vacuum. Rasta didn't turn to Africa out of a vacuum. Reggae growing out of the Rasta experience saw Africa in a positive light. Reggae had a big impact on the aspiring middle class and the working class, who had bought the negative image promoted by colonialism.

"The connection is important in a number of ways. Even though someone of African descent may not know where to find tribal or family people in Africa, they know that those people are there. The person can't shake off his or her Africa-ness. They wonder, 'Why am I so different?' Their failure to understand the root of their difference becomes a deep, abiding anxiety.

"Because Africa is present in the New World, but its connection to the old has been severed, or attempted to be severed, that creates an anxiety of who we are in the present. The sense of where you came from is fundamentally important. The truth is, we value one's identity and place on the basis of origin. African societies have always placed value on ancestors. Then you can imagine the incredible wound of history that takes place when you are cut off from your ancestors.

"We still suffer from that wound of history. This incredible psychic severing has taken place largely through systematic approaches to driving people from the memory of their history through a process of denigrating that history – depriving people of their language, and so on. There is a psychic break that takes place, and it takes place because there is memory of that ancestral tradition. So when you're faced with a cultural situation that seems to have this point of break, that everything began in this new world, we begin to feel as if something has been taken away from us and the sense of time and place is lost.

"The point about colonialism – the point about imperialism – is to say, you people don't have anything, you never created anything, you never had anything. We have all these things, so we are superior to you. It's a tragic deprivation. A fundamental tragedy of slavery is that people of African descent do not look back to [see if] they belong to one tribe or another. They have to look back to Africa. The term Afro-American is as much a term of affirmation as it is an inadvertent articulation of tragic loss. What I mean by that is [that] the Afro-American or the Afro-Caribbean person really has no access to the information of a home town or home place. An African may tell them 'You know, you look just like my relatives,' and then they may get an idea that they might come from that region. Therefore, what we have to do is claim the whole bloody continent, because there is no physical locality we can claim. As Rasta demonstrates, this lack of information opens the door for new mythologies, so something positive and quite fantastic is created."

David Hinds of Steel Pulse voiced the same outlook. "Reggae does help create a communal memory and history among oppressed people everywhere, no matter their colour," he said from his home in England. "The music has very much created that community between the Caribbean and Africa. My last couple of pilgrimages to Africa – especially the one I made just before the end of the last millennium – showed me very much how much commonality the Caribbean –

especially Jamaica – has to Africa. When I was in Ghana I noticed the way they paint their trucks; their arts and crafts are so similar to what goes out in Jamaica.

"Reggae music has played a big part – which was the initial idea – to unify Africans at home or abroad. All of us with African heritage have come out of a psychic trauma of slavery and all kinds of institutions, whether physical or mental. We've been deprived. Then you've got fine guys like Burning Spear comes out talking about Marcus Garvey. Marcus Garvey stood for Africans at home and abroad uniting to become a united front, where there was a respect as a people. He was always saying that a nation without authority, a nation of people that can't go with themselves and do things in the right manner, was a nation without respect.

"You can say that Garvey was all pro-black in every sense of the word; but at the same time, when it comes to humanity, he was helping mankind. I don't think that mankind can strive if one side of mankind is down. You find in the Western world society – which is of the caucasian race – when it comes to technology, the military forces, that society is very high, so to speak. But at the same time we can't have that balance of harmony among mankind if another is down, regardless of colour or creed or gender. This is where Rastafari comes into it. We're saying, 'Yeah, this has happened to us. Let's try to better ourselves so that we can be respected and we can go on and continue with whatever love or business there is to be negotiated to make this world a better place.'

"A lot of people can misinterpret Rasta as being pro-black and pro-African, and therefore to appear to be anti-white. But it's not that, you know. Like in the case of Louis Farrakhan as being anti-white. But Louis Farrakhan is very well versed as to what has been historically happening with his people. He knew, and we know, that we need to establish mankind on a better level than what it is right now. We, as all people, are in a predicament, and we need to sort ourselves out. A lot of people can misinterpret that as being anti-white or being pro-black on the point of superiority. It's not that at all."

18 Capleton's Stampede

Last night I went to another all-night concert, this one at Port Maria. The Lonely Planet guide accurately describes the town of 8,000 as "merely a place to pass through on the way to Port Antonio", but it's the home town of Capleton, the self-styled "prophet" DJ who rules Jamaica at the moment. He was throwing a benefit concert for the hospital and school, and had enlisted his friends for an all-star line-up: Buju Banton, Luciano, Beres Hammond, Bounty Killer, Sizzla, Tony Rebel, Admiral Tibet, Lexxus and 12 other acts. Lady Saw, the only female DJ who goes *macho a macho* with the male DJs, was also on the bill. Her home town is just up the coast from Port Maria.

I should have known early on that the evening was being zapped by an evil eye. Tickets were to go on sale at 7pm. At 7:30pm, soldiers arrived to guard the closed gate. An SUV backed in near the gate to serve as the box office. A handwritten sign under the windscreen wiper said, "Adult $100. Children free." A man realised that the sign was for a different event and used a pencil to convert the $100 into $400.

"That won't work," another man complained. He crossed out the $400 and wrote $100.

"No man can read that," said another man and tore out the chunk of sign with the handwritten $400 over the $100.

The sign was ripped nearly in half, and it folded itself over the windscreen wiper so that no one could read it.

A sizeable crowd was lined up for the advertised 9pm show. At 8:30, people started to shout for tickets. The soldiers, very polite and professional, tried to herd the crowd into a queue. People boldly insulted them, demanding that tickets be produced. The soldiers retired from the field of action. The man in charge, a local fellow completely out of his depth, tried to placate the crowd. "Ten minutes. Ten minutes more," he promised, and retreated behind the zinc fence.

An hour later, and with tickets still not appearing, the crowd were in a lynch-mob mood. Several hundred people jammed around the driver's side of the SUV. Two men slipped into the vehicle from the passenger side. A man in a blue shirt positioned himself next to the driver's window, his back to the pressing crowd. The driver's window was rolled down a couple of inches. People lurched forward, thrusting their money over the shoulder of the blue-shirted man. He randomly grabbed money and handed it through the crack in the window. Tickets were passed back, which the money-taker held in the air to be snatched out of his hand. An estimated 10,000 people were expected to buy tickets in this way.

The full-moon night was fraught with possibilities – in the sense of the Chinese curse "May you live in interesting times."

People trickled inside the fenced-in sports field, where a self-contained sound system, packaged in a three-quarter-ton panel truck (the side panels lifted up to reveal banks of very powerful speakers), pounded the crowd with deafening sound. A few people shuffled, but most didn't demonstrably respond to the music. The dissonance of sound-system music, with the DJ breaking in to override the artist with his own words, and the fragments of rhythms clashing together wasn't meant to unify the crowd into a share-the-good-vibes community. The music had no continuous harmony, but instead had a restless skipping and jumping sound that kept people off balance.

That, apparently, is part of the appeal. The music has a short attention span, which also appeals to an audience accustomed to video bits and soundbites. To a large extent, sound-system music is egomaniacal, not meant to include people; it exists only for itself, which is also part of the appeal. This is throwaway music, not meant to outlast the moment. It takes no responsibility and doesn't expect responsibility from the listener. Its energy is undeniable, but that energy keeps people revved up in a hyper-kinetic running-in-place dance: elbows jabbing and eyes averted, the people around me created their own space and invited no one to share.

The sound system shut down at 12:30am. Marley's 'Everything Going Be All Right' came on, and the crowd's mood noticeably changed. While the sound system had played, everyone had appeared to be wrapped in a cocoon of apparent boredom. With Marley's music, however, people sang together the words of the classical reggae. There was a palpable sense of community, of the sharing of an experience. The tension of the aggressively bombastic sound dissipated. People started to sway and reach out for each other's hands – metaphorically, at least.

Half an hour later, the stage show began with the lesser names that were allotted one song. It was an all-Rasta, all-DJ show. With each passing hour, the more seasoned pros that knew how to work a crowd took the stage, building the energy to a climax for the super stars.

At 3:30am, the show changed from a musical event to a hate performance. Onstage, a Bobo DJ singsong-shouted hot fire, more fire, burn down Babylon. Ten thousand people bounded on spring-loaded knees above the heads and shoulders of each other, ejected out of the cockpit of sanity and into the wild, fiery crackle of the righteous command from Isaacs to give fire, hot fire, more fire, burn down Babylon, give fire to His sons to burn down Babylon. His sons, the chosen few, held aloft extra-large aerosol cans blasting three-foot dragon tongues of flame to salute the DJ crouched over the mic, his throat muscles taut from the strain of pushing people out of control. The sons waved red, yellow and green Rasta-coloured flags emblazoned with "MORE FIRE" bracketing a Lion of Judah jauntily carrying a flag over its shoulder. The daughters twirled white handkerchiefs above their heads, which were easily mistaken for fresh panties, perhaps meant as another flag for the DJ.

Fire! More fire! Burn out the evil. Vaporise the impure. Sodomy is against the Bible, singsong-shouted the Bobo Rasta DJ. All evening the anti-gay songs had been greeted with full-throated howls of approval by the 10,000 people jammed around the stage. Bash batty boys! Burn down batty boys! A virulent anti-gay virus infects Jamaica, a too-well-loved disease for anyone to easily eradicate. The Bobo Rasta sank his teeth into the anti-gay message and shook it hard, like a terrier shaking a rat to death. Verbal blood flew, and the crowd loved it. Man and man, woman and woman: not allowed, sang the DJ. "It's an abomination," he exhorted the crowd. "It's against the Bible." Ten thousand people thrust their fists in the air, flicked their lighters and shouted, "Fire! More fire!" In the Rasta lexicon *fire* means the burning out of impurities; but with this crowd, the message was destruction. Burn 'em up. "Batty boys [gays] should not be allowed!" shouted the DJ. "Bash the batty boys. Rastafari! Haile Selassie!" (Batty is a British term, meaning crazy, weird and strange, outside the norm.)

Kill them in the name of God. Kill them in the name of our righteousness. "We Rastafari the only way," sang the DJ, and the largely non-Rasta crowd cheered.

I looked out over the mass of people and felt a chill of terror. If the batty boy now, who next? Would someone assume that I looked gay in my stylin' white-and-black straw swirl hat? Would they turn against the neighbour who had more money? Would they target anyone with whom they disagreed? Or the fans of a rival DJ? Or members of the opposite political party? Flashes of Germany, 1939.

Zealots are dangerous, as history teaches. The Taliban jailed Afghanistan men who did not grow beards. The Taliban decreed that women who appeared in public without being completely covered by a *burka* were to be beaten – all in the name of righteousness and to save society from itself. Bash the batty boy in the name of righteousness and save society from itself. The night was fraught with possibilities. The DJ continued to whip the crowd, foaming them up, jacking them with frenzy.

Then the stampede happened.

I was standing by the security fence at the side of the stage when I glanced over my shoulder. Four women ran, crouched over, snaking through the crowd as if dodging bullets. Then the mass surged straight at the stage, screaming, pushing and shoving in pell-mell panic. It was like seeing a dam break and watching the water spill forth, at first a graceful flow and then a torrent of uncontrollable force. The human wave hit the security fence and smashed it over. I had three thoughts:

free my leg, which was trapped under the fence; push up, so that the pile of people on top of me didn't crush my lungs; and save my hat.

The stage lights went out to eliminate a target. I scrambled free on knees shaking with adrenaline and retreated as far behind the stage as possible to get out of the human tide. A young woman on the verge of hysteria stood trembling in the arms of her date. I spotted Anthony B crouched behind a protective wall formed by his men. Buju Banton was with him, looking for a way out. The crowd milled about, as nervous as wild cats ready to bolt. Gradually, people cautiously ventured back onto the field. They used matches and lighters to search for lost shoes, shirts and jackets. Sharp shards of broken bottles littered the ground. People limped on sprains and bruises. Fortunately, no one was seriously injured.

I decided to position myself closer to the exit in case a fast departure was necessary. Several hundred other people had the same idea. Then two shots, muffled – *pom! pom!* People in front of me dashed for the open gate. I didn't have to look behind to know what was coming. I sprinted for the gold just to keep up with the running mass of frightened people.

As I ran down the road, I heard the sounds of two more shots. A man running next to me said, "It was such a good concert. Shame it was mashed up. It would have gone until nine this morning."

I later learned that the initial stampede started when a woman hit her man over the head with a bottle because he dared to dance with another woman. No one explained the gunfire.

As I moved down the road in the stream of people running away from the concert site, Capleton, the patron of the evening, took the stage and tried to get the crowd back. Junior Reid joined him. They recaptured several hundred fans, but the show never recovered. The music wasn't worth the danger.

It was ironic that this had happened to Capleton. Ten years ago, he was a rude DJ spouting negativity, and then he was baptised into the Bobo sect, the most conservative of the Rastafari. Two years ago, he put on a concert where he banned lewd, negative and violent lyrics. As an "ital" Rasta, he didn't allow the serving of meat or fish at the concert.

Capleton, "The Fireman", is a strong, outspoken opponent of the vestiges of colonialism and a fierce advocate for equality and justice.

For several days after the concert I collared every Jamaican I could and asked, "What do you think about musicians who urge people to attack members of society?" At the concert, several Rastas I had spoken with were visibly upset that lewd and violent words had been used in the name of Haile Selassie and Rastafari. "We have so much work to do," they lamented. "It's hard to get people to change." They admitted that there are conflicts within the Rastafari movement. "The youth just want to argue," they said. "They want to do things their way, with a lot of negativity. Yes, sodomy is condemned in the Bible, but the Bible also speaks of love and compassion. If Jah is to have meaning, he must exist in all of us."

Other Jamaicans shook their heads in despair. They were not willing to defend the human rights of gays, but they wished them no harm. "They can do what they want in private, but they mustn't try to influence our children," one man said. A woman told me, "Those people are fundamentally wrong. They are the root of much evil. They stay away from me and I stay away from them, then we get along," while another man replied, "Live and let live."

A couple of years ago, a march in Kingston was organised to show solidarity for the rights of all people, including gays. It flopped because no one dared to show their faces in support.

I caught Prezident Brown at his Music Avenue studio in Ocho Rios before he left for Germany. "To stand up to the bashing of women and gays would take courage," he said. "Those in position to stand up and be listened to, they don't want to risk their money position. Cashflow is why those musicians are not taking a stand."

The concert incident highlighted a long-standing issue within the Jamaican music fraternity. The Jamaican musicians with whom I had spoken all emphasised the importance of presenting a positive message. Negativity in the lyrics is destroying our youth, they all told me. A couple of years ago, many musicians – including some of those at the concert – signed a compact agreeing not to pander to violence and lewdness in their music, but still no one stands up and condemns those musicians who advocate hate for their own profit. No one has taken a strong public stand against their fellow musicians who callously inject hatred into the society in order to sell records and boost their own popularity.

Several years ago, Buju Banton released an openly anti-gay song, 'Boom, Bye Bye'. (Read, 'Bang, You're Dead'.) The New York gay community called for a boycott of his records, and Banton, under pressure, issued an apology. No one in Jamaica calls for a boycott of the artists who sing "Bash the batty boys"; no one composes songs that directly address that human rights issue. Instead, they write sappy love songs so sanguine that they could be written for deodorant commercials. There are no warriors willing to lead the crusade for the rights of gays, and by extension for all human rights. If you don't defend the rights of all people, you risk losing your own rights. Marley and the Trench Town reggae artists knew that. They took a stand against the prevalent colonial mind-set that dominated Jamaican society and said, "We do not support that oppression. We are not coconuts, dark on the outside and white on the inside, and you shouldn't be either."

The Jamaican musical community – performers, songwriters and producers – now have an opportunity to put some sorely missing backbone into their message of love and unity and peace. They may even surprise themselves and hit upon a spark of vitality that Jamaican music needs to again take a leadership position on the world stage.

I walked the several blocks with the crowd streaming from the concert site to the bus/taxi stand in Port Maria. All that fear coursing through my system had made me hungry. It was 5am, and nothing was open. Even the street vendors were still in bed. Since I was halfway to Boston Beach, reputedly the home of the best jerk on the island, I decided to go there, catch a nap on the beach, and wake up in time for lunch.

The bus went only as far as Port Antonio, 12 miles before Boston Beach. That's how I discovered what I consider the most pleasant tourist town on the island, a working Jamaican market town with tourist facilities. Cruise ships have bypassed Port Antonio since Hurricane Gilbert destroyed the town's deep-water pier in 1988, and so the town has escaped the rip-off markets, massive developments and hustlers that pollute other resort areas. There are several low-budget and mid-range hotels in the town, while a couple of miles outside of town are the expensive hotels and exclusive rental villas, the most notable being at Frenchman's Cove, San San Beach and Dragon's Bay Beach.

Port Antonio's first tourists were Errol Flynn, the '30s star of swashbuckling films, and his Hollywood pals Clara Bow, Ginger Rogers, Bette Davis, William Randolph Hearst, and JP Morgan. Flynn owned the Titchfield Hotel (now long gone); a farm ten miles from town, where his widow, Pat, lived for years; and Navy Island. Hollywood still comes to Port Antonio; *Blue Lagoon*, *Club Paradise*, *Cocktail* and *Lord Of The Flies* comprise a short list of films made on location here, in this place of pellucid waters and tropical lushness.

In the spirit of a fan gawking at a star's Hollywood house, I took the short boat ride to Navy Island. The island, two city blocks long and a block wide, is mostly covered with a dense tangle of trees. When Flynn owned Navy Island, the only building on it was his boathouse; now there is a restaurant, rental villas and three beaches. Two of the beaches are open to the public, while the third is reserved for the nude bathing of the island resort's guests.

As I walked to Cruisers Beach, I passed a minor historical footnote, a 20-foot-long motor launch lying in the grass. Although falling apart at the seams, it was freshly painted blue and white, with "Errol Flynn's motor boat" written on the stern. The boat served as a planter for a few scraggly flowers. I also passed a "for sale" sign. The island was on the block.

Pangs of hunger reminded me of my mission to find the best jerk in Jamaica. I caught a jitney to Boston Beach, a crossroads with a jerk stand on each corner. The beach, used mainly by fishermen, was a short walk away. I stopped at Sufferers' Jerk Pork Front Line One and met the crew: Skinny ("Jerkman to the stars"), Kojak and Edwin. "I'm the best on the island." Skinny was not shy. "I've cooked jerk for Eddie Murphy and Tom Cruise. People come all way from Kingston for my jerk. You wait until lunch and see."

Skinny, aka Everton Williams, was born and raised in Boston

Beach. He is rail thin, six feet two, and missing two upper front teeth. He started in the jerk business as an eight-year-old boy, scraping the singed hair off pig carcasses. Now he holds the top job of making the jerk sauce. Chefs in five-star hotels vie with street vendors for the title of who makes the best jerk. Recipes for jerk sauce are closely guarded trade secrets. Skinny agreed to let me watch him prepare his sauce, counting on my ignorance of local herbs to protect his ingredients. He sat on a low stool, his knobby knees jack-knifed up like bird wings, and used a shiny, well-worn tree branch as a pestle to pulverise scallions in a bowl made from a hollow log. "The sauce is everything," he said. "I have 21 spices in my sauce. I use nutmeg, green and dried pimento berries [allspice], Scott Bonnie pepper, the hot, hot bird pepper, cinnamon, thyme, lots of things."

While Skinny prepared his sauce, Kojak slaughtered pig. A short, muscular, compact man, whose real name was Vasco Allen, he emanated authority and an intense presence, as if he personally owned the space in a four-foot-wide radius around him. My first impression was that it would be prudent not to enter his space without permission. As it turned out, Kojak proved to be a warm-hearted man with a teasing sense of humour. He had been a taxi driver in Brixton, London, for 21 years before returning to his native Jamaica to become a butcher.

Edwin, the cook, had been making charcoal from freshly cut pimento branches since 4am that morning. Now he shovelled the coals into a 4' x 8' jerk pit and laid poles of pimento "sweetwood" across the top of the pit. He is a solidly built, barrel-chested young man, whose formidable physique is countered by a sweet, soft voice that revealed a lamb in lion's clothing. He wore a white paper toque jammed down on his sweat-stained red baseball cap. "Normally, I wear a white coat, too, but it's dirty," he said, gesturing to his Kelly-green-muscleman T-shirt. "A white coat looks professional. Customers like to see that. Do I look professional?" he asked earnestly. His ambition was to own his own jerk stand, and he was eager to appear as a serious chef.

Kojak rubbed Skinny's sauce into the deeply scored pork and chicken. Getting the sauce directly into the meat, rather than slathering it on top, was the sign of authentic jerk. The meat was laid on the poles of sweetwood over the bed of glowing pimento charcoal. Planks were laid on top of the meat so that the weight forced the dripping fat to fall onto the coals, sending up pungent smoke to cure the meat, which cooked for five hours before Skinny announced that lunch was served.

This definitely wasn't Rasta food. Strict Rastas never eat meat, including pork and chicken, shellfish or scaleless fish – especially predatory fish. They believe that you take on the characteristics of what you eat, a tenet of macrobiotics. Eating flesh, mingling animal blood with human blood, makes the human warlike and aggressive.

An organic vegetarian diet is part of the Rastas' political stance, an effort to stay independent of the overclass that produces unhealthy food for a profit. The rural Rastas learn about medicinal herbs and take great care in preparing their food to promote good health. Central to the idea of ital living is their belief in herbal healing. They tell anyone who will listen that it was never an objective of the colonial or the present Neo-Colonial State to provide a proper balanced diet for the people, then or now.

They also shun salt. The strongly salt-based diet introduced on the estates by the slave "plantocracy" was viewed as a European plan to thwart the Africans' desire to repatriate back to their homeland. Salt was used to corrupt their minds with colonial thoughts. Not eating salt became a metaphor for resisting the overseer's culture.

The ban on salt may have come from Kumina, a central-African cultural and religious tradition linked to the Congo people. A commonly held view among the Kuminists, and many other Jamaicans, is that ancestral spirits do not eat salt. Within the Kumina tradition, Africans who don't consume salt are able to develop the power to "interpret all things", as well as the ability to "fly from Jamaica back to Africa".

The BaKongo people believed that the ingestion of salt prevented them from flying back to Africa, according to Monica Schular's *Social History Of The BaKongo*. In the BaKongo cosmology, a barrier of water called Kalunga separates the living from the dead. The Atlantic Ocean was identified with the Kalunga, after BaKongo crossed to enter the land of the dead, as the Americas were considered. Once across the ocean, there was no way to return to Africa, except through the magical powers in a salt-free diet. Similar beliefs are found in Haiti and Cuba. The common Jamaican expression yu salt, or 'im salt – which refers to a streak of bad luck or misfortune – preserves the tradition, linking salt with the loss of spiritual force.

By this time, a crowd had magically appeared at the jerk pit, and true to Skinny's word some had driven from Kingston just for his jerk. We stood around a long block of cement that served as a table, next to the cooking pit. People ordered by weight – "A pound of pork, mon" – and Edwin sliced off hunks without taking the meat from the fire. He'd flip the order onto a square of butcher paper and serve it up with thick slices of cake-like bread, roasted breadfruit and a bottle of Red Stripe beer.

The spices smacked my lips with a scorpion sting, setting them abuzz after the first bite. The jolt quickly settled into a pleasant tingle. The flavour became richer as the subtleties of Skinny's sauce blended together with each bite. I felt as though a skilful artist was painting my palate in bold primary colours over an undertone of cool pastels. As one taste evaporated, another traipsed along my tongue to the back of my mouth, where it lingered, waving farewell, before bowing offstage.

"What you think of my jerk," Skinny asked.

"The reggae of food."

"Ya, mon. Makes your teeth dance."

I asked Skinny if he played an instrument.

"No, but I sing." And he did.

He wasn't half bad. Reggae jerk. It could be a dance. Or a restaurant.

19 Maroon Music

In the Cockpit, the wildest and most isolated region of Jamaica, is the district known as the Land Of Look Behind, and in that blank space on the map, up the trail from Quick Step, is Me No Sen You No Come. The names sum up the history of the area. Ghostly comings and goings and sneaking around by shadowy men with a murderous glint in their eyes has been the rule of this place. This is Maroon country, the battlefield where runaway slaves fought successful guerrilla warfare against the British and won their autonomy.

Me No Sen You No Come doesn't exist any more as a physical place. It was once a village of nine men, eight women and four children founded by runaway slaves around 1812. The village was destroyed in 1824 when two white men were shot and their friends attacked and routed the villagers.

Jimmy and I were on our way to Accompong to find Maroon drummers. Accompong is the capital of the Maroons, and the site of a big festival of indigenous music held every 6 January. I figured that there had to be musicians in those hills.

The name Maroon is derived from the Spanish *cimarron*, or "wild one". Most of the Maroon leaders, especially in Jamaica, were of the Akan-speaking group from the Gold Coast. The African people from this region were the fiercest and most troublesome of the slaves, so much so that British planters refused to use them. There were Maroon societies in Haiti, Suriname, Panama, Brazil and Mexico. The Maroons in the New World were the first slave group to organise and fight for their freedom.

The Africans placed under the Maroon umbrella didn't come from the same tribes or speak the same language. They were people from the Yoruba, Noko and Soboand Nago nations; Ibo from lower Nigeria; and Coromantee, Mandingo, Hausa and Ashanti from the Gold and Ivory Coasts. They were strangers to each other and each others' ways. However, they did share an African-ness that transcended regionalism or ethnic and linguistic affinities. That African-ness included attitudes on warfare, sex roles, familial arrangements and hierarchy of authority. A belief in ancestral worship, good and evil spirits that could be enlisted by sorcery and a number of gods who exercised control over various aspects of life more than any other single factor united the people. Regardless of ethnicity, the various Africans would invariably invoke the right *loa* ("spirit") before going into war. The Yoruba god of war, loa Ogun, was the most popular.

The Spanish first brought African slaves to Jamaica in 1517 to replace the Arawaks that they had enslaved as a workforce and were killing off through ill treatment, overwork, European diseases and the introduction of cattle, which destabilised the native agriculture. Some of the Africans became hunters of game, wild cattle and wild hogs. They mastered the skills of woodcraft and gained a detailed knowledge of the trail systems through the mountains. This knowledge was the key to the Maroons' ability to defeat a superior British force through guerrilla attacks.

A Spanish census in 1611 accounted for 107 free blacks and 558 slaves in Jamaica. By 1655, when the last of the Arawaks had died off, there were 1,200-1,500 African slaves, nearly equal the Spanish population there. It's estimated that perhaps 60,000 Arawaks lived on the island when Columbus first visited in 1494.

The Spanish never made a serious attempt to develop Jamaica. It was primarily a supply station for the gold-bearing ships carrying lucrative South American plunder. British pirates such as Henry Morgan preyed on these treasure ships. On 10 May 1655, having failed in an attempted conquest of Cuba, a British expeditionary force invaded Jamaica in an effort to save face. The Spanish, who had 500 fighting men out of a population of about 1,400 on the island, decided that prudence was the better part of valour in the face of the 38 ships of the British fleet and their 800 fighting men. Most of the Spanish fled to Cuba without a fight.

Don Cristoval Ysassi Arnaldo, however, saw an opportunity in the retreat. He and some men, along with their slaves, decided to stay and harass the British until reinforcements arrived from Cuba. Then he would have a claim on the governorship. He took to the hills, from which he raided the British fledgling settlements. But after five years, reinforcements hadn't arrived, and Arnaldo and his men lost heart and slipped away to Cuba. However, the Africans stayed behind, having learned valuable lessons in guerrilla warfare. These Africans, now free men, formed the nucleus of the first Maroon society.

There were three main groups of Maroons with recognised leaders. The best known of these groups settled in the hills above Guanaboa Vale, which is now a village a few miles from Spanish Town. Their leader was Juan de Bolas, and a mountain north of the town is named after him.

The second most significant group of Maroons settled in a more isolated and secluded area at Los Vermejales. This band was under the leadership of Juan de Serras, the most astute Maroon leader. His men were largely of the hunting class, the samurai of the early Maroons, who applied their hunting skills to guerrilla warfare. Serras set out three goals, which served as a model for future Maroons: capture slaves from plantations to augment their numbers; steal weapons and supplies from the plantations and hunters; and gain access to the impenetrable north and north-eastern interior of the island.

Jimmy drove up twisting mountain roads deeper into this still largely impenetrable region. A light rain fell. "Bad news," Jimmy said.

"What?"

"The rain. Rain showers can turn an empty field into a duppy dancing ground."

"I'd like to see a duppy dance," I replied, a bit of a smartass.

"You'd get a crick in your neck."

"How's that?"

"Because you'd always have to be looking over your shoulder to make sure no evil spirit or enemy was sneaking up on you. That's why this region is called Land Of Look Behind. And you'd have to walk like a drunk. The best way to confuse a duppy following you is to walk a zigzag. Or find an obeah to cast a protection spell for you."

"An obeah?"

The word obeah comes from the Twi word *obayi*, which means "magic" or "sorcery". Some believe that an obeah can use the power of the spirits of the dead to harm people and influence events, like black magic. It's based on the Ashanti-inspired system of using good or evil. Sometimes obeah is called the dark science. Nowadays, the obeah is mainly a bush doctor, someone who knows the curative powers of plants, but there are rumours of their other powers. An obeah is different from a myalman, who has the ability to neutralise the duppies' evil. Marley was thought of as a myalman, and credited with the ability to will away evil. His grandfather, Omeriah Malcolm, was an accomplished herbalist and myalman, so it ran in the family. Omeriah had been taught the "science" by his father, Robert "Uncle Day" Malcolm, who was descended from the Coromantee of the Gold Coast. Perhaps this is why there is so much of the language, lore and idioms of the country folks in The Wailers' music.

I asked Jimmy where the concept of a myalmen comes from and he proceeded to give me a brief history. Myal was originally an African spirit-based religion not too different from Kumina or Pocomania, but it got mixed up with Baptist. In 1776, at the outbreak of the American War Of Independence, some American planters loyal to the British Crown moved to Jamaica with their slaves. One of those slaves was a Baptist preacher named George Lisle, or Liele. Lisle, along with two other slaves, Moses Baker and George Lewis, began to preach. Lisle founded a Baptist church in Kingston, the first in Jamaica. Myal, already established in the rural churches and belief systems, influenced the Baptist teachings as they spread across the island. Myal refashioned the symbols and teachings of Christianity into its own image – "snatched the Christian message from the messenger", as Jimmy put it.

In Christian teachings, Jesus Christ is the mediator between God the Father and mankind. In Myal, man's primary relationship with God was with the holy spirit rather than with the Father or with Jesus, the Son. Myal placed John The Baptist above Jesus, because it was he who transformed Jesus through the power of baptism. Myal was transfixed by the spirit as possessor, and sought him in dreams and secluded retreats. Christianity placed its emphasis on transmitted knowledge – Bible, doctrine, catechism – for its conversions. Myal placed its emphasis on the expression of the spirit. Possession by the spirit became the quintessential experience of myalised Christianity, replacing prayer and hymn-singing. Worshippers danced and groaned until struck by the spirit. The term "native Baptist" was widely used to refer to the more Christianised forms of Myal.

Myalism played a prominent part in a number of slave revolts. The British enacted laws in 1774 that prescribed death for anyone attending Myal ceremonies. Myal was very anti-obeah, as sorcery performed by the obeahman manipulates symbols in order to harm their victims. Myal was also known for its healing, a tradition that remains today. The same anti-obeah and healing sentiments are expressed in Rastafari. The Myal country remedies preserved by the Maroons are often thought of as a "white witchcraft" that combats the effects of obeah practices.

Myal underwent another important development in 1860, a time of great religious revival that began in Ireland and swept the Anglophone world. Myal as a religion was transformed by the intensity of the Great Revival into two variants, Zionism and Pukumania, both under the general name of Revival Zion. The Great Revival, in which worshippers physically experienced the holy spirit, infused Afro-Jamaican beliefs with a religious fervour that expressed itself in ecstatic music and dance.

"You don't believe in this duppy spirit stuff, do you?" I asked Jimmy.

"I'm a Jamaican," he replied seriously. "But I don't worry about duppies. I know plenty of ways to keep them away."

"How?"

"Sprinkle piss around my yard as a duppy repellent. Or wear a measuring tape around my waist. The tape reminds the duppy of being measured for their coffin. And I avoid any woman who might be Long Titty Susan."

"What!?"

"Oh, yes. You've got to be careful about duppies and sex, especially if you're a woman. A lot of rural Jamaican women always sleep on their bellies and wear panties, bras and slips to bed to discourage a male duppy. Dead girly-girly men are certain to return as duppies to their lovers. I've been told that wearing red or black panties as barriers will keep off the dead lover during the night. A female duppy may visit a man in the night for sex, but the man will probably be too scared to get it up."

"And who is this Long Titty Susan?"

"Evil. Pure evil. She only takes, never gives. Best to avoid women like that."

Now I suspected that Jimmy was pulling my leg.

"She looks like a normal woman during the day, but at night she sheds her skin and walks about raw and sucks the blood of babies, like a woman can suck out a man's money. In the day, she looks like a normal woman. At night, she becomes a cannibalistic vampire, that woman. Eat you right up. She's a witch, and mothers fear her – truly, man, no lie – because she's a baby-hunting monster."

"How do you tell a Long Titty Susan?"

"Her tits sag. Her breasts are empty of milk, so she has nothing to give. She is anti-social because she takes life and refuses to bear children to replenish the society. Long Titty Susan is a very selfish person. Best to avoid women like that. I like women with stand-up titties. That way I know they're safe."

"You're a dirty old man, Jimmy."

"Yeah," he replied with a flick of a smile. "I like it that way."

We crested the Cockpit Mountains. "There is a huge reservoir of water under us," Jimmy said. "Two-thirds of Jamaica's surface is limestone, which can be several miles thick. The porous limestone soaks up the rain and holds it. The water bursts out as springs and rivers. The Martha Brea River that pours out of the Windsor Cave comes from this reservoir."

We curled down the southern side of the mountains to where the land was flat enough for sugar-cane fields and coffee farms. "The coffee from around here is very strong," said Jimmy, forever a font of local information. "It's grown at a lower elevation than the Blue Mountain, but they blend the two together without pointing that out."

We found the road to Maggetty, where the coffee is processed. I was hoping that I'd be lucky and score there, but Jimmy turned just before the town and we climbed back into the hills. We missed the unmarked turn to Accompong, asked directions in Retirement and backtracked a mile to take the first left.

The road was a thin ledge barely clinging to the steep mountainside, a deteriorating track wide enough for only one vehicle. As we crept along, I understood why the Maroons chose this natural redoubt as their base of operations. Actually, this was the home territory of the Leeward Maroons. The Windward Maroons were based at the opposite end of the island, in the Blue Mountains. The two groups were not necessarily allies.

Cudjoe was the most famous leader of the Leeward Maroons, while Nanny was the mythically renowned leader of the Windward Maroons, whose main base was Nanny Town, now a ruin. Cudjoe, or Kwadwo ("a male born on Monday", according to the Akan tradition), was a rather short, uncommonly stout man with strong African features. He was an autocrat who ruled with an iron fist, meted out stern discipline (including execution), was extremely brave and smart, and was an obeahman who, it was believed, could manipulate the supernatural forces of good or evil for the benefit of the community. He demanded that only English was spoken by his people, as a way of unifying the diverse ethnic groups.

Nanny, on the other hand, remains a historical mystery. No firm facts are known about her. She had the reputation of a freedom fighter of the first order and as a master of the obeah "science". It was said that she could spirit away the best slaves from a plantation without being seen. She allegedly kept a huge cauldron boiling continuously without any visible fire, into which enemy soldiers who ventured too close would fall and die of suffocation. The foundation of this myth may be the Macungo River, which drops over a 900-foot precipice, creating a bubbling froth with the appearance of a boiling cauldron.

Local folklore claims that she was the sister of Cudjoe. This seems unlikely, given the differences between the two groups. The Leeward Maroons lived under a despotic system, while the Windward Maroons, with quasi-autonomous towns under different leadership, lived under a more democratic system. The Windward Maroons were more aggressive than the Leeward Maroons in fighting slaveocracy. Nanny, called "the old hagg" by the British, opposed Cudjoe's treaty in 1738 with the British that ended the First Maroon War. The Windward Maroons regarded the treaty as a traitorous sell-out. In exchange for land in the Cockpit and a degree of autonomy, Cudjoe and his people – referred to in the treaty as "friends and assistants" – agreed to collaborate with the British in quelling any slave rebellions, to capture runaways, and to serve in the British militia.

The Windward Maroons were forced to sign a peace treaty in June 1739, three months after Cudjoe cut his deal. The British were not generous with the Windward Maroons. Nanny Town, which once had a population of 300 men, women and children, was destroyed. The Windward Maroons were not given land or self-governing rights accorded to the Leeward Maroons, and were treated as a conquered people.

The treaty didn't put an end to all slave rebellions. In 1760, Tacky, an Akan-speaking slave, led a well-planned, well-organised and widespread slave revolt. He wanted to transform the island into a free society divided into small principalities and governed along traditional African lines, as among the Akan-speaking people. The rebellion was crushed within six months, thanks in large part to the Leeward Maroons.

More revolts broke out in 1761, 1765 and 1766. The Leeward Maroons – especially those from Accompong and Trelawny Town, Cudjoe's main base – were instrumental in putting down these uprisings. The British governing assembly voted a payment of £450 to these Maroons for their expenses in capturing runaway slaves.

Slave rebellions continued to plague the British. Three-Finger'd Jack, a bandit or rebel depending on who wrote the history, operated during the late 1770s and early 1780s before Maroon bounty hunters eventually killed him. 1795 saw the outbreak of the Second Maroon War, also known as the Trelawny Revolt. The fight was triggered when two Leeward Maroons, convicted of killing "tame hogs", were flogged. The Leeward Maroons complained that the punishment violated their treaty. The British rejected the Maroons' demands, and fighting broke out. Very few slaves joined the Leeward Maroons during the five-month, full-scale war; they were generally hated and distrusted by other Africans, both slaves and free men.

In 1819, there were an estimated 2,555 runaway slaves living in the mountains, while the island-wide Revolt of 1831 involved some 20,000 slaves. On 1 August 1834, the British Parliament abolished slavery throughout the British Empire. This Emancipation Day is now a Jamaican national holiday.

Jimmy and I cleared the top, and the vista opened out onto a quaint-looking village nestled in seemingly manicured rolling hills. It could have been the English countryside, except for the surrounding mountains of dense jungle. The place was a natural fortress, with one crummy road as the only access route.

We rolled to a stop in Accompong, a one-street village named after Cudjoe's brother. It was hard to imagine that every 6 January, Cudjoe's birthday, an estimated 20,000 people come to this village for the music festival. The parking and traffic had to be terrible. A group of men were sitting with their backs against the storefront, watching soft drinks being unloaded from a truck.

"Am looking for musicians," I said to one man.

"Am a musician," he replied.

His name was Bill Rolando Peddie, cousin to the Colonel, the elected leader of the Leeward Maroons and a policeman in Montego Bay, who lived in the most handsome house in Accompong. Bill was a talkative, friendly man who was more than willing to share his music. "I'll get boys," he said.

We followed him down the street. He stopped at the house of a stout woman, who waved us in. She made the traditional gomba drum used by the Maroon drummers. The drum is square, in the style of the Ghanaean drums of the Maroons' ancestors. She showed me how to tune the drum with removable wooden wedges. The gomba is used like the fundue drum in Nyabinghi drumming, explained Bill. It's the heartbeat, the holder of the rhythm. Bill picked up a small, hand-made bass drum which had been modelled after a drum used in military marching bands, and took it with him.

We stopped at a couple of other houses, gathering together four drummers. Along the way, Bill explained that there is a movement to have the entire Cockpit area designated as a national park. "There are over 100 species of birds here." He waved an arm at the surrounding forest. "28 of them are on the endangered list. We have the giant swallowtail butterfly – it's threatened, too – and medicinal plants, lots of healing herbs all around – cerasee, cold bush, leaf of life, strongback, tea bush. It's important to preserve these."

We walked to a cane hut on a hilltop, where the drummers sat down with their drums. "Our music is a combination of African and European," Bill explained. "Besides the drums, we use a fife, a scraper, a marimba and, sometimes, a fiddle."

Chanties and folk and drinking songs of the seamen heard in port were incorporated into Jamaican music. An example of the blended music, according to Bill, is the John Canoe, or jonkonnue, songs. In West Africa, at the end of each year, an ordained sect in the community goes from house to house singing derogatory songs, without naming names, about the people who did wrong during the year. In Jamaica, this has survived as the Christmas tradition of "singing on people". The John Canoe celebration (dubbed "Pickaninny Christmas" in slave times by the whites) are re-creations of West African yam harvest feasts dominated by the male masquerader, who pranced to the furious rhythms of the "gombayers". The gombayers struck their square and barrel-shaped drums with one short stick while scraping another along a notched strip of wood affixed to the side of the drum. The dance is a display of magic and spirit. The word jonkonnue has been traced to *dzong kunu*, which means "terrible sorcerer" in the West African Ewe tongue.

The European dance tempi that the slaves overheard at the lavish plantation balls, particularly British reels and the French quadrille, became part of the local music. The John Canoe dances included steps from the English Merry-Andrew and Morris dances, while echoes of the quadrille can also be heard in Jamaican rural music. These intermingling styles would later be the basis for the slaves' and free peasants' songs, ring tunes, digging songs and "sankeys" (Revivalist hymns, named after the evangelist and composer Ira David Sankey, who published the widely used hymnal *Sacred Songs And Solos* in 1873.)

Bill pulled out a ram's horn. "This is an abeng horn," he said. "The abeng horn came with our ancestors from Africa." A small hole was drilled about an inch and a half below the tip. At the horn's base was a blowhole, over which the blower placed his mouth. By opening and closing the small hole with the thumb, the person could control the pitch, range and loudness of the sound. "The Maroons who fought the British used the abeng horn to warn villages of an attack by the British." Bill demonstrated. He played a surprisingly wide range of notes. "See, they could send messages telling of enemy positions, movements, and directing a counter-attack. To divulge the code to a non-Maroon meant death. The very sound of the abeng would scare the enemy. We still use it sometimes to send messages when we're out hunting or in the country." This simple, multitonal warning system, which doubles as a musical instrument, is similar to the Akan abertia.

Bill and the other drummers sat on bits of found wood, propped their drums between their knees and started playing and singing. The drumming was distinctly West African, much faster than Nyabinghi drumming and slightly off the pace of Kumina drumming. The words to the songs were a mixture of original African dialect and Jamaican patois. It was infectious music meant to inspire dancing.

After the songs, Bill said, "Buju Banton, Junior Reid and Black Uhuru have come to record our music. I think there'll be a lot more Maroon music in popular songs."

As we left Accompong, Jimmy asked, "You learn anything?"

"One of the drummers said, 'The young foot wears an old shoe.' What did he mean?"

"The youth walk to the future on the shoe leather of the past. You don't know where you're going if you don't know where you've been."

20 New Music

What new sound is evolving in Jamaican music, if any? I asked Freddie McGregor, who has 37 albums to his credit and who received the Jamaican Living Legend Award in April 2000. We were at his Kingston home sitting on his front veranda on an early Thursday evening. He had just finished a business meeting with four men dressed like Mormon missionaries – black slacks, white shirts, black ties, short hair – to put the final touches to the release party for his new album, *Signature*.

Freddie was curled up on a cast-iron garden lounger too short for his frame, talking on a cell phone. He chewed on a stalk of sugar cane freshly cut from his yard while listening to the other end of the conversation. He introduced me to his beautiful daughter, Yeshemabeth, to keep me occupied while he finished the call.

"Yeshemabeth was Haile Selassie's mother's name, meaning 'Mother Of All Nations'," she told me proudly, "but I've shortened it to Shema, which is my professional name." Shema has musical genes. Her mother is Judy Mowatt, one of the original Wailer's I-Three singers and a successful solo artist. Shema was finishing her third album in her father's studio, Big Ship, which stood next to the house.

Freddie sat up. He had been lying on a compact automatic in a black leather holster. He casually tucked the gun back in his waistband and shook out his long dreads. I asked him to describe what his current music was about.

"I don't write songs particularly for Jamaica," he replied, "but if I was to write about Jamaica, I'd write about the cost of living, the lawlessness, and the undiscipline [*sic*] in the society. That really takes over Jamaica now. Lawlessness and undiscipline, coupled with the political climate and instability. We need to bring back discipline among this generation of youth. Not so much [of] the youth in Jamaica want to keep their African heritage alive. Too many want to tattoo themselves and dress like the woman. We are losing our culture side of ourselves. We are too much like the American way of life, you know.

"If the root-conscious music fades out then the heritage memory will fade. Exactly. That's why it's important to keep the grass roots of the music. Enough of us root performers are here so you don't have to worry about that. You'll hear more singers and less DJs, more instruments and less computer ridims. Capleton, the DJ who rules the island now, does conscious music, a sign that conscious roots is coming back. After a while, people want to hear truth. They want to hear the real truth and the real healing. Regardless, people crave the truth, and the real music come to the fore."

I had asked Jesus Afari, the dub poet, about new Jamaican sound while we sat in the Black Scorpion studio selecting a cover photo for his new album. "Jamaican music is now at a crossroads," he answered. "In the mid to late 1980s and early 1990s, slackness, decadence, disrespect and condemnation as it relates to women and to certain of the fundamental principles came into the music. At the [end] of the '80s and the dawn of the '90s, that was the situation. Therefore, other artists and musicians started to rise up and saw the need for greater substance and direction and upliftment and love and enlightenment and consciousness and a sense of responsibility to be injected into the music to give people direction and hope. I, for one, was part of that resurgence.

"So many artists who started out well became self-centred and egotistic, and that has backfired. Now people are reaching the point where they need something new, some new direction, something that is futuristic that can help us deal more effectively with the inevitable challenges as we go into the 21st century.

"The ridim will change. The music will change based on the influence of African rhythms. Latin music – that will seep into the music. We are at a station in world history and world affairs where these ideas of cross-culturalisation, cross-fertilisation, in music will affect all music. All world music will be a part of that whole scenario.

"If you notice, the dancehall music now has a certain aggression and a certain light-headedness and recklessness, which results in the whole social attitude and behaviour that now prevails. There is a strict relationship between music and art and other creative expression and social behaviour. There is a parallel between violence in the music in film and violence in the society, and in the homes, and in the family.

"I'm experimenting with different sounds – a little bit of jazz, a little bit of hip-hop. I preserve elements of Nyabinghi and Rastafari within the music and natural sounds to keep a focus on the environmental. There is work being done using four or five drums under the reggae ridim. I have rhythms made by Sly And Robbie, Scully and Dean Frazer. We use five bass drums and a lot of percussions associated with Rastafari through the congas. It has a Caribbean feel based on Dean Frazer's horn section. There are other people who are working with such sounds also. More of that sound will soon start to be heard out of Jamaica.

"I'm planning to go into the studio with The Mystic Revelation Of Rastafari to create some rhythms using acoustic instruments and congas. I won't necessarily project a raw Rasta message, but I'll project a world view which will inspire different people from a wide cross-section."

U Roy, the original DJ, "the Teacher", also predicts that the evolving Jamaican music will go back to the roots. "I think it's going to be reggae all along," he said when we spoke at his home. "I think back to the roots reggae because, from the 1980s, I don't hear no new ridim. All of them make over. I know reggae gets some big fights right now. There are some people who don't want too much reggae to take up. Reggae go just right up on its own that like it's been riding along. In the States, so much millions go to promote hip-hop and all them others, and in Jamaica not even a dolla them put up to promote reggae, not even one dolla. So whatever heights reggae reach right now, reggae just ride its own and reach them heights.

"We don't come to certain things with a positive attitude. Some of those don't take the music serious, and that discourages people from coming forward to help promote the music. Some singers and DJs have negative vibes, so [when] people have some big money for production [and] decide to spend some money on promotion, they say, 'No, don't like the vibes at all.'

"Not much is happening right now. Especially right now; things get rough right now. You don't see much stage shows, not even much dance. People don't have much money right now, believe me. A man not going to spend his $300 dancing when his children need that money for school that week. They're not going to go dance with that. The youth has to have some lunch money tomorrow. When the sound systems started, back when I started 40 years ago, people didn't have much money then, but it was much easier. Even though your money was small, things were much easier. Much, much, much, much, much easier. Take it from me. Then, when you wake up with £5, you can do *many things!* Now, when you wake up with $500 (approximately $10 US), you can maybe do two things."

"I don't think reggae lyrics will say the same things. Something new, something also conscious, will come. Jamaicans are some smart people if they only decide to use their brain in the smart form. When you put your brain to stupidness, then you utilise stupidness. If you put your brain to smartness, or something wise, then you're going to go wise. As long as young youth come write some conscious lyrics then conscious reggae will come back. Trust me.

"Rastafari will be an influence all the time. Not for some people, but for me, Rastafari is the biggest thing. Rastafari will be a strong influence all the time, as long as we do this in a conscious form, you know? It will speak about oppression and liberation, but there are lots [of] other things to speak about, too."

The Reverend Danny Dread, a DJ since 1976, doing dancehall and sound systems, had just returned from a Germany tour when I met him in the yard of Sugar Minott's studio. "Where's the music going now?" I asked.

"Back to Studio One music," he replied. (Studio One was Clement Dodson's studio that produced roots reggae.) "Even Sizzla looking back to that root reggae. Root goes back to ska beat. That African sound in the drums and guitar is the most natural for the music. The sounds we're looking for now goes to the original. I've stopped using computers completely in my music. Back to the singer and the acoustic guitar. I've started singing instead of doing the talking DJ stuff. The computers can't give us the natural sound. A computer doesn't have the feeling of an alive musician. I, and other musicians, we're going back to the feeling of the ridim. The computer ridim is always the same. The computer can't take advantage of the space it hears in the sound. It's not flexible enough to move with the music. The world is confused with this one-stage music.

"Back in the 1970s and '80s, when I and U Roy and Sugar were on the dancehall, people danced. Men and women got out there and bumped. There was joy in the music, and that made the people joyful. Dancehall was a happy time to go dancing. Now dancehall is more modelling than dancing. The people with the most expensive fashion are there. The men are over on one side looking, holding a bottle of beer. Women over on the other side, holding a bottle of beer. If a man and woman dance together, everyone looks at them like they're strange. We want to put the dance back in dancehall.

"We, the original writers, wrote about the natural, the earth, sea, tribulations we go through. Not the fantasy, like some dancehall, about getting a big gun and shooting to kill when they only fantasise that danger, or the commercial. The big heads don't like people to get too much consciousness. Those who control the record industry, all business, they feed people the commercial to keep them asleep so they learn nothing. If they don't know nothing, they can't challenge authority.

"The artists are here to keep people awake and wise. We write about the unity between people, not about them shooting each other. The violence come with the music of the 1980s. When people listen to that, 'shoot people dead', it eventually gets to the youths. This sells because it's pushed. Commercial pushes the bad over the good.

"The music is still coming out of the ghetto. There are more songs for positive and against the violence, and more songs against the politicians. The youth, and everyone, more and more don't believe the politicians. The last national elections had the lowest turnout ever. The introduction of the guns was done by the politicians when they armed their followers and sent them to shoot the others. Eddie Seaga and Michael Manley is why Jamaica is like it is now. Seaga is one of the baddest men in Jamaica. They've kept the people poor. A hungry man is an angry man who can't feed his children. Then, in frustration, he might rob to get money and maybe shoot."

Gary Johnson, aka Mr Mutton, a 30-year-old DJ who recently returned from a US tour with Beenie Man, Luciano and Burning Spear, joined in. "Right now the sound of reggae is dancehall mixed with hip-hop because that's what the producers say is the market," he said, "but you start hearing more heartbeat music coming out of Jamaica. More of the *boom-boom*, the one-two beat that was original from Marley. There'll be more Kumina and Nyabinghi drums, and kettle drum, behind the beat. The dancehall beat will keep the music upbeat, and the heartbeat will give it grounding. The music is shifting back to cultural music teaching the youth to forget about crime as a role model. My new song 'Careless' is about not living carelessly so you get taken out. It's about youth not wanting a job or school, just living careless like a cowboy, and how that will get you nothing but trouble."

There's definitely more interest in injecting authentic drumming back into the music. Luciano, Anthony B and Prezident Brown are actively exploring how to use Nyabinghi drumming in their music. Buju Banton and Black Uhuru went to Maroon country to record their drumming based on ancient West African patterns.

Another strong trend in popular Jamaican music now gaining international attention is gospel reggae. This is not new. At the beginning of the reggae era, Bob Marley And The Wailers, Toots And The Maytals and others were very much evangelistic Christian. The lyrics changed into Rasta songs later on, but initially they were very Christian.

However, during the '60s and '70s, the Jamaican Christian churches were antagonistic towards reggae. That music was never heard in church. Even so, the local gospel music – usually called "Christian music" – has close ties with the reggae industry. Jamaican gospel music assimilated both black and rural white gospel styles from the United

States and blended them with various foreign and local influences. Stylistically speaking, much of this music was quite close to reggae, but with certain distinguishing features, such as differently accented drum patterns, a bush tambourine, and sometimes prominent clapping. Some of the gospel music was reggae in all but name.

Judy Mowatt, who first stepped into the international spotlight as one of the original I-Three singers behind Bob Marley And The Wailers, has stopped performing secular reggae. She is now one of Jamaica's leading gospel reggae artists. On a Saturday afternoon, we sat on her veranda in Kingston and talked about the cross-fertilisation of reggae and gospel. Before we began, she said a prayer: "First of all, let's just thank the Lord for this moment. We just want to thank the Lord for His blessings and to bring us together. And, Father, we just pray that the purpose of this work, Lord, will be to establish Your work. The music we're talking about is the music You have blessed us with. We are just giving You the glory and the honour right now. In Jesus' name, amen." Then she settled back, an arm draped over the back of the couch. She was dressed casually, in shorts and a loose-fitting blouse, and without make-up.

"The gospel is really ingrained in our society," she said. "It's getting bigger now. Gospel music is, I'd say, the first music. It's the music that, when you go around the island and you stop at a little church, the music that is being played now, the style of music, is gospel reggae. You have different styles of reggae... Dancehall, it's inside those little churches. It started in there, where you have the musicians that play for praise and worship, and that feel comes out of church. A lot of the musicians who are playing today, they were in the church, so they brought the church feel on the street. They took it to the studio, and they have expanded on it. Originally, the beat came out of the church. Even some of the styles the DJs have, it's coming from that little preacher man, his style of preaching. Most of the DJs' sound is coming out of the church.

"When I was growing up, as a child we listened to the pipe organ music. You never had reggae music playing in the church. You were doing the wrong thing should you introduce reggae music inside the church. What you heard was the European style of music that was inculcated inside of our songs. We find that, in the 1970s and '80s, in the churches the style has changed. We've come into our own because reggae belongs to this island, and originated from this island. It was weird to know that we were playing American and European music, and the music we were blessed with – the music that is uniquely ours – we were ignoring it.

"During the 1980s, I find that the churches were looking towards playing reggae music. They were focusing on the music. We realise now that we are blessed. God did not give reggae only to the secular world. He gave it to Jamaica, to all of us who express ourselves in this music. And so I find that the churches are more receptive to playing reggae music. My church is mostly reggae music. We believe in playing a little ballad, jazz to make it well rounded, to show we are in appreciation of all kinds of music.

"There is a power inside of reggae music. There is something unique inside the music. When you play it, you get a different feeling. You can dance to it. You can worship God on it. You can do anything you want to do with it.

"We are seeing cross-fertilisation, a gospel-influenced reggae. That's what's happening right now. You are soon to hear it more off-island. Many of us musicians have come from the secular into the churches now. We are not allowing the traditional church music to influence us. We are singing our music inside the church. Any church I play at, I play my reggae songs. Most of my gospel songs are gospel reggae. Papa San, he was a DJ who was playing secular before he came into the church. Now he has reggae-ised his gospel, and is playing it into the church. The church people are appreciating it very much.

"There is a group of us from secular music. In 1997, Carlene Davis, Papa San, Lt Stitchie, Chevelle Franklin, Junior Tucker and myself were six key people from secular that went into the church at one time. The Lord showed me what He did. C for Carleen and C for Chevelle, S for Stitchie and S for San, J for Judy and J for Junior. We came two by two – S/S, J/J, C/C, as soldiers for Jesus Christ.

"We consider ourselves soldiers, or warriors, for Jesus Christ, because there is a war between good and evil. Good must overcome evil. We're on the side of good battling evil. Because Jesus Christ was victorious over evil, we who are His children see ourselves as being victorious also. We are battling against injustice, against oppression, against perversion, against lust, against wantonness, against everything that is ungodly.

"Themes in gospel include what I was singing about with Bob and The Wailers: oppression in whatever form must end, because that is ungodly. The songs are written with that specific. The answer is not to look [to] any man but to God.

"The beat doesn't change in gospel reggae. It's hardcore reggae music. The lyrics change. Some of the popular rhythms being played can use those same popular rhythms and have the gospel lyrics to influence the ridims. What has been happening in Jamaica, gospel is now played in the dancehalls. The Grace Thrillers, a very popular gospel group, one of the oldest gospel groups in Jamaica – they are now being played in the dancehall. The Grace Thrillers were one of the first to popularise gospel reggae. They went against what was supposed to be the norm and started playing reggae. They became popular doing gospel reggae. They took this throughout the Caribbean. Their, and others', gospel reggae is being played in the dancehalls."

Hopeton Lewis, Gloria Bailey, Claudelle Clarke, The Gospel Blenders, Evangelist Higgins, The Don Sam Group, Glacia Robinson, Carlene Davis and Otis Wright are a few of the gospel reggae performers popular in Jamaica. Judy Mowatt and Carlene Davis were voted Best Gospel Act at the 19th Annual International Reggae And World Music Awards for their song 'Just To Be Close To You'.

Women in reggae have historically been relegated to the background, the equivalent of the little woman in the kitchen. This is changing dramatically. "Now a lot of female singers rise up," says Marcia Griffiths, one of the trailblazers for women in the Jamaican music industry and an I-Three singer, like Judy Mowatt. "Everything has changed from the days when there were just a few of us female singers. It's not how it used to be when women were put on the back burner. In the male-dominated music business, female singers – and women in general – they just see us for our favours. Not any more. We find that women are the ones really carrying the banner now. The women dominated the award shows in the United States, and the same thing is happening in Jamaica.

"The female singers are writing on the themes of truth and reality. No fantasy. The message of the female singers is love, truth – all reality. They don't speak to the political side. They are more love, you know? More love. You'll be hearing from Shema McGregor, Pam Hall, Angel and Fiona, who is a fantastic singer."

There is another, less obvious development in Jamaican music: rock reggae. This is heard mainly at sessions (pay parties sponsored by producers testing out new music). At one time, sessions were considered scurrilous by parents of teenagers, but now "uptown" sessions are gaining acceptability and moving out of the underground. At uptown sessions, the promoter provides a good venue, free food and sometimes a group from the United States. The difference between the uptown sessions and the rough-and-tumble "downtown" dancehall is like the difference between the suburbs and the ghettos. The group Downstairs, with their CD *Reggae Rock*, is emerging as the best-known rock reggae group.

Dub/reggae fusion is the sound that is coming, the sound that's not even heard much in the studios yet, according to Paul "Lymie" Murray, who was preparing his second album at Freddie McGregor's Big Ship studio. "It will be a slower, fatter sound. Drums and bass. Drumming in dub is more pronounced than in reggae. Four or five drummers make it all fat. You don't walk away from that. You have to come. You sing over the keyboard, but you speak better over the drums. This will give reggae a new distinct sound. A bigger bottom sound. Reggae with a harder edge. Reggae with an attitude. That's what's coming. A fusion of dancehall and reggae. The DJ is not going away, just like the singers never went away. It's still hardcore reggae but with a more world beat flavour. That's how reggae is evolving, the kind of reggae Jimmy Cliff is making. Give it time."

The Ghetto Youths United Crew and Junior Gong, both under the production wing of Stephen Marley, have roots reggae/dancehall fusion CDs under their belts. Luciano (a reggae singer) and Buju Banton (a DJ) joined forces on *Unchain Spirit*. A version of Burning Spear's 'Africa Bound', mixed with Buju Banton, is gaining airplay in Jamaica. Working the two prominent styles of Jamaican music, reggae and dancehall, into a complementary partnership sounds promising. However, expecting DJ fans to give equal loyalty to Burning Spear, for example, is akin to believing that hardcore Metallica fans will spend equal money buying Johnny Mathis CDs.

The Strugglers, five young guys from the Riverton Dump (literally a city dump, where people live), deliver up authentic oppressed reggae. They are below the radar so far, but they have hunger in their bellies. At one gig, two of them had acceptable shirts, two had barely passable shirts, and one had no shirt, so they all went on without shirts. The girls in the audience thought that poverty was just a cool style, and the group had the moxie to make it so. Their solidarity catches the style of the early Trench Town kitchens.

But Jamaican music needs more than talent, which exists in spades. The "pay to play" that musicians consistently complain about is detrimental to the quality and quantity of music. Listen to what Sugar Minott has to say on this: "Right now I have nine songs out and I can't hear none right now on the radio because I'm not paying the DJs to play them. Radio people won't play the music without money. This morning on the radio, the DJ played a reggae series to respect the '90s artists. Within a half hour, she played eight Sanchez within the segment. This sounds like other artists weren't doing shit during the '90s because she played eight of one person. If they played eight of my songs I'd feel the same way, like maybe I'd paid them off. [I'm] not saying that Sanchez did, but things are out of balance."

The payola is "polite violence" (to use Mortimo Planno's term) committed by the music industry against itself, a form of slow suicide, and a form of censorship, which is an expression of fear. The corruption that permeates Jamaican officialdom, from under-the-table payments for a driver's licence to paying off cops, heavy thumbs tilting the electoral process, violence and inhumane treatment within the prison system, the judicial system – this systemic corruption cries out for opposition leadership. The politicians are not providing that leadership. Musicians have the ear of the public. Musicians have the power to direct the public, which is well demonstrated at concerts. On this account, Jamaican musicians are like doctors who only write prescriptions. Writing and performing a song is as different from living the song as pushing pills is different from performing surgery.

Musicians who say they don't create music for Jamaica should dance in their own Yards first, then worry about their international sales. The power of the music for all Jamaican musicians comes from the indignation and outrage of the artist's heart over the neglect suffered by their Yardmates – and Jamaica is one big Yard. The issue of human rights in Jamaica begs for a champion. The success of early reggae sprang from speaking directly to the conditions of the slums and the continuing colonial mentality of Jamaican institutions and its ruling class. Then the music found an international audience. The opportunity exists today for the musician bold enough to proclaim him- or herself a warrior in the struggle for human rights for specific minorities (namely gays and women) in Jamaica.

The Jamaican wit and wordplay needs a voice. What a marvellous and unique gift to give the world! But who's wrapping that package for delivery?

"What's happening in Jamaica now is that the same system that rules the society rules the music with a certain bondage and mind control," said Ken Booth, one of Jamaican music's living legends. "One of the important things of music in Jamaica is to go against the mind-set of racism, of colonialism, of the separation of disrespect because one man has more money than the other. We have the privilege to do so, but we're not doing it. They, the producers and singers that dominate the music, are not leading on the right path.

"The record industry is the Babylon system itself. Babylon is all that is not doing what they are supposed to do. You have to give justice no matter in what capacity you have. If you're not putting out justice, burn you, ya. Some man want it to look like white man is Babylon because the white started it, yes; but the black man took it from him and uses it now. The record producers are telling the artists that they have to do certain music. That's what we're talking about. Nowadays the producer uses the artists, takes part of you, makes the artists prostitute themselves."

Bob Clark, a songwriter active in the music industry, an Irie FM radio personality and a thoughtful, constructive critic, gave this summary of the Jamaican music: "There is no creativity, no new music, right now. If people are fed enough garbage, that becomes the norm. There is a lack of leadership on the part of the music fraternity and the society. The music is becoming stagnant. The quality isn't there. Given the economic situation here, originality has no value. That's why we hear recycled rhythms from 30 years ago. Today, it's about survival, not about creating music. It costs too much money to create and produce original music. That's why there is a slight revolution in the music right now, in that it's going back to the roots sounds that already exist."

Fully Fulwood, founder and bass player of The Soul Syndicate, put his finger on the essence of the issue: "If you're a creator of music, you have to have crazy wisdom, which is all about compassion and generosity. You have to respect your instrument, respect people, respect yourself. You have to be humble and practise what you preach. A warrior has to be genuine from the heart. Don't preach something you're not genuine about."

People will flock to be the chorus of whoever steps forth with bold, creative music of reggae warriorship. The talent is there waiting for the historical moment. The historical moment is here waiting for the leader.

Bibliography

BARRETT, Leonard E: *The Rastafarians* (Beacon Press, Boston, 1997)

CAMPBELL, Horace: *Rasta And Resistance, From Marcus Garvey To Walter Rodney* (Africa World Press, Trenton, 1987)

CAMPBELL, Mavis C: *The Maroons Of Jamaica 1655-1796: A History Of Resistance, Collaboration And Betrayal* (World Africa Press, Trenton, 1990)

CHANG, Kevin O'Brien and Chen, Wayne: *Reggae Routes: The Story Of Jamaican Music* (Temple University Press, Philadelphia, 1998)

CHEVANNES, Barry: *Rastafari Roots And Ideology* (Syracuse University Press, 1994)

DAWES, Kwame: *Natural Mysticism* (Peepal Tree Press, Leeds, 1999)

DAVIS, Stephen and SIMON, Peter: *Reggae Bloodlines: In Search Of The Music And Culture Of Jamaica* (Da Capo Press, New York, 1992)

FOSTER, Chuck: *Roots Rock Reggae* (Billboard Books, New York, 1999)

GUNST, Laurie: *Born Fi' Dead* (Henry Holt And Company, New York, 1995)

JAHN, Brian and WEBER, Tom: *Reggae Island: Jamaican Music In The Digital Age* (Da Capo Press, New York, 1998)

HAUSMAN, Gerald (editor): *The Kebra Nagast* (St Martin's Press, New York, 1997)

MURRELL, Spencer and McFARLANE: *The Rastafari Reader: Chanting Down Babylon* (Temple University Press, Philadelphia)

POTASH, Chris (editor): *Reggae, Rasta, Revolution: Jamaican Music From Ska To Dub* (Schirmer Books, New York, 1997)

SOBO, Elisa Janine: *One Blood: The Jamaican Body* (State University Of New York Press, Albany, 1993)

WHITE, Timothy: *Catch A Fire: The Life Of Bob Marley* (Henry Holt And Company, New York, 1998)

Index